KENNEDY IN VIETNAM

KENNEDY IN VIETNAM

WILLIAM J. RUST
and the Editors of U.S. News Books

A DA CAPO PAPERBACK

Library of Congress Cataloging in Publication Data

Rust, William J.
  Kennedy in Vietnam.

  (A Da Capo paperback)
  Reprint. Originally published: New York: Scribner,
1985.
  Bibliography: p.
  Includes index.
  1. Vietnamese Conflict, 1961-1975 — United States.
2. United States — Foreign relations — Vietnam. 3. Vietnam
— Foreign relations — United States. 4. United States —
Politics and government — 1961-1963. 5. Kennedy, John F.
(John Fitzgerald), 1917-1963. I. U.S. News Books.
II. Title.
[DS558.R87   1987]   959.704′33′73   87-522
ISBN 0-306-80284-8 (pbk.)

This Da Capo Press paperback edition of *Kennedy in Vietnam*
is an unabridged republication of the edition pubished in
New York in 1985. It is reprinted by arrangement with
Charles Scribner's Sons, Inc.

Published by Da Capo Press, Inc.
A Subsidiary of Plenum Publishing Corporation
233 Spring Street, New York, N.Y. 10013

CONTENTS

ACKNOWLEDGMENTS

As the corporate authorship of this volume implies, many people contributed to the preparation of *Kennedy in Vietnam*. My deepest gratitude belongs to Janice R. Hanover and Kevin M. Generous, my research assistants during the book's four-year gestation period. I am only slightly less indebted to the staff of the John F. Kennedy Library, particularly Suzanne K. Forbes and Martin F. McGann for their help in the document declassification process.

Various chapter drafts profited from the scrutiny and substantive comments of George W. Allen, Bui Diem, George A. Carver, Thomas J. Corcoran, William J. Duiker, Edward G. Lansdale, and Charles B. MacDonald—all of whom served as paid consultants to the Book Division of U.S. News & World Report. Other readers, whose uncompensated comments were frequently even more valuable, included: William E. Colby, Lucien E. Conein, Michael V. Forrestal, John J. Helble, Roger Hilsman, Paul M. Kattenburg, Victor H. Krulak, Charles Maechling, Joseph A. Mendenhall, Russell F. Miller, Rufus C. Phillips, Dean Rusk, William H. Sullivan, Maxwell D. Taylor, and William C. Trueheart.

The assistance of these consultants and readers, many of whom played prominent roles in the events described in *Kennedy in Vietnam*, should not necessarily be construed as their endorsement of the entire book. Moreover, they are not responsible for the volume's analysis or any factual errors of commission or omission. I alone bear that responsibility.

Accountability for the prose, however, is another matter. The manuscript underwent several complete revisions, sometimes because of the editorial suggestions of Linda S. Glisson,

viii ACKNOWLEDGMENTS

Peter G. Huidekoper, and Roy B. Pinchot. They have helped make this book more readable.

Finally, I am grateful to Leah Bendavid-Val and Thomas Simonton for their assistance in collecting and selecting the photographs.

WJR
Stamford, CT
Feb. 19, 1985

SOCRATIC QUESTIONS

On Wednesday afternoon, November 20, 1963, President John F. Kennedy summoned Michael Forrestal to the Oval Office and chatted informally with his young White House aide for the Far East. "He talked about some personal things, about Jackie," Forrestal recalled many years later. "He was feeling quite high about the elections the following year."

Turning to business, the president asked Forrestal to go to Cambodia and speak with Prince Norodom Sihanouk, who earlier that day had severed all economic and military ties with the U.S. government. At odds with American officials for years, the neutralist Cambodian leader believed the CIA had been plotting against him—a disturbing conviction undoubtedly aggravated by the recent overthrow and assassination of South Vietnamese President Ngo Dinh Diem. "You go out there and tell [Sihanouk] that this terrible thing has happened in Saigon," Kennedy said while searching his office for an appropriate gift, "but that we think he's still the best solution for his country."

As Forrestal started to leave, the president stopped him: "Wait a minute. When you come back, I want you to organize an in-depth study of every possible option we've got in Vietnam, including how to get out of there. We have to review this whole thing from the bottom to the top."

During the ensuing conversation, Kennedy revealed private doubts about the American commitment to South Vietnam—a commitment he had inherited and increased to $400 million in annual aid and the deployment of 16,000 U.S. military advisers in an essentially leaderless nation. Belatedly, Kennedy asked fundamental questions about U.S. policy: Was South Vietnam a viable state? Could we see it through? "He didn't say, 'It's not going to work,' " remembered Forrestal. "His questions were Socratic, but slightly antagonistic. . . . It was devil's advocate stuff."

It was also Forrestal's last conversation with the president. En route to Phnom Penh, the White House aide stopped over in Saigon on Friday, November 22. Around 1:00 A.M. the next morning, he was awakened with news of the assassination.

Whether John F. Kennedy would have acted on his doubts and charted a different American course in Vietnam is a tantalizing if ultimately futile question. His former advisers are divided over what he might have done had he lived. According to presidential aide Kenneth O'Donnell, Kennedy said that he intended to withdraw American military advisers from Vietnam after the 1964 election. Secretary of State Dean Rusk, however, doubts Kennedy had made any such decision. "I had hundreds of talks with John F. Kennedy about Vietnam, and never once did he say anything of this sort to his own secretary of state," said Rusk.

Robert F. Kennedy, the President's younger brother and closest confidant, uttered perhaps the most insightful—and least revealing—speculation about John Kennedy and Vietnam. In 1964, when asked whether President Kennedy would have committed U.S. combat troops if a South Vietnamese defeat seemed imminent, Bobby replied, "Well, we'd have faced that when we came to it."

Robert Kennedy's answer reflected not only the ad hoc decision-making process of his brother's administration but also the president's fundamental ambivalence toward the American commitment in Vietnam. On the one hand, he unquestioningly assumed that the international and domestic consequences of a Communist victory there would be catastrophic. The specter of falling dominoes throughout Southeast Asia and a divisive search for scapegoats at home haunted him, as it would his successor, Lyndon B. Johnson. Moreover, Kennedy believed that South Vietnam played a significant role in American national security, which required a world of politically diverse nations rather than a bloc of Communist countries united in a hostile ideology. "Our security and strength, in the last analysis, directly depend on the security and strength of others,"

President John F. Kennedy at a January 1963 press conference. *(U.S. News & World Report)*

read a speech he intended to deliver in Dallas. "Our assistance to these nations can be painful, risky, and costly, as is true in Southeast Asia today. But we dare not weary of the task."

Yet despite the stated importance of an independent, non-Communist South Vietnam, President Kennedy, like his predecessor, Dwight D. Eisenhower, had profound reservations about backing the U.S. commitment with American combat troops. Kennedy earnestly believed the struggle could be won only by the South Vietnamese. "In the final analysis, it is their war," he said in September of 1963. "They are the ones who have to win it or lose it. We can help them, we can give them equipment, we can send our men out there as advisers, but they have to win it, the people of Vietnam, against the Communists."

Kennedy's numerous public pronouncements of this sort were

not merely political eyewash. In the fall of 1961, when escalating Communist attacks threatened South Vietnam with slow but eventual defeat, he rejected recommendations to commit U.S. combat troops. Instead, he substantially expanded the American advisory role, a decision that skirted the potential conflict between his belief in Vietnam's importance and his determination to limit the U.S. commitment. The influx of American military and economic assistance postponed the day of reckoning, and Kennedy never had to face the stark choice that confronted Lyndon Johnson: abandoning South Vietnam to communism or embroiling America in a land war in Asia.

While one cannot confidently predict Kennedy's response to South Vietnam's political and military deterioration in the mid-1960s, one can describe with assurance how his presidential decisions set the stage for Lyndon Johnson's war. In addition to stepping up the U.S. advisory commitment, Kennedy authorized modest covert operations in North Vietnam and the Laotian panhandle. The ineffectiveness of these attempts to curb Hanoi's direction of the southern insurgency engendered planning for larger covert and overt operations, which the Johnson administration refined and implemented.

President Kennedy's most far-reaching Vietnam decision was stimulating the overthrow of Ngo Dinh Diem. Assassinated just three weeks after the coup, Kennedy did not live to see its consequences: eighteen months of revolving-door government in Saigon and a continuous reshuffling of local officials in the provinces. Incapable of coping with the country's political and military problems, the succession of ineffectual South Vietnamese leaders required ever-increasing U.S. assistance to contain the insurgents, who were joined on the battlefield by regular units of the People's Army of (North) Vietnam. By the summer of 1965, it appeared that only massive numbers of U.S. combat troops could stave off the complete collapse of South Vietnam.

Ironically, Kennedy backed the South Vietnamese generals who overthrew Diem in hopes of bolstering the indigenous counterinsurgency effort. Instead, his complicity in the coup d'état increased U.S. obligations to South Vietnam and drew America ever deeper into a long, divisive, and misunderstood war. Like his immediate predecessors, President Kennedy had bequeathed to his successor a larger and more hazardous commitment to an alien land of no inherent value to the United States.

One of the world's oldest nations, Vietnam has a history marked by foreign domination. Neighboring China governed the country from the second century B.C. until the tenth century A.D. This thousand-year rule left the Vietnamese with both an enduring cultural legacy and an abiding hostility toward the Chinese. During the nineteenth century, France absorbed Vietnam into its colonial empire. French hegemony lasted until World War II, when the Japanese controlled and then ousted the Vichy regime in Vietnam.

The Allied victory over Japan created a political vacuum in Vietnam that Communist revolutionary Ho Chi Minh eagerly filled. A nationalist who had long struggled for Vietnamese independence, Ho and his Viet Minh forces seized Hanoi in August of 1945 and proclaimed the Democratic Republic of Vietnam (DRV). Within a month, the French began their military and political efforts to reassert control in Indochina. After a year of guerrilla warfare and inconclusive negotiations between Ho and the French, the French–Viet Minh War finally erupted.

Initially, the U.S. government took a relatively disinterested view of the struggle. The choice between French colonialism and Vietnamese communism seemed unappealing and the combatants' differences largely irreconcilable. "Frankly, we have no solution to the problem to suggest," a State Department policy directive advised. "It is basically [a] matter for [the] two parties to work out themselves."

The Cold War, however, pushed U.S. policy toward support of the French. In the wake of the Communist victory in China and the Soviet Union's recognition of the DRV, the State Department recommended that "all practicable measures be taken to prevent further Communist expansion in Southeast Asia." In May of 1950, one month before the outbreak of the Korean War, the Truman administration announced that the U.S. would supply the French with economic assistance and military equipment. That summer the first elements of the U.S. Military Assistance and Advisory Group (MAAG) arrived in Saigon.

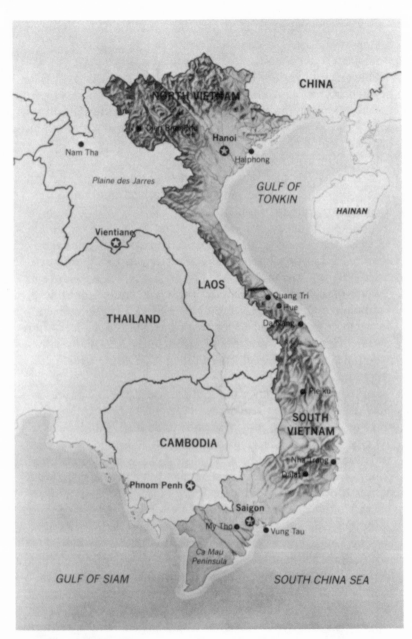

Map of Indochina.

In 1951 the tall, bushy-haired, thirty-four-year-old representative from Boston's Eleventh District visited Vietnam during a tour of the Far East. At the time the U.S. government was financing 40 percent of the French war effort. Wined and dined by the colonial authorities, Congressman John Kennedy visited the combat zones where Foreign Legionnaires fought the Viet Minh. Although he admired the courage of the French fighting men, Kennedy considered U.S. policy in Vietnam disastrous. "We have allied ourselves to the desperate effort of a French regime to hang onto the remants of an empire," he wrote in his trip report. "There is no broad, general support of the native Vietnam government [by] the people of that area."

To Kennedy and other U.S. officials, the key to defeating communism in Indochina was complete independence for Vietnam, Laos, and Cambodia. He amplified this belief three years later, when the Eisenhower administration considered U.S. military intervention to rescue the besieged French garrison at Dien Bien Phu. During the floor debate over Indochina, Kennedy, now a U.S. senator, warned that in the face of continued colonial rule the Vietnamese population would remain apathetic toward the Communists. Reminding his colleagues that the U.S. government was currently underwriting 80 percent of the war, Kennedy declared: "I am frankly of the belief that no amount of American military assistance in Indochina can conquer an enemy which is everywhere and at the same time nowhere, 'an enemy of the people' which has the sympathy and covert support of the people."

Despite his doubts about defeating the Viet Minh, Kennedy conditionally supported U.S. military intervention in Vietnam. If France granted Vietnamese independence and clearly turned the struggle into a war against communism, Kennedy told the Senate, he would favor "united action" against Ho Chi Minh's forces, "realizing full well that it may eventually require some commitment of our manpower." Kennedy apparently believed that the Vietnamese shared the sharp American distinction between nationalism and communism; that the population would enthusiastically respond to Western ideology even though Communists had taken the leading role in the fight for independence; that the people would readily distinguish between a foreign colonial army and a foreign anti-Communist army.

To put it harshly, Kennedy suggested that by changing the name of the war, it might somehow be easier to win.

President Eisenhower decided against unilateral U.S. intervention to rescue Dien Bien Phu, which fell to the Viet Minh just as the Geneva conference on Indochina began. The Eisenhower administration's view of the conference was one of barely disguised hostility. The Panmunjom talks in Korea had convinced U.S. officials that meaningful negotiations with the Communists were virtually impossible. And in view of the weak French military position, the Geneva conference could only result in a net loss for the non-Communist world. On July 21, 1954, the French and Viet Minh military commands signed the cease-fire agreements ending the war. The conference's unsigned final declaration called for a temporary partitioning of Vietnam at the 17th parallel and a plebiscite to reunify the country within two years.

After Geneva, Eisenhower sought to bolster the fledgling government of Prime Minister Ngo Dinh Diem. Although his prospects for survival in South Vietnam's political jungle seemed poor, there appeared to be no non-Communist leader with a better chance of success. And even if South Vietnam did eventually collapse, reasoned Secretary of State John Foster Dulles, support for Diem would buy time to strengthen other non-Communist countries in Southeast Asia. Elbowing the French out of Vietnam, the Eisenhower administration began providing direct economic and military assistance to Diem's government.

To the astonishment of his friends and foes, Diem successfully consolidated his position. By 1956 a temporary administrative zone had become a political fact of life. In the process an American holding action against communism in Southeast Asia had turned into a significant commitment. "This is our offspring—we cannot abandon it, we cannot ignore its needs," Senator Kennedy told the American Friends of Vietnam, an organization to which he belonged. "And if it falls victim to any of the perils that threaten its existence . . . then the United States, with some justification, will be held responsible; and our prestige in Asia will sink to a new low."

With the U.S. solidly committed to South Vietnam, the second Indochina war began slowly, almost imperceptibly. After the French–Viet Minh War, North Vietnam had initially been preoccupied with its own internal reorganization. Exhausted by the seven-year struggle, Ho Chi Minh's lieutenants ordered "stay behind" cadres in South Vietnam to follow a reunification strategy of "peaceful political struggle." However, Diem's unanticipated political survival, his refusal to hold the scheduled plebiscite, and his attempt to suppress communism led to renewed violence. In 1957 Communist terrorist attacks and assassinations of Diem's rural officials began on a modest scale. The reunification strategy of violence was affirmed and amplified by Hanoi's Lao Dong (Communist) party two years later. In 1960 Communists in the south began conducting large-scale guerrilla warfare against the Diem government.

Despite the renewed fighting, Vietnam had slipped to the bottom of American foreign-policy priorities. Berlin, Cuba, and the Congo were the principal Cold War battlefields; even in Southeast Asia Vietnam took a backseat to neighboring Laos. With Vietnam a non-issue in the 1960 campaign, President-elect Kennedy undoubtedly paid little attention to a seemingly trivial event in Saigon that occurred three days after his election: an unsuccessful coup d'état against South Vietnamese President Ngo Dinh Diem. Lost in the shuffle between administrations, the abortive 1960 coup was a symptom of serious sickness within the South Vietnamese body politic, the base upon which Kennedy would build his counterinsurgency effort. "It was a firebell warning which few noticed," reflected the CIA's George Carver many years later. "Its not being heeded made probable, if not inevitable, much tragedy that was historically soon to follow."

CHAPTER ONE

KILL ALL THE PARATROOPERS!

It was 3:30 A.M., November 11, 1960, when armored vehicles loaded with South Vietnamese troops rumbled down the tree-lined Saigon boulevard leading to Independence Palace, home and office of President Ngo Dinh Diem. The soldiers, members of the elite airborne brigade of the Army of the Republic of Vietnam (ARVN), had been told by their officers that the presidential guards had betrayed Diem and seized the palace. The paratroopers' stated mission was to liberate the president.

Although a high wall and fence surrounded the palace grounds, a spacious open area in front of the cream-colored, two-story building gave the paratroopers a clear field of fire. Shattering the morning stillness with the stuttering roar of machine-gun fire, the battalion-strength assault force stormed the main gate. Sharp fighting raged along the fence as a company of sixty presidential guards within the palace grounds resisted fiercely. The few paratroopers who managed to scale the fence were cut down before reaching the palace.

After thirty minutes of furious combat, the paratroopers' assault stalled. Pausing before they launched another rush, the soldiers posted armored cars in the middle of every intersection adjacent to the palace. Harassing fire pinned down the presidential guards, and more combat-ready troops poured in to the area.

Hundreds of curious Saigon residents risked the sporadic shooting and ventured into the tree-shaded mall in front of the palace grounds. Mingling with the soldiers, the spectators wandered by the bodies of slain paratroopers and the bullet-riddled vehicles littering the streets. At approximately 7:30 A.M., firing

1

erupted again, scattering the crowd and killing at least two bystanders.

To the surprise of most of the soldiers surrounding the palace, at 8:00 A.M. Colonel Nguyen Chanh Thi, commander of the airborne brigade, issued a communiqué announcing a coup d'état. Widely regarded as a Diem loyalist, Thi was fiercely anti-Communist. Although his combat record was excellent, the mercurial thirty-seven-year-old colonel had been described by some CIA sources as an "opportunist and a man lacking strong convictions." One U.S. military observer characterized him as "tough, unscrupulous, and fearless, but dumb."

Although Colonel Thi was the nominal leader of the rebellion, two of his subordinates had masterminded the coup: Lieutenant Colonel Vuong Van Dong, chairman of the rebels' Supreme Revolutionary Committee, and his brother-in-law, Lieutenant Colonel Nguyen Trieu Hong, who was killed in combat during the first minutes of the coup. The conspiring colonels were exasperated by Diem's inability to suppress the burgeoning Communist-directed insurgency in South Vietnam and by a promotion system based on personal loyalty to the president rather than military competence. The rebel leaders believed that if they ousted Diem, most of the country's military establishment and non-Communist politicians would enthusiastically rally to their side.

In the months preceding the coup d'état, the plotting officers had quietly marshaled a force of five airborne battalions, an artillery battalion, and two companies of marines. Among these units, usually only the commander or his deputy was aware of the planned coup. The conspirators had sought out officers who were outstanding individual leaders and whose troops would follow them anywhere.

The plotters made the final "go" decision during the second week in November, when all of the key airborne battalions were in the Saigon area. The November 8 election of John F. Kennedy also influenced the timing of the coup, according to George Carver, then a CIA operative in Saigon:

The military coup planners were a bit hazy on the finer points of U.S. constitutional procedure and more familiar with European parliamentary practice in which one government's "fall" was promptly followed by the opposition's acquisition of power. They wanted to give President Kennedy's incoming administration a fresh Vietnamese hand to play. They also wanted to pre-empt any risk that a new Catholic American president might throw the full weight of American support irrevocably behind the Catholic Ngo Dinh Diem.

Although they had failed to capture Diem in their first attack, the rebels successfully secured their other objectives in and around Saigon, including Joint General Staff Headquarters, the police station, and Tan Son Nhut Airport. The paratroopers also captured Radio Saigon, but only after Diem had broadcast a message to Fifth Military Region Commander Colonel Tran Thien Khiem to move his Second Armored Battalion, stationed forty miles southwest of the capital in My Tho, to the outskirts of Saigon, where he was to wait for further orders.

At 11:30 A.M. Radio Saigon broadcast the Revolutionary Committee's Order of the Day instructing the troops to maintain discipline. Denouncing Diem's "feudal totalitarianism," the rebels publicly announced the success of their revolution and the formation of a new caretaker government. This declaration would prove to be premature.

Inside the palace, Ngo Dinh Diem had miraculously escaped death. During the initial moments of the attack, .50-caliber machine-gun fire had ripped through his bedroom window and slammed into the wall only an inch or so above the bed. Had he not been getting a soft drink from a nearby refrigerator, the South Vietnamese president would have been killed.

The rebel attack was neither the first nor the last attempt on Diem's life by his own countrymen. The South Vietnamese president was an honest, anti-Communist nationalist, but he was also authoritarian, nepotistic, and stubborn. After a meeting with him in 1954, an American embassy official in Saigon prophetically observed: "Diem showed a curious blend of heroism mixed with narrowness of view and egotism which will make him a difficult man to deal with."

Born in the former imperial capital of Hue in 1901, Diem was the third of six sons and a devout Catholic who briefly

South Vietnamese President Ngo Dinh Diem. *(U.S. News & World Report)*

studied for the priesthood. After graduating from the School of Public Administration and Law in Hanoi, he received an appointment to the French colonial bureaucracy and quickly earned a reputation as an incorruptible administrator and an ardent anti-Communist. In 1933 Emperor Bao Dai appointed him minister of interior. Diem quit the post less than a year later after the French refused greater Vietnamese participation in the government. He charged the emperor with being "nothing but an instrument in the hands of the French authorities."

Diem returned to Hue and lived reclusively for nearly a decade. During World War II, he unsuccessfully sought Japanese assistance for the creation of an independent Vietnam. Diem was captured by the Communists in 1946 and taken to Ho Chi Minh's mountain stronghold in northern Vietnam. Ho, who needed the support of non-Communist nationalists in his struggle against the French, asked his captive to join the DRV government. Diem appeared interested in the offer. Demanding access to all decisions and information, he sought the Ministry of Interior and control of the police. After several weeks of deliberation, Ho refused the request. Diem was later released with a warning that he would find the Vietnamese countryside "hostile."

Finding the choice between French colonialism and Vietnamese communism odious, Diem left the country in 1950 and eventually arrived in the United States. Ostensibly studying the "mechanics of the American government" and researching ecclesiastical matters, Diem championed the cause of non-Communist Vietnamese independence and impressed such influential Americans as Senators John Kennedy and Mike Mansfield. Throughout the French–Viet Minh War, Diem repeatedly refused Emperor Bao Dai's request to return to Vietnam and participate in the government. The French, unable to defeat Ho Chi Minh, had been negotiating Vietnamese independence with the more malleable monarch, who, according to the U.S. intelligence community, was "weak, venal, infused with a sense of his own grandeur, and wholly incapable of consistently responsible action." Only after the French defeat at Dien Bien Phu did Diem anticipate real Vietnamese independence and accept the emperor's call to return as prime minister.

To the U.S. government Diem seemed an encouraging change in the non-Communist Vietnamese leadership. Unlike his predecessors, described by one American diplomat as "suave, Europeanized, money-seeking, dilettante[s]," the new prime minister had not been co-opted by the French. He appeared to be the only non-Communist leader who could possibly attract the support of the xenophobic Vietnamese peasantry. Yet U.S. officials also recognized Diem's liabilities as a political leader. "He impresses one as a mystic who has just emerged from a religious retreat into the cold world," observed C. Douglas Dillon, the American ambassador in Paris. "He appears too unworldly and unsophisticated to be able to cope with the grave problems and unscrupulous people he will find in Saigon."

Prime Minister Diem had been in office less than two months when his army chief of staff, General Nguyen Van Hinh, threatened a coup d'état. Reportedly in collusion with the French, who sought to retain their influence in Vietnam, the politically ambitious general contemptuously ignored Diem's attempt to fire him. American officials helped thwart the conspiracy by enticing several of Hinh's coconspirators out of the country and warning the general that "U.S. support most probably would stop" if his coup succeeded.

Despite extensive U.S. backing for Diem, American officials maintained lingering doubts about his competence. In the spring of 1955 General J. Lawton "Lightning Joe" Collins, the special U.S. representative to South Vietnam with the rank of ambassador, charged that Diem had a "marked inability to understand the political, economic, and military problems associated with Vietnam." At a meeting in Washington the former Army chief of staff declared: "Diem must be replaced. . . . [A] plan of action should go into effect immediately."

While instructions from Secretary of State John Foster Dulles endorsing Collins's view were drafted and sent to Saigon, the struggle between Diem and the Binh Xuyen gangsters—river pirates who controlled Saigon's gambling, prostitution, and police force—exploded into urban warfare. With help from the CIA, Diem scored an unexpected victory. U.S. policy immediately flipped back to supporting Diem, and the State Department quickly rescinded the secretary's earlier instructions.

With the U.S. government back on board, Diem further

consolidated his power. In October of 1955 he unseated Emperor Bao Dai in an election to determine South Vietnam's chief of state. Although American advisers assured him that a plurality of 60 percent would be sufficient, the South Vietnamese prime minister won an incredible 98.2 percent of the vote. In Saigon, where there were some 400,000 registered voters, Diem managed to win more than 600,000 votes.

Despite such apparent popularity, Diem encountered growing opposition from the non-Communist urban elite, who objected to his authoritarian rule and their exclusion from meaningful participation in the government. In April of 1960 eighteen of South Vietnam's leading politicians gathered at Saigon's Caravelle Hotel. Charging Diem with arbitrary arrests and "oppressions against the population," they petitioned him to "liberalize the regime," a request Diem dismissed as absurd in the light of the struggle against the Communists.

The South Vietnamese president also faced burgeoning dissatisfaction in the senior ranks of the army. Like the rebel colonels, the general officers of the Army of the Republic of Vietnam objected to a politicized promotion system and resented Diem's meddling in military matters. "It's funny," recalled Army Chief of Staff Brigadier General Nguyen Khanh, who staged his own coup d'état in 1964. "When civilians reach a certain position in the government, they want to play soldier; when a soldier reaches a certain position, he wants to play at politics."

During the 1960 paratroopers' coup, most of the army's senior officers kept a low profile. With cautious opportunism, they waited to see who would win before taking sides. Diem, horrified by the failure of his top commanders to assist him, would forever be suspicious of Major General Duong Van "Big" Minh for scheduling a meeting of several leading generals on the day of the coup. While Diem and a handful of presidential guards were surrounded by the rebels, according to Carver, "the generals all sat calmly in Minh's garden watching his orchids grow."

CIA Chief of Station William Colby had a rude awakening in Saigon on the morning of November 11, 1960. His home on the Alexandre de Rhodes was only one block from Independence Palace and parallel to the rebel paratroopers' line of attack. As bullets zipped through his house, Colby barricaded his wife and children in a hall on the ground floor. When the fighting flared up again at 7:30 A.M., Colby peered over his balcony and was astonished to find John Helble, a young Foreign Service officer, hiding behind a wall in front of the house. Helble, who had come down to the palace to keep the embassy informed about the disturbance, had been talking to some paratroopers when the shooting erupted. Caught in the cross fire, he sought refuge behind the trees in the mall. "I ducked behind tree after tree, but most of them were already occupied by paratroopers," he said later with a chuckle. "So I just threw myself over a residential wall."

During a lull in the fighting, Helble scrambled into the Colby residence. The CIA station chief asked him to remain there and wait for a chance to get his family to safety. Colby then slipped out of the house and walked three-quarters of a mile to the American embassy.

William Egan Colby, forty, was nominally an embassy first secretary. Like many officials in the CIA's Directorate of Plans, the somewhat misleading name of the agency's Clandestine Service, he had served in the Office of Strategic Services (OSS), America's wartime intelligence agency and the forerunner of the CIA. Slim and bespectacled, Colby had been a "Jed"—a member of one of the three-man, multinational Jedburgh teams that had organized resistance behind enemy lines. After the war, he earned a law degree and joined the firm of OSS commander William "Wild Bill" Donovan. Colby signed up with the CIA after the outbreak of the Korean War and served in Stockholm and Rome before arriving in Vietnam in 1959.

As Saigon station chief, Colby directed some seventy CIA officers, whose principal tasks were assisting the Diem regime with intelligence collection and paramilitary operations against North Vietnam. Some of Colby's officers also kept tabs on the host government and its opponents. The week before the paratroopers made their move, the Saigon station had received reports of an imminent coup d'état. Such rumors were common in Saigon's seething atmosphere of political intrigue, and Colby spent several days arguing with CIA officer George Carver about the significance of this information. "A report was cabled to Washington on the afternoon of November 9," according to Carver. "The station considered it properly balanced, but I thought it downplayed the allegations."

Ostensibly an Agency for International Development employee, Carver was a case officer (a CIA official handling foreign agents) who maintained contact with Diem's civilian opposition. By his own description "impassioned," the thirty-year-old Carver agreed with the rebels that Diem's style of rule was quickly becoming the Communists' principal asset in South Vietnam. "I hadn't prompted the coup or been involved with the planning of it," said Carver later, "but I was absolutely convinced that to achieve American objectives in Vietnam, Diem had to be ousted."

Within hours of the initial assault on the palace, Carver began phoning his Vietnamese contacts. After a few calls, he reached Hoang Co Thuy, the uncle of the slain rebel Colonel Hong and slated to be vice premier in the new government. Anxious to assure the Americans that the coup was not Communist inspired, Thuy invited Carver to his home, where a meeting of the Civilian Revolutionary Committee was in progress. After checking with Colby, Carver accepted the invitation.

While Carver met with the civilian leaders of the coup, another CIA officer, Russell F. Miller, made contact with the rebellion's military leaders. An airborne veteran of World War II, Miller worked on the agency's paramilitary operations. Under military cover, the thirty-eight-year-old CIA official had been in Vietnam two years and knew many of ARVN's leading officers. Like several other U.S. political, military, and intelligence officers, Miller had gone into the streets of Saigon to report on the coup. At the palace he spoke with several paratroopers and located the rebels' radio post. With the help of a Vietnamese-speaking CIA employee, he eavesdropped on the rebels' communications between the palace and their headquarters. "Where is your command group?" Miller asked the paratroopers.

The soldiers replied that if he wanted to know what was going on, he should go to Joint General Staff (JGS) Headquarters at Tan Son Nhut, approximately three miles from the palace. Somewhat appalled by the lax Vietnamese security, Miller left for JGS. On the way to rebel headquarters, he picked up an American CIA employee who was from the analytical, rather than the operational, side of the station. While driving down a side street, Miller stopped his Ford sedan to look around. Machine-gun fire erupted nearby and so unnerved Miller's passenger that he tried to dive under the dashboard, where he became stuck. Finding the covert operator's life a little too "sporty," an agency euphemism for frightening, Miller's companion asked to be dropped off a few blocks away.

Later that morning, Colby informed Ambassador Elbridge Durbrow that the CIA was in touch with the rebels. Durbrow also received a call from President Diem seeking the U.S. attitude toward the coup. Embassy officials publicly declared that they were "of course, not in a position to mediate or even comment upon" the differences between the rebels and Diem. In reality the ambassador was secretly urging both the paratroopers and the South Vietnamese president to negotiate. The embassy's political section had recommended an evenhanded approach to the contesting sides, both of which were considered friendly to the United States. With the outcome of the coup still in doubt, it would be disastrous to future U.S.–South Vietnamese relations to back the losing side.

Elbridge Durbrow, fifty-seven, was a scrappy, gravel-voiced diplomat prone to language more commonly heard in a barracks under fire than at an embassy reception. A career Foreign Service officer, "Durby" had served in the Moscow embassy during the thirties and forties, an experience that, in his own words, left him "a 100-percent containment man." Despite their mutual militant anticommunism, Durbrow was ambivalent about Ngo Dinh Diem. The ambassador considered Diem the "best available Vietnamese leader" but feared that his authoritarian rule and growing unpopularity were jeopardizing the war effort against the Communist guerrillas. In September of 1960 the diplomat warned the State Department: "It may become necessary for [the] U.S. government to begin consideration [of] alternative courses of action and leaders to achieve our objective."

The following month, Durbrow met privately with Diem to discuss steps the South Vietnamese president should take to bolster his deteriorating political position. The ambassador suggested that Diem delegate more authority to his ministers, appoint token non-Communist political opposition to the cabinet, and disband the Can Lao, a semi-covert political party that inspired fear and suspicion throughout the country. Diem replied that most of Durbrow's suggestions conformed with his basic ideas, but as much as he would like to put them into effect, the war against the Viet Cong made it most difficult.

Durbrow then begged the South Vietnamese president's indulgence and asked if he might bring up "a most sensitive and delicate matter": Ngo Dinh Nhu, Diem's younger brother and principal adviser, and his wife, Madame Nhu. Much of the discontent with the South Vietnamese government focused on the Nhus. The regime's theoretician, Nhu controlled the Can Lao and the government's various intelligence organizations. His perpetually smiling countenance masked an apparently limitless appetite for intrigue. Madame Nhu was as unpopular as her husband. A five-foot-tall, eighty-pound spitfire, she had sponsored a "family bill" imposing strictures on marriage, divorce, and sexual relations. Although consistent with the Ngo family's Catholicism, the bill violated traditional Vietnamese customs in these emotionally charged areas.

After discussing the growing national criticism of the Nhus, Durbrow suggested they be assigned to government duties abroad. Diem's expression became grim, and Durbrow detected a slightly hurt manner. "These rumors about the Nhus [are being] spread by the Communists" was the South Vietnamese president's only reply.

"It was pretty damn tough on him," Durbrow recalled. "He didn't like a goddamned word I said."

Despite Diem's failure to follow his advice, Durbrow sought to discourage coup plots, which might create opportunities the Communists could exploit. During the paratroopers' coup, the ambassador instructed Colby to try to persuade the rebels to negotiate with Diem. The CIA chief of station passed the order to his men in the field. Russ Miller dutifully saluted, but Carver raised objections. "I was convinced that my orders were not in the rebels' interest and not in the U.S. interest," said Carver later. "I bitched and moaned and explained why I thought my orders were stupid. . . . Basically, Bill [Colby] said, 'George, I know your position. I don't agree with you, and we haven't got time to discuss it now.'"

Reluctantly, Carver acceded to Colby's order.

By early afternoon on the eleventh, Miller and Carver had delivered a simple message to the leaders of the coup: The U.S. government would like the rebels to settle their dispute with Diem without further bloodshed. The leaders of the coup, well aware that U.S. military assistance was the lifeblood of South Vietnam's defense against the Communist insurgency, heeded the suggestion.

Some of the rebel leaders welcomed the opportunity to keep bloodshed to a minimum. They regarded the troops defending Diem as comrades-in-arms, and bitter fighting between rebels and loyalists would only sow discord in the army after the coup had been successfully concluded. Other rebels questioned the wisdom of breaking off the attack and negotiating with Diem. The civilian leaders turned to Carver for his personal opinion, but the CIA officer refused to be drawn into any such discussion. Years later, Carver could still recall his urge to encourage the paratroopers to press the attack: "Every fiber of my being wanted to say, 'For Christ's sake, will you guys get off your ass and get this thing finished?'"

Army Chief of Staff Brigadier General Nguyen Khanh acted as the Vietnamese mediator between Diem and the paratroopers. Khanh had formed Vietnam's first airborne company in 1949 and knew most of the rebel officers. One of South Vietnam's most aggressive military commanders, the diminutive thirty-three-year-old general lived five blocks from Independence Palace. Awakened by the shooting, Khanh at first thought Communist guerrillas were attacking Diem. Before leaving for the palace, he ordered two general reserve battalions to report to the rear of the Saigon Cathedral, just two blocks from the palace. When Khanh's operations officer dutifully passed this order to the airborne brigade, one of the rebels replied, "Don't worry, we have already sent two battalions over there."

With the chief of staff's flag flying on his car, Khanh drove to the rear entrance of the palace. The presidential guards recognized him but refused to open the gate. "If you want to get in," said one of the guards, "you will have to climb over the wall."

After scrambling over the fence, Khanh checked on President Diem's physical safety and began directing the defense of the palace, a task greatly facilitated by the arrival of Ky Quan Liem, the deputy director of the Civil Guard. Although the rebels had seized Radio Saigon and the army radio network, they had neglected the Civil Guard network, an oversight for which they would pay dearly. Liem, posing as a rebel negotiator, had bluffed his way through the paratroopers' lines and into the palace. Once inside, he used the Civil Guard radio network to establish communications with Colonel Tran Thien Khiem's armored battalion.

Early in the afternoon, Khanh received a phone call from the chairman of the rebels' Supreme Revolutionary Committee, Lieutenant Colonel Vuong Van Dong, who wished to meet with the general. Khanh, realizing that the first elements of the armored column would be arriving momentarily, replied, "All right, I will meet you in one hour."

At 2:30 P.M. an armored column of twelve tanks, two half-tracks, and an armored car lumbered down the boulevard in front of the palace, rolled through the paratroopers' perimeter, and encircled the palace. The cannons of the tanks pointed menacingly at the building. While the new arrivals casually mingled with paratroopers and curious civilian spectators, the commander of ARVN's Second Armored Battalion convinced the rebel leaders he was sympathetic to the coup. In fact, he did not know which side he was supporting. His instructions from Colonel Khiem were to surround the palace and await orders from Khanh and from Khanh alone.

After refusing to speak to Diem, the battalion commander met with General Khanh. "The first thing," said Khanh with a swirling motion of his finger, "you've got to turn your guns around. Number two, don't fire unless you are attacked. Number three, I will go to meet the rebels over there in a few minutes."

Shortly after the armored column's arrival, many of the paratroopers, assuming they had been relieved by friendly forces, picked up their gear and filed out of the area at a brisk march. As the last paratrooper departed from sight, the tanks turned their guns away from the palace and pointed them toward the rebels. From this moment on, the rebels' chances for an easy victory over the hopelessly outnumbered presidential guards vanished. Although the coup leaders could still launch an assault on the palace, the battle would now be extremely bloody.

Having shifted the balance of power, Khanh met Colonel Dong in the middle of the wide boulevard that only hours earlier had been the axis of the rebel attack. The lean, thirty-year-old Dong complained about Diem's ineffective prosecution of the war. The rebel leader demanded that Diem step down from office and that the military be allowed to form a provisional government. Sympathetic to Dong's point of view, not to mention intrigued by the possibilities of a military government, the wily Khanh said he would see what could be done.

Inside the palace, Khanh discussed Colonel Dong's demands with Diem, Nhu, and Madame Nhu. The Vietnamese general advised Diem to step down: "It is the will of the population and all the armed forces."

"No, no, never!" exclaimed Madame Nhu. "You have to kill all of the paratroopers."

General Khanh, insulted by the outburst and convinced there was no reasoning with her, rose from the table and said, "All right, if you want to take my place, take command. I'm leaving now."

Diem asked Khanh to stay and turned to his sister-in-law: "Madame Nhu, you are tired; we fought too much last night. You'd better get some rest."

Diem appeared to agree in principle with the rebel demands. He charged Khanh with organizing a provisional government and conciliating any differences between the paratroopers and the army. Negotiations between Diem and the rebels began that afternoon and continued into the night. At 9:00 P.M. rebel-controlled Radio Saigon broadcast that an agreement had been reached that included a cease-fire, Diem's resignation, and the formation of a new military provisional government. Ten minutes later a rebel press conference confirmed the success of the coup.

Both announcements were premature. General Khanh had found few of South Vietnam's senior commanders, and the rebels had not nailed down an agreement with Diem. Although willing to dissolve his government, Diem stubbornly refused to resign. Throughout the night, rebel skeptics kept urging an end to talks and a rush on the palace, but Diem kept offering one more concession—or offering to talk about one more conces-

Madame Ngo Dinh Nhu, Diem's sister-in-law. *(U.S. News & World Report)*

sion—and the negotiating process limped along. The American embassy, urging both sides to compromise in the negotiations, encouraged the rebels to retain Diem as chief of state.

During the early hours of Saturday, November 12, Diem and the leaders of the coup managed to hammer out an agreement. The rebels agreed to keep Diem if he would dismiss his government and entrust the Supreme Revolutionary Committee with forming a provisional military government. To show his good faith, the South Vietnamese president even taped a surrender statement for the rebels to broadcast later in the morning.

But the negotiations had been an elaborate charade. Throughout the previous day and night, Diem had been in constant radio contact with loyalist units in the countryside. Units from the Twenty-first Infantry Division had been ferried across the Saigon River into the city, and elements of the Fifth and Seventh Infantry divisions were just outside the capital, poised to counterattack.

At dawn rebel, loyalist, and uncommitted ARVN troops mingled in downtown Saigon. Except for the immediate vicinity of Independence Palace, there were few clearly demarcated rebel or loyalist lines. Although the rebels were supposed to wear red neckerchiefs, many did not, and it was impossible to visually determine the loyalties of the identically dressed, combat-ready soldiers. The troops were edgy and confused, and any fast-moving vehicle or person was apt to draw fire, often from both rebels and loyalists.

For the second straight morning, hundreds of civilians had gathered in front of the palace. The mob, many of whom were carrying "Diem Must Go" signs, had been summoned to the palace by rebel radio broadcasts urging a mass demonstration against the South Vietnamese president. After an emotional harangue by Colonel Thi, leader of the coup forces, the crowd surged toward the palace fence. At this some of the loyalist armored vehicles and troops fired into the civilians, killing thirteen and wounding scores more.

Despite the previous night's agreement between Diem and the rebels, the bloodbath the American embassy had sought to avoid now appeared inevitable. Around 9:00 A.M. Colonel

Khiem's relief force began rumbling into the city. Almost immediately reports of troop movements streamed into the embassy. Ambassador Durbrow, who had assumed Diem's negotiations were in good faith, decided he "must speak firmly" with the South Vietnamese president. At 9:20 A.M. Durbrow phoned Diem and reminded him that the embassy had worked all day and night urging the rebels to negotiate. "After all these efforts," said Durbrow, "I [am] extremely perturbed, particularly after [the] announcement of [the] agreement with [the] rebels." In a "most emphatic manner," according to his report to the State Department, Durbrow warned Diem of the "disastrous effects" for all concerned if the loyalist troops planned to shoot it out with the rebels.

While agreeing that bloodshed should be avoided, Diem charged the coup leaders with negotiating in bad faith. He reminded Durbrow of rebel broadcasts inciting the population to protest in front of the palace. The rebels, said Diem, were the ones who had broken the cease-fire.

Durbrow reiterated that Diem "must negotiate immediately with [the] rebels to avoid further shooting." If a bloodbath were to occur, predicted the ambassador, the "entire population would rise up against both loyalists and rebels, and [the] Communists would take over [the] city."

Diem promised Durbrow he would see what he could do.

Meanwhile, Khiem's relief force moved steadily toward the palace. At a press conference held at rebel headquarters, Colonel Dong declared the troop movements a "flagrant violation" of the agreement with Diem. Dong naively added that he still expected Diem to honor the agreement. Fifteen minutes after Dong's statement General Khiem announced over Radio Saigon the reoccupation of all the capital's public buildings and ordered the rebel troops to surrender. In a subsequent radio broadcast Diem addressed the nation: "To protect the people's [lives] and interests, I have ordered the insurgents to surrender, but they failed to obey the right cause. I therefore give orders to the Vietnamese armed forces to settle the matter with them."

Khiem's counter-coup forces quickly crushed the rebellion. The first loyalist rockets scattered the paratroopers from their camp in the fifty-acre park behind the palace. Rebel troops frantically abandoned their positions around the palace, tearing off their neckerchiefs and even their uniforms as they tried to blend into the civilian population. Realizing they had been duped by Diem, the coup leaders were enraged. Some argued for a final assault, no matter how futile. They could still shell the palace with artillery under rebel control. Russ Miller was at JGS as the Twenty-seventh Artillery Battalion trained its 105-mm howitzers on the palace. Over a CIA network, Colby radioed Miller that "the howitzers ought not to be fired."

Keenly aware of the inevitable errant rounds and of the many American residences in the palace vicinity, Miller appealed to the rebels' honor. He reminded them that many civilians and even their own soldiers would be killed in such an attack. The CIA officer also chided the rebels for their unsuccessful assault on the palace. "If you couldn't succeed with a battalion of paratroopers," said Miller, "what do you expect to accomplish with artillery?"

The rebel guns remained silent. Years later Miller, with characteristic understatement, admitted the situation had been "touch and go."

By early afternoon, the rebel leadership gave up the fight and ordered their forces to disperse and flee as best they could. Colonels Thi and Dong and about ten fellow officers made a mad dash for Tan Son Nhut Airport. They boarded a C-47 and fled to Cambodia, where Prince Sihanouk gave them asylum.

Shortly after the coup had been crushed, one of the rebel civilian leaders, and evidence indicates it may have been Hoang Co Thuy, appeared at George Carver's home begging for protection from Diem's retribution. Carver smuggled him out of the house under a blanket and drove him to an agency "safe house." With the CIA's reputation for protecting its sources at stake, Durbrow and Colby arranged for the rebel to be flown out of the country. Several days later, hidden in an APO mail sack, he was loaded aboard the air attaché's plane. Eventually the agency relocated him in Europe.

Although American mediation had enabled Diem to save himself physically and politically, the South Vietnamese president was deeply disturbed by the embassy's evenhanded approach to the contesting sides during the coup. In the past the U.S. mission had bailed Diem out of one crisis after another.

Now, however, it appeared to the South Vietnamese president that he would receive the same consideration as any one of his mutinous military commanders. "I think President Diem interpreted [U.S. evenhandedness] as disloyalty to him," Colby later said. "I think he felt we should have been much more supportive, much more positive."

Diem and Nhu were also unhappy about the presence of two Americans with radios at the rebel command post during the coup. Of particular concern to the palace were the activities of George Carver. By Sunday, November 13, leaflets began to appear in Saigon blaming "colonialists" for the coup. Diem and Nhu hinted to American officials that Saigon's unfriendly atmosphere would be materially improved by the departure of Carver. Brother Nhu met with Colby and alleged that Carver had been encouraging the rebels. "All nations conduct espionage, and this is not a matter to get upset about," said Nhu. "But what no nation can accept, and our government no less, is interference with its political authority and processes."

Colby ritualistically denied Carver's employment with the CIA and assured Nhu that Carver was only reporting on the rebel activities, not encouraging them. The two governments quickly reached an impasse. On November 20 Carver received a "death warrant" written in French and ostensibly sent by surviving remnants of the rebel organization. The warrant claimed that a rebel court had sentenced Carver and his family to death for "betrayal of the rebel cause."

To the Saigon CIA station the document appeared to have the metaphoric fingerprints of Nhu all over it. Although doubting the authenticity of the threat, Colby believed it offered a solution to the Carver problem. "The death threat looked like a real easy answer," recalled Colby. "I took it to the [Diem] government and said, 'One of our officers has had this terrible threat from the people who used to be in the rebellion. We've decided to move him and his family out of the country.' Everybody's face was saved."

Three weeks after the attempted coup, Durbrow reported to Washington that on the surface life in Saigon had returned to normal. He was relieved that Diem had not adopted a "vengeful attitude" against the rebels and was encouraged by Diem's stated intention to reorganize his military command

and cabinet. Despite these promising gestures, the ambassador warned of a "quite serious undercurrent [of] malaise and skepticism" among South Vietnamese officials who doubted that Diem would make effective reforms quickly enough.

The ambassador concluded his message by warning that the steadily increasing Communist guerrilla movement and mounting popular dissatisfaction with Diem posed a highly dangerous threat to U.S. interests. Foreshadowing the issue that dominated Kennedy's relationship with the South Vietnamese government, Durbrow wrote: "We should help and encourage [Diem] to take effective action. Should he not do so we may well be forced in [the] not too distant future to undertake [the] difficult task of identifying and supporting alternate leadership."

CHAPTER TWO

WE MUST CHANGE
OUR COURSE

The phone call summoning Brigadier General Edward G. Lansdale to the White House came early Saturday morning, January 28, 1961. "Get down here right away," Secretary of Defense Robert S. McNamara tersely ordered. Lansdale had no idea why he had suddenly been called before the new president. A Pentagon liaison with the CIA and McNamara's deputy assistant for special operations, he monitored several paramilitary and unconventional warfare activities. One plan under consideration, which he viewed with skepticism, was a CIA-sponsored invasion of Cuba. Over the next three months, this operation evolved into the Bay of Pigs debacle.

A former advertising man, the fifty-three-year-old general had served in the OSS during World War II. Brimming with ideas about intelligence activities, Lansdale joined the newly created U.S. Air Force after the war. In the early 1950s he worked for the CIA in the Philippines, where he helped the government suppress the Communist-led "Huk" rebellion. Imparting his flair for unconventional warfare, Lansdale armed the Philippine government with a psychological warfare capability. One combat "psywar" unit capitalized on the local fear of vampires. After spreading rumors that a vampire inhabited a certain area, the Filipinos punctured two holes in a dead Huk's neck and drained the blood from his body. The psywar unit then left the bloodless corpse on a trail for his comrades to find. Within hours the insurgents had fled from the area.

Lansdale's assistance to the Philippine government also included political advice. He became a friend and confidant to Ramón Magsaysay, the dynamic secretary of national defense

21

who later became president of the Philippines. Impressed by Magsaysay's understanding of guerrilla warfare, Lansdale tutored him in military and political affairs. "Each night we sat up late discussing the current situation," Lansdale later reflected. "Magsaysay would air his views. Afterwards, I would sort them out aloud for him while underscoring the principles or strategy or tactics involved. It helped him select or discard courses of action."

Lansdale's success in the Philippines impressed Central Intelligence Director Allen Dulles, who suggested sending the unconventional warfare officer to Vietnam to help salvage something from the collapsing French effort against the Viet Minh. Nominally the American embassy's assistant air attaché, Colonel Lansdale arrived in Saigon on June 1, 1954, one month after the French defeat at Dien Bien Phu. His instructions were to assist the Vietnamese—rather than the French—in waging paramilitary and political-psychological operations against the Communists.

The American immediately threw himself into the thick of South Vietnam's chaotic political scene. The day after Ngo Dinh Diem's arrival in Saigon, Lansdale sought out the South Vietnamese prime minister to offer advice about generating popular support for his government. The two men quickly established a close relationship, meeting regularly at the palace. Lansdale counseled and supported Diem throughout his struggle to consolidate his authority. In October of 1954 Lansdale and his team, the Saigon Military Mission, thwarted General Hinh's planned coup by luring the chief of staff's top lieutenants out of the country. And during the 1955 struggle with the sects and Binh Xuyen gangsters, Lansdale and the CIA were virtually at war with the French intelligence service, which sought to topple the South Vietnamese prime minister. For his assistance to Diem—one of the most successful political action programs in the CIA's history—Lansdale was awarded the National Security Medal.

Although his rapport with non-Communist Vietnamese leaders was excellent, the uninhibited Lansdale frequently ran afoul of U.S. officials. In the face of J. Lawton Collins's attempt to replace Diem, Lansdale's activities earned him a reputation as an unprincipled adventurer, eager to undermine the ambassador's authority. "I was convinced he was not a wheeler-dealer; he was not an irresponsible swashbuckler," Deputy Defense Secretary Roswell Gilpatric recalled. "[But] the State Department distrusted him because they felt he would work around them."

Returning to the United States in 1956, Lansdale resumed his military career in the Pentagon's Office of Special Operations. With increasing dismay, he followed the State Department's blunt demands that Diem reform politically. Appalled by Durbrow's equivocal support for Diem during the unsuccessful paratroopers' coup, Lansdale believed the ambassador's usefulness in Saigon had come to an end: "Diem cannot help but wonder at U.S. objectives as voiced by such a spokesman. . . . The most charitable view that Diem could take would be that our ambassador is a badly informed man, but he would also then believe that the ambassador has been far too prone to listen to the wrong people in Vietnam, people who are Diem's enemies."

Lansdale returned to Vietnam in the waning days of the Eisenhower administration. The idea for the trip was his own. Years later he sheepishly admitted that the motive for the journey was to distance himself from the planned Cuban invasion: "I took a dim view of it from the beginning, and I wanted to be out of town when it happened."

His reputation as a covert operator bred speculation among Vietnamese and Americans about the purpose of the trip. Beyond a vague explanation that he wanted to look around, Lansdale remained inscrutable. The CIA suspected his journey was the first step in a Pentagon attempt to take over agency activities in Vietnam. Station Chief William Colby described a CIA briefing to Lansdale as a "shambles": "He obviously thought he was being subjected to some form of shell game and said hardly a word during the whole evening."

Traveling with the interpreter from his mid-fifties team, Lansdale toured the countryside and discovered the war was going much worse than he had been led to believe by official reports. He estimated that between 3,000 and 15,000 Communist guerrillas dominated much of the First and Fifth Military regions, an area stretching from the jungle-covered foothills north of Saigon to the Gulf of Siam.

During his visit, Lansdale renewed his friendship with Diem, who seemed suspicious of the American. "In our first meeting, he was a bit cautious with me," Lansdale wrote in his trip report. "I suspected that he was waiting for me to drop Washington's other shoe as a follow-up to the ambassador's demands that he reform his ways."

After reminiscing about their past experiences together, Diem warmed up to Lansdale and gave his version of the attempted coup. "He showed me where [the rebels] had shot some .50-caliber machine-gun bullets in the bedroom and how high off the bed it was," recalled Lansdale. "He was trying to get my sympathy and showing me a little bit of what he'd gone through."

Lansdale returned to Washington a few days before the inauguration of John Kennedy. In his report the general described Vietnam as a "combat area of the cold war . . . requiring emergency treatment." He warned that unless the South Vietnamese mobilized their total resources, they "probably will be able to do no more than postpone eventual defeat." Lansdale also vigorously defended Ngo Dinh Diem, recommending friendship and understanding as the most effective approach to the South Vietnamese president: "If the next American official to talk to President Diem would have the good sense to see him as a human being who has been through a lot of hell for years—and not as an opponent to be beaten to his knees—we would start regaining our influence with him in a healthy way."

Sharply critical of the Foreign Service in Vietnam, Lansdale charged that "many of the Americans in Saigon perhaps subconsciously believed in defeat." While excluding the CIA and MAAG chiefs—both of whom staunchly supported Diem—from this criticism, Lansdale concluded that "too much time and energy had been spent on the political situation in Saigon instead of on the very real Viet Cong menace." In a personnel recommendation undoubtedly resented by the State Department, he urged the transfer of Ambassador Durbrow: "He has been in the 'forest of tigers' which is Vietnam for nearly four years, and I doubt that he himself realizes how tired he has become or how close he is to the individual trees in this big woods."

Lansdale suggested dispatching to Saigon "an unusual man" capable of influencing Asians through understanding and a team of Americans that sounded suspiciously like his old Saigon Military Mission. To many U.S. officials these recommendations seemed an exercise in self-promotion. "It did not take much to conclude," Deputy Assistant Defense Secretary William Bundy later observed, "that Lansdale hoped that he himself might be picked to head such a team, presumably as ambassador."

The general's trip report bubbled up through the bureaucracy until it finally landed on the desk of the new president. Shocked by the paper, Kennedy asked that the next White House meeting on Southeast Asia be devoted to Vietnam. Informed of the president's "keen interest" in the Lansdale memorandum, Defense Secretary McNamara ordered the general down to the White House for the Saturday morning meeting.

After a brief wait—CIA officials were finishing up their presentation of the planned Cuban invasion—Lansdale was ushered into the Oval Office, where the president, vice president, secretaries of state and defense, the chairman of the Joint Chiefs of Staff, and the director of Central Intelligence had already assembled. Kennedy thanked Lansdale for his memorandum. For the first time, said the president, it gave him "a sense of the danger and urgency of the problem in Vietnam."

Assistant Secretary of State J. Graham Parsons opened the meeting by presenting the Counterinsurgency Plan (CIP), a joint project of the Departments of Defense and State designed to shift South Vietnam's military emphasis from defense against a conventional invasion by North Vietnam to internal security against the Communist-supported insurgency. The $42 million plan would pay for a 20,000-man increase in ARVN and a 32,000-man increase in the Civil Guard, South Vietnam's provincial paramilitary force. Parsons, a former ambassador to Laos and a holdover from the Eisenhower administration, had received the CIP only a few days before. "I found myself trying to brief this august assemblage on a very complex document that had just come in," he later recalled. "But no matter how inadequately I portrayed it, it was obvious that the president and others present were very much interested in this approach. . . . "

A key element of the Counterinsurgency Plan involved a reform of Diem's chaotic military command structure. Violating the fundamental principle of "unity of command," thirty-eight province chiefs, three regional field commanders, and a chief of staff reported independently to the South Vietnamese president. Although decreasing the likelihood of any officer becoming powerful enough to launch a successful coup d'état, the overlapping lines of military authority hindered the war against the Communist guerrillas. The civil side of the CIP called for the introduction of non-Communist opposition leaders into the South Vietnamese government and stressed the need for political reform.

President Kennedy asked his advisers whether the proposed increase of 20,000 men in ARVN "would really permit a shift from the defense to the offense." Despite assurances that this increase would free a significant number of soldiers for counterinsurgency operations, Kennedy remained unconvinced. He later scribbled on the flyleaf of the CIP's summary and conclusions, "Why so little?"

The president asked Lansdale for his estimate of the prospects in Vietnam. "The Communists," replied the general, "regard 1961 as their big year." Only a maximum American effort could frustrate them and allow the South Vietnamese to move on the offensive in 1962. To accomplish this, Lansdale said, "the Americans in Vietnam must themselves be infused with high morale and a will to win, and they must get close to the Vietnamese; secondly, the Vietnamese must, in this setting, be moved to act with vigor and confidence; third, Diem must be persuaded to let the opposition coalesce in some legitimate form rather than concentrate on the task of killing him."

Lansdale reported Diem's confidence in the CIA and MAAG chiefs and distrust of certain State Department officials, whom the South Vietnamese president believed were "very close to those who tried to kill him on November 11." Lansdale said he had found it impossible to dissuade Diem on this point. Secretary of State Dean Rusk, defending the Foreign Service, interjected: "Diplomats in Vietnam face an extremely frustrating task. They were caught between pressing Diem to do the things he did not wish to do and the need to convey to him American support. It was a difficult balance to strike, and Diem was extremely sensitive to criticism."

During the meeting, the president asked Lansdale, "Did

Dean tell you I want you to go to Vietnam as ambassador?"

"No, he didn't," sputtered the general. While mumbling what a great honor it would be, Lansdale wondered whether Kennedy's casual mention of the appointment was a serious job offer.

The president ended the meeting with a call for action. He directed CIA chief Allen Dulles to prepare guerrilla operations against North Vietnam and ordered the formation of a Vietnam task force similar to the committees monitoring the administration's other crisis areas: the Congo, Cuba, and Laos. "We must change our course in these areas," said Kennedy. "We must be better off in three months than we are now."

Shortly after the meeting, Kennedy approved the Counterinsurgency Plan, his first presidential decision on Vietnam. He also endorsed several of the recommendations in General Lansdale's report. A new ambassador would soon be sent to South Vietnam with instructions to sympathize with Diem and build up his confidence in the United States. The president, however, reversed himself on Lansdale's appointment as ambassador.

The catalyst for this reversal was J. Graham Parsons. A few days after the January 28 Vietnam meeting, the assistant secretary of state raised the subject of Lansdale with Dean Rusk. "[Do you] realize the implications of having a prominent CIA agent being given this position of prominence and great responsibility in a critical area of the Far East?" Parsons asked. "Was this the kind of image that the president and [you] would want?"

According to Parsons, Rusk seemed rather startled by the implications. "It may be quite difficult," said the secretary of state. "I want to think this over."

After mulling it over, Rusk apparently advised against the appointment. Although the president favored Lansdale, the bureaucracy was filled with the general's enemies. "He was in the doghouse with both [the Defense and State Departments]," recalled Deputy Defense Secretary Roswell Gilpatric. "Lansdale was fascinated by the political scene. That's one of the reasons that his activities and views raised the hackles in the State Department. And he didn't take the same degree of interest or concern in what his military colleagues were doing on the counterinsurgency training program and development of new techniques, equipment, weapons, and so forth for coping with guerrilla-type activities."

On February 27 Lansdale was promoted to special assistant to the secretary of defense. Later in the spring Gilpatric proposed sending him to Saigon as the operations officer for the Vietnam task force. The recommendation was torpedoed by military and civilian officials in Saigon, who feared that Lansdale's closeness to Diem might compromise their own influence with the South Vietnamese president. Moreover, Lansdale's uninhibited personality antagonized national security bureaucrats in Washington. Chairing a meeting of the Vietnam task force, he announced to the State Department representatives: "We will begin with a ten-minute session for you to say what a dirty bum I am."

"It was a fight from the word go," Lansdale recalled many years later. "There seemed to be great resentment toward my mannerism, toward a mystique or something, which I didn't think I had."

Although Vietnam captured the president's attention early in his presidency, neighboring Laos was his first full-blown foreign policy crisis. On March 23, 1961, Kennedy held a televised press conference in the State Department auditorium to dramatically portray the recent military gains of the Pathet Lao, the local Communist forces. Using three large maps, he charged that in violation of Laotian neutrality, "large-scale" Soviet airlifts and North Vietnamese "combat specialists" had been providing ever-increasing support to the Pathet Lao: "It is this new dimension of externally supported warfare that creates the present grave problem."

Kennedy implicitly warned that the U.S. was prepared to go to war: "If these attacks do not stop, those who support a truly neutral Laos will have to consider their response. . . . No one should doubt our resolution on this point."

The "Land of the Million Elephants" was an unlikely spot for a Cold War confrontation. A divided kingdom presided over by three princes whose political leanings were respectively to the right, center, and left, the former French protectorate exhibited few characteristics of an integrated, sovereign nation. Perhaps the diverse Laotian population's only unifying trait

At a televised press conference, Kennedy pledged U.S. support for a truly neutral Laos. *(U.S. News & World Report)*

was a conspicuous lack of interest in killing one another. "I remember one report of the two Laotian sides leaving the battlefield to attend a water festival together," said Dean Rusk.

Kennedy's quest for a neutral Laos was a shift in policy from the Eisenhower administration, which viewed neutrality as a naive and even "immoral" concept. Secretary of State John Foster Dulles, who sought to surround the Soviet Union and China with nations allied to the United States, extended Western military protection to Laos—and South Vietnam—through the Southeast Asia Treaty Organization (SEATO), the collective security alliance formed after the Geneva conference. To combat internal subversion, the Eisenhower administration overtly and covertly undermined a coalition government.

By the end of the 1950s the U.S. government had pinned its anti-Communist hopes in Laos on Colonel Phoumi Nosavan, who with CIA support and approval took effective control of the government. A diminutive man with an affable smile and constantly running eyes, Phoumi was a different breed of Laotian: shrewd, tough, and opportunistic. A "right-wing strong man" in the parlance of the times, he was a particular favorite of U.S. military advisers in Laos, despite the fact that his anti-Communist fervor far exceeded his effectiveness as a combat commander.

The aggressive, overt U.S. support for Phoumi, combined with corruption in the Royal Lao Army, triggered a neutralist coup d'état in August of 1960. Later in the year, when threatened by Phoumi's march on Vientiane, the neutralists accepted a Soviet offer of military equipment. Abandoning the capital, they joined forces with the Pathet Lao, who were supported and directed by the North Vietnamese. In January of 1961, the Pathet Lao-neutralist forces seized the strategically located Plaine des Jarres in central Laos.

At a preinaugural meeting with Kennedy, President Eisenhower underscored the strategic importance of an independent, non-Communist Laos. Calling that country the "key to Southeast Asia," Eisenhower warned of inexorably toppling dominoes: "If Laos should fall to the Communists, then it would just be a question of time until South Vietnam, Cambodia, Thailand, and Burma would collapse." Adamantly opposed to Communist participation in a coalition government, the outgoing president advised the pursuit of a political settlement but warned that a military solution might be necessary. "The United States should accept this task with our allies, if we could persuade them, and alone if we could not," Eisenhower said. "Our unilateral intervention would be our last desperate hope."

The new president took a hard look at Laos and quickly concluded that it was a particularly unpromising area to engage U.S. military power. A logistical nightmare, the landlocked nation bordered on two Communist countries with powerful armies. Moreover, the Laotians' highly questionable fighting abilities made them an unreliable ally. "We came to the conclusion that we ought to try to get everybody out of Laos—ourselves, the French, the North Vietnamese, the Russians—get everybody out," Rusk said later, "and let the Laotians manage or mismanage their own country in their own way, confident they wouldn't kill each other off."

Although Kennedy was determined to seek a political solution, Pathet Lao victories threatened to make the question of Laotian neutrality academic. Supported by U.S. advisers, Phoumi's forces vainly tried to improve their bargaining position. In early March Deputy National Security Adviser Walt Rostow informed the president: "As we have feared, the Communists launched a probing offensive against Phoumi's men. Without much fight, our boys fell back beyond the crucial crossroads."

The failure of Kennedy's initial efforts in Laos triggered a "new phase" in the administration's planning that raised the specter of Western military intervention. Following Eisenhower's advice, Kennedy explored united action with America's SEATO allies. He quickly discovered that the British and French considered the "prospect of [a] large-scale injection [into] Laos of Western armed forces . . . appalling."

Unable to enlist European allies, Kennedy prepared for unilateral U.S. military intervention. A few days before his televised press conference, he authorized sending helicopters and a small force of Marines to Thailand, the first steps in a planned series of gradually escalating U.S. military actions. "In the short run," Rostow later reflected, "the problem was to orchestrate persuasively American military moves, which would make Kennedy's ultimate commitment credible, with the diplomatic process he wished to set in motion."

Walt Whitman Rostow, forty-four, was Kennedy's principal White House aide for Southeast Asia. Part of the president's Charles River brain trust, Rostow had formerly taught at the Massachusetts Institute of Technology. An authority on international development and economic history, he theorized that underdeveloped nations were particularly susceptible to Communist subversion and guerrilla warfare. "Communism," he declared, "is best understood as a disease of the transition to modernization."

Although an academic by profession, Rostow did not shrink from the practical application of military power. He chafed at the restrictions placed on the use of U.S. helicopters and Special Forces units in Vietnam. "It is somehow wrong to be developing these capabilities but not applying them in a crucial active theater," Rostow observed to the president. "In Knute

Rockne's old phrase, we are not saving them for the Junior Prom."

Rostow's academic manner sometimes clashed with the pragmatic style of the president. An admirer of succinctness, Kennedy scrawled on one Rostow memorandum he had found particularly abstruse: "too difficult to read." The White House aide, on the other hand, discovered the president's limited interest in theoretical speculation and long-range planning. According to Rostow, "[Kennedy's] most typical response to an idea was: 'What do you want me to do about it today?' "

In the midst of the unfolding Laotian drama, President Kennedy gave the green light to launch Operation Zapata, the CIA-sponsored invasion of Cuba. In the early hours of April 17, 1961, 1,500 Cuban exiles splashed ashore Blue Beach and Red Beach at *Bahía de Cochinos*—the Bay of Pigs. Although the attackers achieved tactical surprise, Castro's forces reacted with unanticipated speed and vigor. Within seventy-two hours, the exile army had been annihilated; the planned popular uprising against Castro failed to materialize.

A stinging defeat for Kennedy, the Bay of Pigs catastrophe dashed the new administration's ebullient confidence. The shaken president was privately furious with the CIA for advocating the plan and reportedly threatened to scatter the agency to the winds. In a pointed observation to Richard Bissell, chief of the Clandestine Service, Kennedy said that under a parliamentary system he would have to resign; under our system someone else would have to. Months later Bissell, Allen Dulles, and Deputy Director of Central Intelligence Charles Pearre Cabell quietly retired from the agency.

The Cuban disaster also jolted President Kennedy's confidence in the Joint Chiefs of Staff, who had approved the plan. The Chiefs, feeling unjustly blamed for an operation over which they had virtually no control, suffered a consequence that would plague them throughout the Vietnam War: unprecedented civilian involvement in operational details. "Never thereafter," reflected William Bundy, "would civilian leaders and advisers accept military and professional judgments without exploring them so fully as to make them, in effect, their own."

A more immediate result of the botched invasion was a new

look at the military planning for Laos. Earlier in the spring the Joint Chiefs had proposed a variety of conventional operations that revealed a disturbing lack of consensus on military strategy. After the Bay of Pigs, the Joint Chiefs were more unified but extremely conservative in their military advice on Laos. In general they urged an all-or-none approach to the use of force. "We cannot win a conventional war in Southeast Asia," declared Army Chief of Staff General George H. Decker. "If we go in, we should go in to win, and that means bombing Hanoi, China, and maybe even using nuclear weapons."

Admiral Arleigh Burke, Chief of Naval Operations, was of a similar mind: "We would have to throw in enough to win—perhaps the 'works.' "

The extreme alternatives implied by the Chiefs' proposals, either immediate Communist domination of Laos or nuclear war, further undermined Kennedy's confidence in them. "I never saw the American military less clear in mind, less helpful to a president than in the first four months of Kennedy's administration," Rostow later observed. "It had a distinctly unsettling effect on Kennedy in his first year."

The Laotian crisis of 1961 was finally resolved without the use of apocalyptic military action. The North Vietnamese, not wanting American intervention in Laos to interfere with their designs on South Vietnam, agreed to a cease-fire. On May 16 the Geneva conference reconvened to consider Laos. Circumstances had enabled Kennedy to avoid direct U.S. military involvement in Southeast Asia. Like the unanswered question of what he might have done in Vietnam had he lived, Kennedy's commitment to the forcible prevention of a Communist victory in Laos remains a mystery. According to White House aide Theodore Sorensen, the president's commitment "contained bluff with real determination in proportions he made known to no one."

The Laos negotiations and the Cuban fiasco raised doubts about Kennedy's leadership ability. Domestic critics charged that he had lacked resolution in dealing with communism. America's Asian allies could not understand Kennedy's apparent inability to cope with Communists only ninety miles from America. Moreover, pro-Western Asian leaders viewed

Laos as a symbolic test of strength that the Communists were clearly winning. To Kennedy administration officials, the eroding confidence in the president demanded a demonstration of American firmness, particularly in Southeast Asia. During the Laotian crisis, Attorney General Robert Kennedy had asked, "Where would be the best place to stand and fight in Southeast Asia?"

The answer was Vietnam.

"[President] Kennedy had decided, out of these first four months of experience, that if he had to engage American forces in Southeast Asia, he would do so in Vietnam rather than Laos," said Rostow. "Vietnam appeared to have relative advantages, which Kennedy once tersely ticked off to me in these terms: Relatively speaking, it was a more unified nation; its armed forces were larger and better trained; it had direct access to the sea; its geography permitted American air and naval power to be more easily brought to bear; there was the cushion of North Vietnam between South Vietnam and the Chinese border."

To demonstrate U.S. resolve, Kennedy sent Vice President Lyndon B. Johnson on a trip to Asia to meet with pro-Western leaders. Arriving in Saigon in May, Johnson delivered a presidential letter to Diem that pledged U.S. readiness "to join with you in an intensified endeavor to win the struggle against communism. . . . "

The vice president raised the possibility of sending U.S. combat troops to Vietnam. The Joint Chiefs of Staff had recommended that "President Diem be encouraged" to request U.S. forces. These units would help train ARVN, provide the support nucleus for future military operations, and establish a U.S. presence in Vietnam that would deter the North Vietnamese from invading the south. Although Diem welcomed additional military advisers and equipment, he did not want U.S. combat troops. To invite Western forces into Vietnam to defend the government would compromise his nationalist reputation and give credence to the Communist slogan "My-Diem," or American Diem.

Johnson believed that his talks with Diem and other Asian leaders had arrested but not restored lost confidence in U.S. commitments. He warned Kennedy that deeds must follow

Vice President Lyndon B. Johnson, left, doubted whether his visit with Diem restored lost South Vietnamese confidence in U.S. commitments. *(The Library of Congress, U.S. News & World Report Collection, 1952–72)*

words—and soon: "If these men I saw at your request were bankers, I would know—without bothering to ask—that there would be no further extensions on my note." (Johnson's curious choice of metaphors not only confused the identities of the lender and borrowers in Southeast Asia, but also suggested the degree to which U.S. officials had become prisoners of their client states.)

While the vice president toured Southeast Asia, Kennedy formally approved several tangible military, political, economic, psychological, and covert actions designed "to prevent Communist domination in South Vietnam [and] to create in that country a viable and increasingly democratic society." By later standards of U.S. involvement, the authorized military steps were modest: an immediate 100-man increase in the U.S. Military Assistance Advisory Group (MAAG) and the deployment of a 400-man Special Forces group. The president also instructed the Pentagon to determine "the size and composition of forces which would be desirable in the case of a possible commitment of U.S. forces to Vietnam."

In a June 9 letter to Kennedy, Diem followed through on Vice President Johnson's suggestion that he list his most urgent needs. (In an earlier letter, Diem had needled: "I was most deeply gratified by this gracious gesture by your distinguished Vice-President, particularly as we have not become accustomed to being asked for our own views as to our needs.") Diem, greatly troubled by the "threat from southern Laos," sought a 100,000-man increase in his own army. He estimated this program would cost $175 million and require a "considerable expansion of the United States Military Advisory Group."

Kennedy, deferring a response, replied noncommittally: ". . . [T]he Department of Defense is urgently studying your request."

Before further expanding the growing American commitment to Vietnam, the president and his advisers wanted answers to a number of questions: Would an increase in ARVN be militarily effective? Had Diem reformed his chaotic military command structure? Was he making a serious effort to win the allegiance of the peasantry? "[W]e must find out whether the foundation exists for enlarging this struggle," Rostow wrote to Kennedy. "We must know whether we have ground beneath our feet—or, at least, how much ground. I confess that I am distinctly uneasy about the position in Vietnam and the grasp our men there have upon it."

A CERTAIN DILEMMA

The attack began at 1:00 A.M., September 18, 1961. Three battalions of the People's Liberation Armed Forces (PLAF), more commonly known as the Viet Cong, stormed the low earthen rampart and tangled barbed wire surrounding Phuoc Vinh, a small provincial capital sixty miles north of Saigon. Armed with rifles and machetes, the 1,000-man force immediately overwhelmed the 50-man Civil Guard company that garrisoned the village. Forty-two Phuoc Vinh residents died in the attack, and another thirty-five were wounded.

Two ARVN ranger companies patrolling near the provincial capital were of little help to the villagers. Confronted by the superior force, the rangers retreated into the jungle. Their commander later claimed he "intended to ambush the guerrillas when they withdrew."

The attackers captured 100 rifles and 6,000 rounds of ammunition, and they freed 250 suspected Communist prisoners. Before returning to their jungle redoubt in War Zone D, a notorious Communist stronghold since the French–Viet Minh War, the PLAF staged a trial in the marketplace. The province chief and his assistant were found guilty of "crimes against the people" and publicly beheaded.

Although they held the village for only a few hours, the Viet Cong scored a spectacular victory at Phuoc Vinh. By demonstrating the Diem government's limited ability to protect the peasantry, they had advanced their strategy of depressing civilian and military morale. Vietnamese Communist leaders believed that a combination of guerrilla warfare and political subversion would ultimately spark a "general uprising" against the Diem regime.

Communist strategy and tactics were largely dictated by the military weakness of the PLAF, which in the fall of 1961 included some 17,000 conventionally organized main-force units and an unknown number of guerrilla and local militia forces. Directed by Hanoi, the insurgents were almost entirely local recruits. The other units were cadre personnel who had infiltrated from North Vietnam through the network of mountain trails in southern Laos known as the Ho Chi Minh Trail. Despite limited numbers and few modern weapons, the PLAF managed to keep Diem's army off balance. In a form of military judo, the Communist forces frequently provoked heavily armed ARVN units into firing on the rural population they were ostensibly protecting. War-weary peasants described their plight as being "on the anvil and under the hammer."

The Viet Cong also used ruthless and selective terror to advance their strategy. To prove their solidarity with the peasants, the Communists assassinated cruel and corrupt local government officials. The insurgents' principal targets, however, were effective anti-Communist officials and citizens. "[The Viet Cong] bumped off exactly the person who was blocking their success in the villages," recalled Charles Maechling, Jr., staff director of the National Security Council [NSC] Special Group (Counterinsurgency). "One very savage thing they did was bumping off refractory schoolteachers who didn't peddle their line."

Whereas military operations and terrorism were the Viet Cong's iron fist, political warfare was the velvet glove. Seeking willing supporters rather than cowed subjects, the PLAF stole supplies when necessary but paid fair prices when possible. Land redistribution in "liberated" areas helped the Viet Cong recruit peasants, who generally operated in their native area. Moreover, simple effective propaganda manipulated the rural population's xenophobia. A Communist political operative might assemble the villagers, break an egg into a bowl, and deliver a parable about Western "imperialism" and Viet Cong invincibility: "We are yellow, surrounded by white." While beating the egg with chopsticks, he would declare, "This is how we

Communist forces traversing the rugged Ho Chi Minh Trail—a journey that in the early 1960s took six months. *(Vietnam News Agency)*

will win." With great effect, the operative then revealed the yellow scrambled egg.

Confident of eventual victory through a blend of political and military struggle, the Central Office for South Vietnam (COSVN), Hanoi's southern headquarters, warned party members and the armed forces "to avoid going down the road to complete war." Communist leaders were wary of U.S. military intervention—"a complex problem which we must follow and find ways to limit, guard against and be prepared to cope with in a timely fashion"—but they believed that fear of Russian and Chinese countermoves and disapproval by America's European allies would deter such a step. In October of 1961 a COSVN resolution wishfully observed: "[T]he ability of U.S. imperialism to send troops to directly intervene in the South has many limitations."

Contrary to the expectations of Vietnamese Communists, the U.S. government was busily preparing plans to dispatch troops to Southeast Asia. To Kennedy administration officials, the Phuoc Vinh attack was part of a disturbing trend indicating the war's escalating scale and tempo. In September the number of Communist attacks was triple the average of previous months. And despite substantial reported combat losses, Viet Cong main-force units had increased by 30 percent in only three months. On October 5 a Special National Intelligence Estimate noted Communist control of the Ca Mau peninsula on Vietnam's southern tip and predicted that the PLAF would seek to liberate another area in the Central Highlands: "It is probable that the Bloc intends to build up the eastern part of South Laos, improving the roads, mountain trails, and airfields, as a major supply channel to support a stepped up Viet Cong campaign in north and central Vietnam."

That same day White House aide Walt Rostow summarized for President Kennedy the growing official consensus for some form of military action in Vietnam: "We must move quite radically to avoid perhaps slow but total defeat. The sense of this town is that, with southern Laos open, Diem simply cannot cope."

Rostow suggested deploying troops along South Vietnam's 250-mile border with Laos. Although unsure of its military effectiveness, he believed a border force would free ARVN to pursue guerrillas, discourage North Vietnam from invading the south, and hearten Diem. Most importantly, Rostow speculated that a U.S. military presence in Vietnam could be a bargaining counter in negotiations with the Communists. "If we go in now," he concluded, "the costs—human and otherwise—are likely to be less than if we wait."

At Kennedy's request, the Defense Department passed the Rostow proposal to the Joint Chiefs of Staff for a military evaluation. They concluded it was "not feasible." Troops deployed along several hundred miles of border, predicted the Chiefs, would either be attacked piecemeal or bypassed completely. Moreover, soldiers on the Laotian border would be weakly positioned should North Vietnam or China intervene. The JCS also shot down a civilian-inspired plan to station a border force along the 17th parallel, the dividing line between North and South Vietnam. They observed that this border was not a principal infiltration route for the Communists. Labeling the proposal "militarily unsound," the Chiefs speculated that the North Vietnamese might interpret it as preparation for an invasion and try to destroy these troops.

In their analysis of the civilian plans, the JCS repeated their conviction that the defense of South Vietnam must be viewed in the larger context of Southeast Asia: "[A]ny concept which deals with the defense of Southeast Asia that does not include all or a substantial part of Laos is, from a military standpoint, unsound."

Instead of a force within South Vietnam, the Chiefs recommended a "concentrated effort in Laos." Dusting off a contingency plan they had recommended during the previous spring's Laotian crisis, the JCS urged the implementation of SEATO Plan 5, which would deploy troops in the Mekong Valley in Laos. Originally designed to shield Thailand, this plan could be modified to cut across the Laotian panhandle and sever the North Vietnamese infiltration routes into the south.

Aware of Kennedy's extreme reluctance to send troops into Laos, the Joint Chiefs halfheartedly recommended an alternative proposal if SEATO Plan 5 were "politically unacceptable." The new plan, termed "less desirable" by the JCS, called for placing 10,000 to 12,000 troops in South Vietnam's Central Highlands astride active Communist infiltration routes and operational targets. The Chiefs did not believe their alternative proposal would be very effective, but they considered it preferable to either of the civilian plans.

The day after the Chiefs submitted their recommendations, Deputy Under Secretary of State U. Alexis Johnson advanced yet another suggestion for committing U.S. combat troops to South Vietnam. Entitled "A Concept for Intervention in Vietnam," this plan blended Rostow's border patrol force with the

JCS proposal for deploying troops in the Central Highlands. Johnson, director of the interagency Vietnam task force and a former ambassador to Thailand, conceded that even if Communist infiltration through Laos were sharply reduced, "there is no assurance that . . . the GVN [South Vietnamese government] will in the foreseeable future be able to defeat the Viet Cong." Envisioning an initial commitment of 22,000 troops, he warned that more would be necessary: "The ultimate force requirements cannot be estimated with any precision."

On Wednesday, October 11, 1961, the president and his senior advisers reviewed the rapidly multiplying plans for sending U.S. combat forces to Southeast Asia. Skeptical of all the military proposals, Kennedy made no major decisions that day. He approved the deployment of an Air Force "Jungle Jim" squadron to train South Vietnamese airmen in counterinsurgency tactics and authorized U.S. advisers to accompany ARVN guerrillas on operations against selected targets in Laos. Kennedy also ordered a delegation of U.S. officials to proceed to South Vietnam and recommend a military and political course of action. Included in the group were Walt Rostow, General Lansdale, and representatives from the State Department, Pentagon, and CIA. The leader of the mission, and the man personally responsible for its recommendations, was the president's military representative, General Maxwell Davenport Taylor.

Max Taylor was Kennedy's kind of general. They not only agreed on many substantive military matters, but the army general also possessed style, an attribute greatly admired by the president. "He talked with an elegance unexpected in a soldier," a State Department official observed, "and he looked exactly as a general should—clean-cut, scholarly, handsome, and resolute."

Born in 1901, Taylor began his distinguished military career at West Point, where he graduated fourth in a class of 102 cadets. During World War II he commanded the 101st Airborne Division and parachuted into Normandy on D day. After the war, Taylor served as superintendent of West Point, commander of the Eighth Army in Korea, and, finally, Army chief of staff. Within the Pentagon, he waged a lonely war against the Eisenhower administration's New Look strategy. Seeking "more bang for the buck," the New Look emphasized nuclear weapons, at the expense of conventional forces, to deter or defeat communism. Taylor, noting the limited utility of nuclear weapons during the Korean and Indochinese conflicts, championed a strategy of "flexible response," which he defined as a capability "for coping with anything from general atomic war to infiltrations such as threaten Laos."

The Eisenhower administration turned a deaf ear to General Taylor's proposals. In the twenty-three split JCS decisions during his term, Taylor found himself on the losing side twenty times. "While I never particularly minded the conflict with my Pentagon peers," Taylor reflected, "I felt keenly the increasing coolness of my relations with the president and regretted being a disappointment to him as I was sure I was."

Taylor retired from the army in 1959 and wrote *An Uncertain Trumpet*, a critical analysis of the Eisenhower administration's defense policies. Published in 1960, the book attracted the attention of presidential candidate John Kennedy, who praised it as "most persuasive" and helpful in "shap[ing] my own thinking." Taylor joined the Kennedy administration in April of 1961. Three days after the Cuban brigade surrendered at the Bay of Pigs, the president asked him to investigate the causes of the operation's failure. With the help of Robert Kennedy, Allen Dulles, and Admiral Arleigh Burke, Taylor interviewed fifty witnesses, including virtually every top administration official. He delivered a single copy of the Bay of Pigs report to the president on June 13, 1961. In addition to analyzing the military causes of failure, the report criticized the ad hoc task forces favored by Kennedy, who believed the advantages in flexibility and timeliness outweighed the disadvantages of such a makeshift decision-making process. Taylor and his colleagues urged the formation of a permanent committee to guide and coordinate Cold War strategy. Tentatively named the Strategic Resources Group, this committee would consist of representatives from State, Defense, CIA, and a chairman appointed by the president.

Although Kennedy politely ignored this recommendation, he asked Taylor to serve as the new director of Central Intelligence. The general turned down the job, offering to put his military experience at the president's disposal. A short time later, Kennedy appointed him to the newly created position of military representative to the president—a temporary slot for Taylor until the expiration of General Lyman L. Lemnitzer's term as chairman of the Joint Chiefs of Staff. As a White House aide, Taylor would advise the president on military and intelligence matters, with particular emphasis on Berlin and Southeast Asia.

Taylor's new responsibilities cut across the turf of several U.S. officials. The very existence of his position was a slap in the face to the Joint Chiefs, whose principal responsibility was advising the president on military matters. Some White House staffers took a dim view of an additional voice competing for the president's ear on national security affairs. Critical of Taylor's devotion to form and method, they charged that the general spent more time making organizational charts than contributing to policy.

But to Kennedy, Max Taylor was a reassuring source of military advice. The president could be certain that the hard-nosed military intellectual would not make unwanted recommendations about employing nuclear weapons in Southeast Asia. Kennedy could also rely on Taylor's sensitivity to the president's reluctance to commit U.S. combat troops to South Vietnam. In a letter to Taylor prior to his October trip, Kennedy pointedly instructed the general to "bear in mind that the initial responsibility for the effective maintenance of the independence of South Vietnam rests with the people and government of that country."

Before leaving for Saigon on October 15, 1961, General Taylor assembled the mission members in his office. He explained that the president had asked for his personal views and advice about Vietnam. While inviting his colleagues to assist in preparing the trip report, Taylor stressed that the final conclusions and recommendations would be his own. The other officials' views would be included in appendices to the report. During the flight to Saigon, he asked each member of the task force to list the most useful contributions he could make. With the help of Walt Rostow, Taylor formalized each official's responsibilities, a situation the White House aide later compared to "two professors going over the outlines for a series of student term papers."

One of their pupils was Ed Lansdale. The Air Force general compiled a list of typically innovative military, political, and psychological suggestions. One idea he wanted to explore was the "human defoliation" of the hardwood forests in War Zone D. Instead of using chemical defoliants, Lansdale suggested awarding a timber concession to a Nationalist Chinese firm that would employ veterans and arm them. "They might very well have to fight to get to the trees," said Lansdale, "so they would clean up the Viet Cong along the way."

General Taylor took a dim view of the suggestion. "Lansdale was an idea man," Taylor later recalled, "and he could turn out ideas faster than you could pick them up off the floor, but I was never impressed with their feasibility."

During the flight, Taylor informed Lansdale that he would not be among the mission members visiting Diem. "Well, I'm an old friend of Diem's," Lansdale protested. "I can't go to Vietnam without seeing him. I'll probably see him alone. Is there anything you want me to ask him?"

Taylor, who believed it was his job to consult with Diem—and without an intermediary—refused to discuss the matter further.

After stopping at Commander-in-Chief Pacific (CINCPAC) headquarters in Hawaii for a briefing by Admiral Harry D. Felt, commander of all U.S. forces in the Pacific, the Taylor mission landed in Saigon, a city suffering from a palpable collapse of morale. South Vietnam's Mekong Delta had recently suffered a serious flood that destroyed hundreds of thousands of tons of rice and an unknown quantity of livestock. And while the country reeled from the natural disaster, Communist terrorists had kidnapped, tortured, and murdered a well-known South Vietnamese military officer.

Diem's personal secretary was among the Vietnamese officials welcoming the American delegation. He approached Lansdale and invited him to dinner at the palace. Conveniently unable to inform Taylor, who was talking with reporters, Lansdale told Rostow about the invitation and left for the palace. Diem, Nhu, and Lansdale spent much of the evening disussing the possibility of introducing U.S. combat troops into Vietnam. One week earlier Diem had indicated to the American embassy his interest in U.S. combat units. According to a South Vietnamese official, Diem wanted a "symbolic" U.S. military presence near the Demilitarized Zone separating North and South Vietnam. At dinner Diem asked Lansdale whether he should request U.S. troops. The American, using characteristic indirection, answered the South Vietnamese president's question with questions: "What do you want U.S. troops for? Are things that bad here?"

During the evening, Lansdale noticed a change in the relationship between Diem and Nhu since his last visit to Vietnam. When the American questioned Diem, Nhu would frequently answer for his brother. "It got obnoxious after a time," recalled Lansdale. "I finally said to Diem, 'Can't the two of us talk together? Your brother can be in on this, but is he running things or are you?' "

Although Diem did not acknowledge it, Ngo Dinh Nhu had increased his already considerable power since the abortive paratroopers' coup d'état. Weary of the constant plotting against him, Diem had given his brother a free hand in rooting out suspected opponents of the regime. Nhu had responded with a vengeance, stepping up domestic intelligence activities and imprisoning dissidents. "It shocked me to see Nhu taking over the place," Lansdale said later. "That worried me."

The day after Lansdale's meeting with Diem, General Taylor and Walt Rostow conducted the mission's first official action, a call on the president at Independence Palace. Purring French in somnolent tones and chain-smoking cigarettes, Diem delivered a monologue about Vietnam and its people. Toward the end of the four-hour meeting, Taylor said that he understood there had been discussions of introducing U.S. combat forces into South Vietnam. Why, he asked, had the South Vietnamese government reversed its long-standing opposition to foreign troops?

"Because of [the] Laos situation," Diem replied with unusual succinctness.

Diem informed his guests that the Vietnamese people were worried by the lack of a formal U.S. commitment; they feared the U.S. would abandon them. At no time during the meeting did Diem directly ask for U.S. combat troops. "He avoided the subject until near the end of the interview," according to Taylor, "and then dealt with it with deliberate ambiguity." The

Americans left the meeting with the impression that the inscrutable South Vietnamese president wanted a defense treaty with the United States and preparations for introducing combat forces should they become necessary.

During his visit, Taylor met with Major General Duong Van Minh, one of Diem's harshest military critics. Athletic, barrel-chested, and nearly six feet tall, the forty-five-year-old general was known to all as "Big" Minh. Trained by the French, Minh fought against the Japanese during World War II. Reportedly, an enemy soldier's rifle butt had mangled his front teeth, giving him a distinctive gapped-tooth smile. As army field commander, Minh had an imposing title but no direct command responsibility. Diem and Nhu, fearing a coup d'état masterminded by the charismatic general, were determined to prevent him from directly leading troops.

In his meeting with Taylor, "Big" Minh bitterly denounced President Diem's interference in military matters. Not only had the Viet Cong grown alarmingly, declared Minh, but the Vietnamese armed forces were also losing the support of the people. "I was somewhat startled by his willingness to criticize his president to a foreigner like me," Taylor later reflected. "I had not yet acquired experience with the Vietnamese bent for running down their closest associates to the casual passer-by."

After touring the Demilitarized Zone and the flood-ravaged Mekong Delta, General Taylor and Walt Rostow made a final visit to Diem. Taylor summarized his initial conclusions, advancing them as personal ideas. On the crucial question of U.S. troops, he suggested introducing an American "flood relief task force" into Vietnam. Such a force, said the general, might contain engineering, medical, signal, and transportation personnel as well as combat troops for the protection of the relief force.

To Taylor, a flood relief task force seemed to offer several advantages. It would demonstrate to friends and foes the U.S. commitment to South Vietnam. At the same time the task force's humanitarian mission would avoid the suggestion of responsibility for the country's security. Thus, the task force could withdraw from Vietnam after completing its mission without a loss of U.S. prestige. Although Taylor mentioned no specific figures to Diem, the general cabled Washington: "The strength of the force I have in mind [is] on the order of 6–8,000 troops."

President Diem, apparently sharing Taylor's reasoning, "expressed satisfaction" with the idea. Although there was no formal proposal or agreement, Diem assumed U.S. troops would soon be arriving in Vietnam. The Taylor mission left Vietnam on October 25. After stops in Thailand and Hong Kong, the U.S. officials arrived at Clark Air Force Base in the Philippines. Determined to return to Washington with a finished report, Taylor and his colleagues drafted their papers at the summer capital of Baguio, a cool resort 5,000 feet above the steamy tropical lowlands.

On November 1 General Taylor summarized his conclusions and recommendations in two top-secret, "eyes only" cables to President Kennedy. South Vietnam, Taylor wrote, suffered from a "double crisis in confidence." The population doubted both U.S. resolve in Southeast Asia and the Diem government's ability to defeat the Communists. The general recommended "a massive joint effort" between the United States and South Vietnam to mobilize the Diem government to cope with the insurgency. Proposing a shift in the American-Vietnamese relationship to "limited partnership," Taylor suggested inserting U.S. civilian and military officials in all levels of the South Vietnamese government and armed forces.

Taylor also amplified his proposal for deploying a flood relief task force to Vietnam. He emphasized that "this force is not proposed to clear the jungles and forests of Viet Cong guerrillas. . . . However, the U.S. troops may be called upon to engage in combat to protect themselves, their working parties, and the area in which they live." Candidly laying out the risks involved, the general warned that sending troops to South Vietnam would further commit American prestige to the country's uncertain fortunes and risk escalation into a major war: "If the first contingent is not enough to accomplish the necessary results, it will be difficult to resist the pressure to reinforce."

Despite these "disadvantages," Taylor optimistically, if not very presciently, concluded: "The risks of backing into a major land war by way of SVN are present but not impressive. NVN is extremely vulnerable to conventional bombing, a weakness which should be exploited diplomatically in convincing Hanoi to lay off SVN."

On Friday, November 3, the Taylor mission returned to Washington and presented its final report to the president. Kennedy thanked the task force members for their report but deferred any decisions until the government had digested their recommendations. After the meeting, he asked to speak privately with General Lansdale, whose return to Vietnam Diem had specifically requested. Although many U.S. officials agreed that Lansdale would be of unique value in Vietnam, the president had more important work for him. "Drop everything else you're doing," said Kennedy. "I want you to work on Cuba."

Later that month the president appointed Lansdale chief of operations for Mongoose, the ill-fated covert attempt to "get rid of" Fidel Castro. Lansdale eventually returned to Vietnam in the summer of 1965 as a special assistant to Ambassador Henry Cabot Lodge. By then the war had long since passed the point where his special talents might have made a major contribution to U.S. policy. To some of the younger CIA officers he seemed a pathetic figure, out of touch with the "young Turks" who ran the government. Many Vietnamese, however, remained in awe of the covert operator. In early 1966, more than two years after the assassination of Diem, General Huynh Van Cao pulled the American aside and said that it was now safe to bring the South Vietnamese president out of hiding. Certain that Lansdale had somehow safely stashed him away, General Cao asked: "When are you going to reveal Ngo Dinh Diem?"

As Taylor had anticipated, his recommendation to send a U.S. military task force to Vietnam triggered a sharp debate in Washington. No one in the government cared much for the half-in, half-out nature of the proposal. Secretary of State Dean Rusk questioned the value of a "relative handful" of American troops if Diem refused to reform administratively and politically. Reluctant to commit additional U.S. prestige to a "losing horse," Rusk believed the critical question was "whether Diem is prepared to give us something worth supporting."

Defense Secretary McNamara and the Joint Chiefs had a

different objection to the Taylor proposal. Admitting that an 8,000-man task force would be of "great help" to Diem, they doubted whether these troops would convince the Communists that "we mean business." McNamara and the Chiefs would support the Taylor recommendation only if the U.S. pledged to defend South Vietnam "by the necessary military action," a commitment that Pentagon officials estimated could involve as many as 205,000 ground troops should North Vietnam and China overtly intervene. (In light of the inability of more than 500,000 U.S. troops to defeat the Viet Cong, the figure of 205,000 might seem absurdly optimistic. CINCPAC contingency plans, however, called for these forces to be armed with tactical nuclear weapons.)

But perhaps the man least enthusiastic about the Taylor troop recommendation was the president himself. To John Kennedy, committing U.S. combat troops to Vietnam appeared extremely dangerous. It might not only unhinge the Laotian ceasefire but might also risk escalating the Vietnamese conflict into a full-scale ground war. Furthermore, pulling a military task force out of South Vietnam might be harder than General Taylor had suggested. "If we commit 6–8,000 troops and then pull them out when the going gets rough," one White House aide noted, "we will be finished in Vietnam and probably all of Southeast Asia."

President Kennedy also disliked the idea of sending combat troops to Vietnam to boost the morale of Southeast Asians. "They want a force of American troops," said Kennedy in early November. "They say it's necessary in order to restore confidence and maintain morale. But it will be just like Berlin. The troops will march in; the bands will play; the crowds will cheer; and in four days everyone will have forgotten. Then we will be told we have to send in more troops. It's like taking a drink. The effect wears off, and you have to take another."

The mere mention of the gloomier implications of the Taylor proposal could spark an angry presidential reaction. When Under Secretary of State George Ball warned Kennedy that the general's recommendation would lead to sending hundreds of thousands of U.S. soldiers to Vietnam, the president snapped with uncharacteristic sharpness: "George, you're crazier than hell. That just isn't going to happen."

Under Secretary of State George Ball. *(U.S. News & World Report)*

Despite Kennedy's aversion to the Taylor troop recommendation, the consequences of a Communist victory in Vietnam seemed equally unacceptable. The rest of Southeast Asia would probably "move to complete accommodation with Communism, if not formal incorporation in the Communist bloc," predicted Rusk and McNamara. "The loss of South Vietnam would not only destroy SEATO but would undermine the credibility of American commitments elsewhere."

The secretaries of state and defense also warned Kennedy of domestic political repercussions: "[The] loss of South Vietnam would stimulate bitter domestic controversies in the United States and would be seized upon by extreme elements to divide the country and harass the administration."

On November 11 Rusk and McNamara presented the president with a joint memorandum that conveniently charted a course through the unacceptable Vietnam alternatives facing Kennedy. A Pentagon analyst later speculated the memorandum was "drawn up to the president's specifications." Urging a U.S. commitment to prevent "the fall of South Vietnam to communism," the secretaries of state and defense recommended immediate military, economic, and political assistance identical to Taylor's concept of "limited partnership." Acknowledging that U.S. combat units might be necessary in the future, their recommendations included *preparing* plans for sending troops—a proposal that tacitly killed the Taylor troop recommendation.

President Kennedy accepted the Rusk-McNamara recommendations virtually verbatim. Approving a "sharply increased joint effort" with the Diem government, Kennedy agreed to send U.S. military advisers to "show [the South Vietnamese] how the job should be done—not tell them or do it for them." At the time neither Kennedy nor his senior advisers realized the exact number of soldiers involved in the decision. Ironically, after refusing to commit 8,000 troops to Vietnam, the president embarked on a course that would send nearly 16,000 American military men to Vietnam within the next two years.

Although the troop debate in Washington had been temporarily settled, the secretaries of state and defense had raised "a certain dilemma" that would persist throughout the decade: "If there is a strong South Vietnamese effort, they [combat troops] may not be needed; if there is not such an effort, United States forces could not accomplish their mission in the midst of an apathetic or hostile population."

In other words, if the U.S. had to send combat troops, the guerrilla war would already be lost.

Frederick E. Nolting, Jr., the American ambassador to South Vietnam, first learned of the presidential decisions arising from the Taylor mission on November 15, 1961. A top-secret, "eyes only" State Department cable conveyed the negative decision on U.S. combat troops and informed Nolting that Diem must make administrative, political, and social reforms "recognized as having real substance and meaning." Moreover, the U.S. government intended "to share in the decision-making processes in the political, economic, and military fields as they affected the security situation."

Nolting had earlier advised against a similar proposal from Washington. Official American participation in South Vietnamese decision making, he predicted, would be interpreted by both Diem and the population "as handing over" the government to the United States.

A career Foreign Service officer, fifty-year-old "Fritz" Nolting had received B.A., M.A., and Ph.D. degrees from the University of Virginia. After serving in the Navy during World War II, he held a variety of diplomatic posts, principally in Europe. By the time of his February 1961 appointment as ambassador to Vietnam, Nolting had earned a reputation as a "comer" in the State Department. "Fritz was considered at that time as sort of one of the fair-haired fellows," recalled one State Department official. "He had a hell of a good record in NATO and elsewhere."

Ambassador Nolting arrived in Saigon in May of 1961 and began carrying out his instructions to improve the strained U.S. relations with President Diem. Like General Lansdale, Nolting believed U.S. influence on Diem was proportional to his confidence in U.S. support. The ambassador quickly discovered that he liked and admired Diem, who seemed "a man dedicated to high principles." Sympathizing with Diem's reluctance to undertake reforms during a war, Nolting urged Washington to strike "a very careful balance . . . between the ideal and possible."

Notwithstanding his fondness and sympathy for Diem, Nolting recognized the South Vietnamese president's administrative weakness and political vulnerability. "It seems to me clear that in some way the Diem government must make a 'breakthrough' to regain popular support," the ambassador warned. "If the situation drags on in an inconclusive manner for many more months, either a military coup, or an open proclamation of a Communist government and widespread civil war, is likely."

Complying with his November 15 instructions, Ambassador Nolting sought an "immediate appointment" with Diem, who interrupted a trip in central Vietnam to hear the results of the Taylor mission. Nolting began his demarche by stressing the theme of partnership and warning of the "far-reaching and difficult measures on both sides" required to defeat the Communists. As had been anticipated by U.S. officials, Diem asked first about combat troops. Nolting responded negatively, adding that the stepped-up American advisory effort would commit "a substantial number of U.S. military personnel for operational duties in Vietnam."

You realize, said Diem, the American "proposals involved the question of the responsibility of the government of Vietnam. Vietnam [does] not want to be a protectorate."

"This [is] well understood," replied Nolting. "We . . . do not wish to make it one."

The ambassador emphasized that the increased American assistance would depend upon South Vietnamese reforms. Diem parried unconvincingly by claiming that his government was "constantly in the process of making reforms." Reminding Nolting there was a war to be won, Diem implied that major reforms would sabotage the fight against the Communists: "[The] object [is] to restore order not to create disorder."

The South Vietnamese president then launched into his standard monologue about the debilitating effects of eighty years of French colonial rule on the Vietnamese population and the dearth of qualified people who would accept responsibility for its leadership. Nolting concluded the two-and-one-half-hour meeting by urging Diem to respond to the U.S. proposals as soon as possible.

"On the whole, I am not discouraged at Diem's reaction," Nolting cabled the State Department. "In fact, he took our proposals rather better than I had expected."

On the same day as Nolting's meeting with Diem, an imposing U.S. official much less sympathetic to the South Vietnamese president arrived in Saigon: John Kenneth Galbraith, the six-foot-eight-inch American ambassador to India. A longstanding friend of President Kennedy, Galbraith had been in Washington during the debate over General Taylor's recommendations and had volunteered to return to New Delhi by way of Saigon.

An economist, teacher, and author, Galbraith had first met John Kennedy at Harvard University, where the former was a young tutor, the latter an undergraduate. During his Senate career, Kennedy occasionally solicited Galbraith's advice on economic legislation. A Kennedy floor manager at the 1960 Democratic convention, Galbraith contributed drafts to the president's inaugural address and his first State of the Union message. Iconoclastic in economic and political thought, Galbraith viewed his ambassadorial appointment with a mixture of self-aggrandizement and self-deprecation: "Kennedy, I've always believed, was pleased to have me in his administration but at a suitable distance such as India. This saved him from a too close identification with my now extensively articulated economic views."

Ambassador Galbraith quickly established himself as a scathing critic of U.S. military intervention in Southeast Asia. He considered the president's decision to seek the neutralization of Laos as the best of bad alternatives. In a May 1961 letter to Kennedy, Galbraith declared: "As a military ally the entire Laos nation is clearly inferior to a battalion of conscientious objectors from World War I."

The ambassador also opposed sending U.S. troops to Vietnam. Characterizing General Taylor's proposed flood relief task force as "exceedingly half-baked" intervention, Galbraith sarcastically predicted: "Once there, they would use a shovel with one hand and deal with the guerrillas with the other."

After preparatory research in Washington, a military briefing at CINCPAC headquarters, and three days in Saigon, Galbraith cabled his analysis to the president. Disturbed by the heavy military emphasis in Diem's struggle against the insurgents, he observed: "A comparatively well-equipped army with paramilitary formations numbering a quarter million men is facing a maximum of fifteen to eighteen thousand lightly armed men. If this were equality, the United States would hardly be safe against the Sioux."

To Galbraith, the "key and inescapable" cause of Communist success in South Vietnam was "the ineffectuality" of the Diem government: "He holds far too much power in his own hands, employs his army badly, has no intelligence organization worthy of the name, has arbitrary or incompetent subordinates in the provinces, and some achievements notwithstanding, has a poor economic policy."

Terming Kennedy's current policy a "hopeless game," Galbraith argued that it was "politically naive" to expect reforms from Diem. Self-preservation, reasoned the ambassador, would prevent Diem from relinquishing power to his military and civilian enemies. As a policy alternative, Galbraith advocated radical political surgery: ". . . [T]he only solution must be to drop Diem."

Galbraith optimistically speculated that "dropping Diem" would be neither "difficult nor unduly dangerous." Although generally opposed to covert action, the ambassador recommended "mak[ing] it quietly clear that we are withdrawing our support from him as an individual. His day would then, I believe, be over. While no one can promise a safe transaction, we are now married to failure."

Most U.S. officials opposed Galbraith's extreme prescription. William Jorden, a State Department representative on the Taylor mission and author of the trip report on South Vietnam's internal politics, conceded that "the arguments in favor of a change, almost any change, are impressive" but warned: "Engineering or backing a coup involves large risks in both the local situation and in the broader framework of world opinion. It is not something we do well. It has little to recommend itself."

Galbraith, who later in the decade became a prominent antiwar spokesman, modestly admitted in his memoirs that his November 1961 observations to President Kennedy were not completely prescient. Characterizing himself as "the victim of my own evasion," Galbraith rationalized, almost apologetically, his unwillingness to urge a total U.S. withdrawal from Vietnam: "I came close to saying, 'Let the insurgents take over.' But that no one could say. Such an admission was all that those arguing for intervention needed to put me in my place. A sell out. My effectiveness would be at an end."

Diem's hostility toward Ambassador Nolting's demarche surfaced slowly and indirectly. On November 20 an inquiry about follow-up discussions with the South Vietnamese president triggered a long and gloomy appraisal of the American proposals by Nguyen Dinh Thuan, secretary of state to the presidency and the most important member of the South Vietnamese cabinet. To Thuan, Diem seemed "very sad and disappointed" and acted as if the U.S. had asked for great concessions in

Vietnamese sovereignty in exchange for little additional help. Thuan warned Nolting that Diem "would not accept anything that looked to [the] public as a sweeping reorganization under U.S. pressure."

Thuan's pessimism did not seem too serious to Nolting, who suspected that it was merely a negotiating ploy. "I think my best tactic is to wait a few days for Diem's response," the ambassador cabled Washington. "I do not want to seem to be pressing him to buy our proposals."

Four days later the Diem government responded to Nolting's reticence with a series of shrill newspaper articles attacking conditional American assistance. "Vietnam Not a Guinea Pig for Capitalist Imperialism to Experiment On," read one editorial headline. "Is It Time to Reexamine U.S.–Vietnamese Cooperation?"

The ambassador considered the anti-American newspaper campaign "foolish and dangerous" but was not completely surprised by the antagonistic articles. The CIA had already reported Brother Nhu's order to the director general of information shifting the South Vietnamese propaganda line to criticism of the United States. On November 26 Nolting met with Diem to protest the newspaper attacks. He pointed out that the articles bore a clear resemblance to what he understood to be the views of the president's brother. Nolting warned that a continuation of this "emotional, incorrect, and damaging line" would complicate, and perhaps make impossible, the joint effort against the Communists.

Diem denied any government involvement in the current newspaper campaign. However, he said, the articles did reflect the "latent feelings" of most Vietnamese toward conditional American assistance. Throughout the conversation, the South Vietnamese president declared that the "quid pro quo" nature of U.S. aid "played right into the hands of the Communists" by giving them "a monopoly on nationalism."

The public rift between the two governments triggered intensified South Vietnamese criticism of Diem and a new round of coup rumors. Forewarned of the hostile articles, "Big" Minh had sought out the U.S. Army attaché on the first day of the anti-American press campaign. Reportedly fearing Nhu's agents more than the Viet Cong, Minh arrived with a bodyguard. The

Vietnamese general urged the U.S. to take a firm stand with
Diem. He characterized the recent military reorganization as
a "sham" to fool the Americans and charged that Diem was
now a "puppet of Nhu." The following day an ARVN colonel
also bitterly denounced Diem's brother to the Army attaché.
Alleging that Nhu was planning his own coup d'état, the
Vietnamese officer warned: "Something must and will be done
very soon, possibly by December 1."

Like most coup rumors in Saigon, there was little hard information about the conspirators' identity or their military
backing. American intelligence officials concluded that Diem's
non-Communist opponents were attempting to discover if U.S.
support for the South Vietnamese president had softened: "Their
estimate of U.S. intentions could strongly influence a decision
to undertake a coup."

Despite Diem's infuriating stubbornness and questionable
effectiveness against the Communists, the Kennedy administration tried to discourage conspiracies against him. Fearing
the uncertain, and potentially disastrous, consequences of a
coup d'état, the State Department instructed Nolting to warn
all U.S. mission personnel about "irresponsible gossip" and
"agents provocateurs."

But U.S. patience was wearing thin. The president and his
senior advisers had become increasingly concerned by Diem's
foot-dragging over their proposals and by the hostile Vietnamese newspaper articles. On November 27 Kennedy convened
a meeting to discuss whether further delay would weaken the
psychological impact of the U.S. program. He decided to order
Nolting to meet with Diem immediately and clarify any possible
misunderstandings about the U.S. proposals. The ambassador
should discuss "concrete measures to improve the efficiency of
the GVN and its image before the world." If these talks were
"clearly not satisfactory," the ambassador should promptly return to Washington to discuss a new, and presumably ominous,
course of action. To emphasize U.S. displeasure, the State
Department authorized Nolting to inform Diem of his instructions.

Nolting, unhappy with Washington's hard-line approach, met
with Diem on December 1. After a "marathon discussion,"
the ambassador believed an agreement acceptable to both gov-

ernments could be reached. Although still unwilling to permit U.S. participation in South Vietnamese decision making, Diem did agree to "closer consultation with U.S. advisers . . . in planning the conduct of the security effort." He also consented to take "all practical and feasible steps" to develop South Vietnam's democratic institutions and "to consider suggestions of the U.S. government in this regard."

These concessions seemed to satisfy Kennedy, who congratulated Nolting for doing a "good job." On December 7 the State Department "clarified" the ambassador's original instructions to conform with his agreement with Diem. Despite tough talk, Kennedy had retreated from his initial position and enlarged the U.S. military commitment to Diem without establishing the South Vietnamese political base needed to support the effort. William Bundy speculated that the momentum of approved military programs—U.S. helicopters were en route to Vietnam, and America's allies had already been informed of the proposed plan—precluded effective bargaining: "To carry the matter to a full showdown with Diem would . . . have been hard to carry off at best."

But there was another, more fundamental reason for Kennedy's limited leverage with Diem, and it was a problem that plagued the U.S. government throughout the 1960s. Because of the perceived international and domestic consequences of an American withdrawal, U.S. officials could never credibly threaten the various South Vietnamese governments with the ultimate sanction—abandoning the country to the Communists. "[The Americans] gave the impression that no matter what, they have to go ahead and win the war," recalled Bui Diem, South Vietnam's ambassador to the United States. "And some [South Vietnamese officials] got the wrong impression that, 'Well, no matter what we do, the Americans are going to be here to help us.' "

A SLOWLY ESCALATING
STALEMATE

Towering over nearby rice paddies, the U.S. aircraft ferry *Core* steamed slowly up the muddy Saigon River. More than thirty banana-shaped CH-21 helicopters, neatly arranged in rows, and several propeller-driven T-28 fighter-bombers jammed the ship's 450-foot flight deck. Completing a forty-five-mile journey through Viet Cong-infested territory, the *Core* docked at the pier in front of Saigon's Majestic Hotel. Some 400 U.S. Army pilots and ground crewmen grinned and waved at thousands of curious Vietnamese spectators lining the riverbanks.

Arriving in Saigon on December 11, 1961, the men and machines aboard the *Core* were the vanguard of the stepped-up U.S. effort to boost the effectiveness of South Vietnam's armed forces. After his October visit to Vietnam, General Taylor had recommended providing U.S. aerial reconnaissance and photography to help find the elusive Viet Cong and helicopters to ferry ARVN forces into battle. To beef up South Vietnam's firepower, the Kennedy administration supplied armor-plated T-28s and glass-nosed B-26 light bombers. Although U.S. military assistance was theoretically limited to intelligence, logistics, and advice, many U.S. servicemen engaged in combat as part of their training mission.

The man orchestrating the American military buildup in Vietnam was Secretary of Defense Robert S. McNamara, perhaps the brightest star in Kennedy's constellation of advisers. A brilliant administrator and statistician, he dazzled other officials with his energy, intensity, and, above all, mastery of quantifiable facts. Rufus Phillips, an old Vietnam hand who worked for the CIA and the Agency for International Development, recalled one meeting in Honolulu where "there must have been 300 slides of every aspect of every supply that was being provided to the Vietnamese: how many planes were flying; how many bombs were dropped. It was all statistics. We came to the end of the slide presentation—about three slides from the end—and McNamara said, 'Stop! Slide 319 does not agree with slide 5.' So they put slide 5 up, and sure enough, there was some mistake."

Born in San Francisco in 1916, McNamara earned a Phi Beta Kappa key at the University of California and an M.B.A. from the Harvard Business School. Rejected by the Navy because of poor vision, he trained Army Air Corps officers in statistical control during World War II. Applying modern management techniques, he shaped mountains of data to get men and equipment to multiple destinations at appointed times. After the war, he joined the Ford Motor Company as part of a team of "whiz kids," so-called for their youthful executive accomplishments. Over the next fifteen years, he rose to the top of the company, becoming president at the age of forty-four.

Tapped by John Kennedy for a top cabinet post, McNamara and his hand-picked civilian staff took the Pentagon by storm. Centralizing decision making in his own office, he mercilessly imposed economic analysis and program budgeting on the American military establishment. In his quest for efficiency, he unified the three service intelligence agencies and tried to reduce service rivalries for limited defense resources. Occasionally brusque and tactless with his subordinates, McNamara was an activist defense secretary, who insisted on examining basic military data himself. "He didn't like flip charts, didn't like men in uniform with pointers reading off things," recalled his deputy, Roswell Gilpatric. "He wanted to ask his own questions, and he wanted unstereotyped answers."

In November of 1961 McNamara "volunteered" to be Kennedy's point man on Vietnam. While supremely confident of his ability to manage the war, McNamara was often insensitive to the conflict's intangibles. Several years later, George Carver, then chief of the CIA's Vietnamese affairs staff, warned the defense secretary of the dubious relevance of quantifying the Asian war. "It was as if I had been talking to a devout Catholic and had questioned the Virgin Birth," said Carver.

Secretary of Defense Robert S. McNamara. *(U.S. News & World Report)*

Less than a week after the *Core*'s arrival in Saigon, McNamara met with top military commanders and Ambassador Nolting at CINCPAC headquarters. The meeting was the first Secretary of Defense Conference. Held in either Hawaii or Saigon, the monthly gatherings became a bureaucratic institution that insiders irreverently dubbed "McNamara's band concerts." At the first conference McNamara stressed President Kennedy's desire to avoid deploying combat troops to Vietnam. Despite the limited U.S. role, the defense secretary wanted "the first team there." He led the discussion of placing U.S. advisers down to the battalion level of ARVN and guaranteed money and equipment for pacification, the joint military-civilian effort to win the loyalty of the rural population. Calling South Vietnam the government's "number one priority," McNamara left no doubt of his intention "to win this battle."

Top military men in the Pentagon, some of whom viewed McNamara and his civilian staff as an "occupation force," applauded the defense secretary's determination but questioned whether the limited measures approved by Kennedy would be adequate. Throughout the Kennedy and Johnson administrations, the Joint Chiefs of Staff faced the problem of policymakers' objectives and rhetoric exceeding the military means they were willing to employ. In a January 1962 memorandum to McNamara, General Lemnitzer, chairman of the Joint Chiefs of Staff, advised that if the current program in Vietnam failed, the Chiefs saw "no alternative to the introduction of U.S. military combat forces. . . ."

To the JCS, who paid slight attention to local Vietnamese factors, the war was no less than "a planned phase in the Communist timetable for world domination." A Viet Cong victory would inevitably lead to the collapse of Southeast Asia. Should the U.S. enter combat, the Chiefs envisioned "a peninsula and island-type of campaign—a mode of warfare in which all elements of the Armed Forces of the United States have gained a wealth of experience and in which we have excelled both in World War II and Korea."

The Joint Chiefs asked McNamara to pass their memorandum to the president. In a covering note to Kennedy the defense secretary matter-of-factly wrote: "I am not prepared to endorse the views of the Chiefs until we have had more experience with our present program in SVN."

Although Kennedy shared the JCS perception of a Communist monolith, large-scale combat waged across the entire Southeast Asian mainland was precisely what he sought to avoid. The president saw the insurgency as a pernicious threat, which U.S. nuclear and conventional forces could not effectively combat. Countering the Communist insurgents' tactics of terrorism, subversion, and guerrilla warfare required a mixture of military, political, and socioeconomic programs, both overt and covert.

On January 18, 1962, Kennedy formally established the Special Group (Counterinsurgency), an NSC subcommittee responsible for emergency programs to prevent or defeat Communist insurgencies in friendly countries. The Special Group (CI)—so-called to distinguish it from the Special Group monitoring clandestine operations in hostile nations and the Special Group Augmented overseeing the attempt to "get rid of" Fidel Castro—paid particular attention to CIA paramilitary programs in Southeast Asia.

Initially chaired by General Taylor, the Special Group (CI) included the chairman of the Joint Chiefs of Staff, the director of Central Intelligence, and other top officials. The real measure of the group's importance, however, was the presence of Attorney General Robert Kennedy. Fiercely protective of his older brother, thirty-six-year-old Bobby Kennedy was determined to prevent spectacular covert action failures like the Bay of Pigs. The administration ramrod, he prodded, browbeat, and roughly questioned bureaucrats throughout the government. "If you have seen Mr. Kennedy's eyes get steely and his jaw set and his voice get low and precise," a CIA official later told a Senate committee, "you get a definite feeling of unhappiness."

President Kennedy charged the Special Group (CI) with ensuring U.S. government recognition of subversive insurgency as "a major form of politico-military conflict equal in importance to conventional warfare." His obvious interest in unconventional warfare triggered a government-wide counterinsurgency fad that masked the bureaucracy's stubborn resistance to change. The military developed crash training programs and exotic hardware such as the "infrared target detector" and "hand-held air gun firing pellets with lethal and paralyzing effects on human targets." Not to be outdone, the State Department scheduled mass indoctrination meetings that, in effect, warned: You've got to watch out! There's insurgency everywhere! "People would look down and see if there wasn't an insurgent sitting under their seat," recalled Charles Maechling, Jr., staff director of the Special Group (CI).

More thoughtful approaches to counterinsurgency had many different names but the same fundamental objective: winning popular support for the central government through a combination of self-defense and civic action. In South Vietnam the CIA had started the Civilian Irregular Defense Groups (CIDG) program on December 15, 1961, when fifty volunteers from the Rhade tribe traded in their crossbows and spears for Swedish-made submachine guns. With U.S. Army Special Forces providing tactical assistance, the CIDG program grew over the next thirteen months to include 38,000 armed civilian irregulars.

The Rhade were Montagnards, the primitive tribespeople who inhabited South Vietnam's rugged Central Highlands. Dark-skinned religious animists who propitiated evil spirits by sacrificing buffalo and drinking rice wine, the Montagnards seldom ventured more than a day's walk from their villages. Dimly aware of the country of Vietnam, they had only the haziest understanding of why the Diem government maintained an army on their soil. CIA operatives assured the Montagnards that if they drove out the Viet Cong, there would be no need for the ARVN presence.

The CIA and Special Forces trained and equipped protective strike forces, provided medical help, and developed educational programs. To foster a sense of national unity, the CIA flew Montagnard leaders to different parts of South Vietnam. Clad in scanty loincloths that earned them the nickname "BAMs" (an acronym for Bare-Assed Montagnards), the tribespeople made many wondrous discoveries, including the existence of the sea. After their first dip in the ocean, several Montagnards complained: "Why had the gods dumped so much salt in all that water when salt was so badly needed in the Highland?"

Despite its promise and demonstrated effectiveness, the CIDG program was plagued by the mutual hostility between the tribespeople and the Diem government. Most South Vietnamese considered Montagnards unreconstructable savages, and government officials were deeply suspicious of U.S. motives. American "resistance to corruption angered many South Vietnamese officials up and down the line," according to a CIA evaluation of the program. "A great deal of time and energy was spent in politically neutralizing elements of the Vietnamese government which wish[ed] to change, dilute or eradicate the program either because of selfish interests, fear of the Montagnards or apprehension that the United States was encouraging Montagnard autonomy."

Although unenthusiastic about the Civilian Irregular Defense Groups, the South Vietnamese government eagerly embraced the conceptually similar strategic hamlet program. Sparked by a proposal from British counterinsurgency expert Robert Thompson, the former secretary of defense in Malaya, strategic hamlets were fortified villages surrounded by barbed wire, bamboo parapets, and earthen ramparts bristling with spikes. On President Diem's sixty-first birthday in early 1962, counselor Ngo Dinh Nhu publicly announced the government's plan to include the entire rural population in the program.

Strategic hamlets appealed to the Ngo brothers for several reasons. In addition to physical protection of the rural population, the program extended the government's influence down to the smallest unit of Vietnamese society. At the hamlet level, so the theory went, the Diem regime could politically contest the Viet Cong. To Nhu, the program's spark plug, strategic hamlets were nothing less than the dawn of a whole new Vietnamese society, free of both Western and Communist influence.

The ideological basis of Nhu's revolution was Personalism, a confusing philosophy that melded individualism and collectivism and stressed self-reliance. He repeatedly tried to explain the strategic hamlets' ideological underpinnings to thoroughly bewildered province chiefs, whose primary concerns were physically constructing the fortifications and pleasing the central government. "They couldn't figure what the hell he was talking about," William Colby said later. "He wasn't that clear—let's face it—because what he was really saying underneath is, 'We're going to replace all you guys.' "

Although equally mystified by Nhu's abstruse philosophical monologues, U.S. officials supported the strategic hamlet program, which dovetailed with prevailing counterinsurgency theories. In a report submitted to General Taylor, State Department Director of Intelligence and Research (INR) Roger Hilsman observed: "This struggle . . . must be won by cutting the Viet Cong off from their local sources of strength, i.e., by denying them access to the villages and the people."

Hilsman, forty-one, considered himself an authority on guerrilla warfare. A West Point graduate, he had fought with Merrill's Marauders in the China-Burma-India theater during World War II. After leaving the Army, he earned a Ph.D. in international relations at Yale University and pursued a varied career in academia and government. Abrasive and voluble, Hilsman had no reservations about challenging the military on strategy, tactics, and doctrine. According to White House aide Michael Forrestal, "Hilsman was a very sharp and outspoken person who had the knack of driving the military up the wall."

At the request of President Kennedy, who was impressed by his views on guerrilla warfare, Hilsman visited Vietnam in January of 1962. In addition to formal briefings, flights over the countryside, and a six-hour meeting with Diem, Hilsman spoke with Robert Thompson, who believed the South Vietnamese government's primary objective should be winning the loyalty of the population rather than killing insurgents. Hilsman also witnessed a U.S.-planned antiguerrilla operation that dramatized the pitfalls of a purely conventional military approach to the war.

According to intelligence reports, there were Viet Cong troop concentrations and munitions facilities in the village of Binh Hoa, some seventeen miles west of Saigon near the Cambodian border. At 8:00 A.M., January 21, B-26 and T-28 aircraft carrying mixed U.S.-Vietnamese crews bombed and strafed the suspected sites for forty-five minutes. After a fifteen-minute lull, four prepositioned ARVN infantry battalions joined by an airborne battalion moved in to trap the guerrillas, who had fled from the area about one hour before the attack. The net result of this phase of the operation: no contact with enemy, five dead civilians, and eleven others wounded. And due to a navigational error, some aircraft had accidentally bombed a Cambodian border village, killing one person and wounding three others.

In his trip report Hilsman characterized the engagement as "well and efficiently executed" but "inappropriate" for anti-guerrilla operations. Prepositioned troops and preliminary air strikes gave the Viet Cong advance warning, enabling them to slip away. Moreover, preparatory air attacks ran the risk of killing innocent or persuadable villagers, "thus recruiting more Communists than were killed." Citing his World War II experiences in Burma, Hilsman declared: "Counterguerrilla forces must adopt the tactics of the guerrilla himself."

Returning to Washington, Hilsman first briefed General Taylor, then the president. The insurgency, he reported, was more a political problem than a military one. Acknowledging his debt to Thompson, Hilsman proposed the strategic village concept, which Kennedy quickly endorsed. Directed by the president to brief top civilian and military officials, Hilsman made another trip to Vietnam in March of 1962. In a hangar at Saigon's Tan Son Nhut Airport, he met with General Paul D. Harkins, who had just returned from an inspection tour in central Vietnam. Harkins, the recently appointed commander of the new U.S. Military Assistance Command-Vietnam (MACV), was encouraged by what he had seen. The South Vietnamese seemed well-trained and energetic fighters. Just the previous night a Viet Cong attack against a fortified hamlet had been successfully repulsed by local self-defense forces.

After an hour's conversation, Hilsman and Harkins were joined by Ambassador Nolting. Although the U.S. mission in Saigon considered the strategic concept sound, there was concern over Brother Nhu's involvement in the program. Rejecting the "oil spot" principle of building fortified villages in secure areas, then gradually expanding into contested territory, Nhu apparently planned to indiscriminately apply the program throughout the country. "This would of course kill everything," Hilsman observed.

The assembled officials also had deep reservations about Operation Sunrise, which called for a belt of strategic hamlets in the Ben Cat district of Binh Duong Province. Flanked by heavy concentrations of Viet Cong in War Zone D and Tay Ninh Province, Binh Duong was the keystone of the so-called arc of insurgency surrounding Saigon. Hilsman and others feared the Communists would overrun these hamlets, discrediting the program. Both Nolting and Harkins had urged Diem to cancel the operation, but their efforts—complicated by earlier U.S. military support for the plan—were in vain.

On March 22, 1962, ARVN's Fifth Infantry Division and other units began a military sweep to drive the Viet Cong out of the populated regions of Ben Cat. After clearing the area, South Vietnamese security forces rounded up the remaining population. Only 70 of 200 families voluntarily moved to the site of the new hamlets. Moreover, there were disconcertingly few able-bodied males present, suggesting either voluntary or coerced defections to the Viet Cong.

Undeterred by this inauspicious beginning, the U.S. and South Vietnamese governments plunged ahead with the strategic hamlet program. Stockades, moats, and other fortifications began sprouting up throughout the countryside. By April of 1962 the Diem government reported that 1,300 strategic hamlets had been constructed. The emphasis on the tangible, comfortingly quantifiable aspects of the program masked its ideological and political sterility. "Diem's mystical philosophy was too abstract and amorphous to be understood and embraced by the non-Catholic peasant masses," according to George Allen, a career intelligence officer who specialized in Indochinese affairs. "The U.S. and South Vietnamese counterinsurgency program rested on the concepts of civic action, security, and apolitical anti-communism, rather than on principles of freedom or of Vietnamese societal values. The ideological and psychological initiative remained almost entirely with the Communists and was never effectively and directly contested by our side."

The strategic hamlet program, reflected Charles Maechling, "became more of a sham than was realized at the beginning. It was not realized that you could have all this visible apparatus of control outside and at the same time not be controlling anything inside."

From his vantage point at the U.S. embassy in New Delhi, Ambassador John Kenneth Galbraith worried over the growing

U.S. military commitment in Vietnam. He considered the Diem government a disaster and feared the U.S. was replacing the French as the colonial military force in the area. In a letter to the president, he facetiously asked: "Incidentally, who is the man in your administration who decides what countries are strategic? I would like to have his name and address and ask him what is so important about this real estate in the space age."

On Sunday, April 1, 1962, Galbraith voiced his fears directly to Kennedy at Glen Ora, the president's temporary retreat in the hunt country near Middleburg, Virginia. The ambassador urged keeping the door open for a neutralist political solution and measurably reducing the U.S. commitment to Diem personally. He also warned of the political dangers of a highly visible U.S. presence in Vietnam. Kennedy, listening sympathetically, asked Galbraith to write out his ideas for consideration by the bureaucracy.

Later that week Galbraith submitted a four-page memorandum to the White House. At the ambassador's request Kennedy discussed the paper with Assistant Secretary of State W. Averell Harriman, who shared many of Galbraith's views. Harriman agreed the U.S. should keep the lowest possible profile in Vietnam. He had recently advised the Saigon embassy of his concern over constant press implications that the struggle was a U.S. war. Particularly troubling was a *New York Times* article reporting the inspection of an Operation Sunrise stockade by large numbers of U.S. military and civilian officials. "Why," Harriman had scolded, "do large numbers of Americans inspect anything?"

A blunt, tough-talking patrician, seventy-year-old Averell Harriman was the son of railroad industrialist E. H. Harriman. A Republican until his mid-thirties, he eventually became a Democratic party doyen whose distinguished career included top diplomatic posts in London and Moscow and the governorship of New York. President Kennedy, somewhat concerned by his age, did not offer Harriman a senior position in the new administration. His vigor and counsel as roving ambassador, however, quickly won the president's confidence. Appointed chief of the U.S. delegation to the Geneva conference on Laos and later assistant secretary of state for Far Eastern Affairs, Harriman received private instructions from Kennedy "to get us out of [Laos] whatever way you can," a task he pursued coldly and single-mindedly. Foreshadowing U.S. strong-arm tactics with Diem in the fall of 1963, Harriman pressured General Phoumi Nosavan to accept a coalition government by cutting off economic aid and recalling a CIA officer close to him. Harriman was only slightly less subtle with bureaucrats who resisted the neutralization of Laos. CIA operative Stewart Methvin recalled his and a U.S. military adviser's impassioned pleas for more weapons and support for anti-Communist forces: "Harriman turned to us, smiled, and asked politely what we had been talking about, showing us that his hearing aid had been turned off."

At his April 6, 1962, meeting with Kennedy, Harriman concurred with Galbraith's pessimistic assessment of Diem. Although characterizing the South Vietnamese president as a "losing horse in the long run," Harriman opposed actively working against Diem. Despite his shortcomings, there was no competent leadership to replace him. Our policy, Harriman advised, "should be to support the government and people of Vietnam, rather than Diem personally."

On the question of a negotiated settlement in Vietnam, Harriman approved of an indirect approach to Hanoi to determine if mutual reductions in Viet Cong and U.S. activities were feasible. He was not, however, in favor "of an attempt to reconvene the Geneva Conference or to seek a neutral solution in Vietnam."

The prospects for a satisfactory negotiated settlement in Vietnam were almost nonexistent. Determined to unify the country under Communist rule, Hanoi was unwilling to admit publicly its direction of the insurgency, much less withdraw its support from the Viet Cong. And while the Diem government was in no position to dictate terms at the conference table, Kennedy was unwilling to abandon an ally who still had the capability and will to resist communism.

Despite the unpropitious circumstances, Kennedy favored a political solution to reduce the burgeoning U.S. presence in Vietnam. Still a relatively small national security problem when compared with Berlin or Cuba, Vietnam was becoming increasingly unmanageable. A recent "operational experiment"

Assistant Secretary of State W. Averell Harriman, left, with Kennedy. *(The Library of Congress, U.S. News & World Report Collection, 1952–72)*

with defoliation had been a typically annoying fiasco. Designed to help detect the Viet Cong, the herbicide test had been largely a failure, yet the Communists still managed to score propaganda points by charging the U.S. with "chemical warfare." Why, Kennedy asked with exasperation, had the defoliant not been tested elsewhere?

The president also faced a slowly accelerating drift toward war in Vietnam, where the distinction between a U.S. advisory and combat role was becoming largely academic. After the appearance of unidentified aircraft over the Central Highlands, presumably Communist planes on resupply missions, Kennedy had authorized in late March 1962 the deployment of U.S. jet interceptors to South Vietnam. Should American pilots shoot down a Communist plane, the administration planned to say the craft had simply crashed. According to a State Department policy directive, U.S. officials were "confident the Communists will in any event receive [the] message loud and clear."

Caught between his conflicting desires to counter subversive insurgency and to avoid entanglement in an Asian land war, the president told Harriman the U.S. government should "be prepared to seize upon any favorable moment to reduce our involvement, recognizing that the moment might yet be some time away."

In the spring of 1962 there was a new crisis in Laos. Despite U.S. advice and Communist warnings, General Phoumi had reinforced the provincial capital of Nam Tha, located only twenty miles from China and near Pathet Lao base areas. On May 6 North Vietnamese and Pathet Lao forces seized this tempting political and military target, driving out 4,500 Laotian army troops. The predictably pitiful performance of the government forces prompted Major General Reuben H. Tucker, the newly appointed MAAG chief, to report that the commanding general "couldn't lead a squad around the block."

The attack on Nam Tha, a flagrant violation of the previous year's cease-fire agreement, virtually eliminated government influence in northern Laos and opened up the provinces bordering Burma and Thailand to Communist domination. To the American intelligence community, the attack seemed to be a nibbling operation designed to test U.S. resolve: "In the absence either of an effective military response to the Nam Tha action or significant progress toward a coalition government, there will be an increasing likelihood that the Communists will undertake offensive operations on the scale of Nam Tha elsewhere in Laos."

President Kennedy, facing a replay of the 1961 crisis, again publicly invoked the specter of U.S. military intervention. Playing the current crisis in a lower key, he explained at a news conference: "Now, I agree [political negotiations are] a very hazardous course, but introducing American forces, which is the other one—let's not think there is some great third course—that also is a hazardous course, and we want to attempt to see if we can work out a peaceful solution."

Kennedy's advisers offered conflicting recommendations about how to respond to the Communist attacks. Harriman and Hilsman urged ordering the Seventh Fleet to the Gulf of Siam and a small ground force to the Thai border opposite Vientiane. These military moves would demonstrate U.S. commitment to a neutral government in Laos and give the Communists the opportunity to consider the consequences of their actions. "The purpose was to signal Moscow and the world that it was a serious matter," Hilsman later explained. "We were going to raise the crisis level."

The Joint Chiefs of Staff, uncomfortable with mere political posturing with military force, asked what would happen if the Communists called the Americans' bluff. Before deploying a small U.S. ground force to the Laotian border, the Chiefs wanted advance authorization to meet any contingency, including nuclear attacks against China. Without such assurances, they generally confined their recommendations to nothing more belligerent than diplomatic notes of protest.

With Rusk, McNamara, and General Lemnitzer in Asia, Kennedy postponed any major decisions on Laos and approved only the lowest common denominator of the two proposals: ordering the Seventh Fleet to the Gulf of Siam. After a hurried meeting on May 10 at the White House, Harriman and Hilsman worried that this step alone was a dangerously inadequate signal of resolve. Sending the fleet without the proposed limited troop deployments might not only tempt the North Vietnamese and Pathet Lao into launching a general offensive but might also trigger domestic political attacks against the administration for responding so feebly to a Communist challenge. Until the president decided whether to deploy troops to Thailand, Harriman and Hilsman thought it best not to engage U.S. prestige by sending the fleet.

Acting on behalf of Harriman, Hilsman called the White House to ask if the president would reconsider his decision. Kennedy, on his way out the door to a public appearance, casually agreed with the State Department position. Hilsman immediately informed General Decker, the acting chairman of the Joint Chiefs of Staff. "My God," Decker exclaimed, "the message has already gone out!"

"Well, I can't help it," Hilsman replied.

"Okay, but surely you will give me a little memo."

Within an hour the president—who had presumably heard from the military about receiving operational orders from the State Department's director of Intelligence and Research—had second thoughts. Phoning the State Department, he snapped at William Sullivan, Harriman's deputy at Geneva: "What the hell is going on there? Do you know that Roger Hilsman has just stopped the fleet?"

Summoning Hilsman to the phone, Kennedy said, "Tell me about this fleet thing." After listening to the INR director's analysis, the president replied that something had just happened that would strengthen his position on dispatching the fleet to the Gulf of Siam. General Eisenhower, whom Kennedy representatives had just briefed, agreed to support whatever decision the president made. Eisenhower's endorsement would not only help overcome objections to putting a limited force into Thailand but would also protect Kennedy's political flanks.

With Hilsman's concurrence the Seventh Fleet was ordered back to the Gulf of Siam. On May 12, when Kennedy's top advisers returned to Washington, the president approved the deployment of U.S. air and ground forces to Thailand. Eventually totaling 3,000 servicemen, this show of force deterred an unimpeded North Vietnamese-Pathet Lao advance to the Mekong River and Thai border. As they had the previous spring, the North Vietnamese apparently feared that open U.S. military intervention might jeopardize their primary objective in Laos: a secure corridor through the panhandle to South Vietnam.

One month later the three Laotian factions finally agreed on a coalition government under the leadership of neutralist Souvanna Phouma that paved the way for an international agreement in Geneva. One potential stumbling block, however, was South Vietnamese President Ngo Dinh Diem, who threatened to boycott the conference. He feared the settlement would not only facilitate Viet Cong activities but would also presage an attempt to neutralize his own country. As a precondition to signing the agreement, he demanded that the coalition government refuse diplomatic recognition to North Vietnam, a gesture designed to bolster Diem's dubious claim as the only legitimate government of all Vietnam.

Once again the Kennedy administration found itself trying to haul its "balky satrap" back into line. On July 9 the State Department instructed Ambassador Nolting to "urgently" deliver a letter to Diem from President Kennedy. Pledging to "continue to help your country defend itself," Kennedy assured the South Vietnamese president that "Lao territory will not be used for military or subversive interference in the affairs of other countries."

The State Department instructed Nolting to "stress in the strongest terms" the importance of a Geneva agreement and to inform Diem of Soviet promises to end infiltration through Laos into South Vietnam. "We are aware of the danger that the Communists will not honor their pledges," wrote Kennedy. "But the only alternative to a neutral Laos appears to be making an international battleground of Laos. This would not help the Lao people and it would not contribute to the security of Laos' neighbors."

Reluctantly, Diem agreed to sign the Geneva accords, which fourteen nations ratified on July 23, 1962. Harriman, having temporarily countered the Communist advance in Laos, was ready to expand the agreement into larger areas of Western-Communist understanding. Near the end of the conference he had asked Kennedy's permission to speak secretly with the North Vietnamese to see if there were any prospects for negotiations. The president agreed, and in a small hotel room near the railroad station in Geneva, Harriman conducted an awkward trilingual conversation with North Vietnam's foreign minister and his interpreter. According to William Sullivan, who handled the English-French translations, the North Vietnamese had no interest in negotiations of any kind: "It was a relatively useless conversation. We got absolutely nowhere."

North Vietnam's inflexibility in Geneva not only suggested the depth of its commitment to reunification but also foreshadowed its noncompliance with the Geneva agreements. Despite the guarantees of the Soviets, who were either unwilling or unable to restrain their satellite, North Vietnam withdrew only one-third of its 9,000 combat troops and advisers from Laos. Moreover, infiltration through the mountain trails into South Vietnam continued unabated at a rate of several hundred troops per month. "[The North Vietnamese] broke the '62 agreements before the ink was dry," Harriman said later.

On the same day the Geneva accords on Laos were signed Robert McNamara convened the monthly Secretary of Defense Conference in Hawaii. The reports from the field were encouraging; the statistical trends were favorable. Citing the "tremendous progress to date," McNamara declared the time had come to develop a long-range plan for phasing out major U.S. advisory and logistic programs. He asked General Harkins how long it would take to eliminate the Viet Cong as a "disturbing force."

"About one year from the time that we are able to get . . . [the South Vietnamese] fully operational and really pressing the VC in all areas," the MACV commander replied.

U.S. military optimism in mid-1962 reflected both genuine progress in Vietnam and profound ignorance of many underlying forces there. The infusion of U.S. advisers and equipment had arrested the military deterioration, but there were still far too few Americans—particularly those who spoke Vietnamese—to collect firsthand information at the "rice roots" level of the war. The raw data that fueled McNamara's optimism had been provided by South Vietnamese officials, many of whom had political and economic incentives to falsify their reports. After Diem's overthrow, U.S. officials learned that his government had allocated money to the provinces in proportion to reported success in the war.

Upbeat South Vietnamese reporting found a particularly receptive audience in General Paul D. Harkins, whose every briefing, meeting, and interview exuded optimism. Soft-spoken and invariably polite, Harkins was a picture of meticulously groomed military elegance, complete with swagger stick and cigarette holder. A West Point graduate, he had served as a staff officer to General George S. Patton during World War II and as chief of staff to General Taylor in Korea. Although McNamara would later judge him "not worth a damn," the defense secretary endorsed Harkins to President Kennedy as "an imaginative officer, fully qualified to fill what I consider to be the most difficult job in the U.S. Army."

Harkins arrived in Vietnam in February of 1962 and quickly discovered the limited loyalty of Diem's politicized military. From his temporary quarters at Saigon's Caravelle Hotel, Harkins watched as two South Vietnamese pilots bombed and strafed Independence Palace. The damage to the building was extensive, but Diem and Nhu were unhurt. A conversation with Major General Tran Van Don, a corps commander and ringleader of the coup that ultimately toppled Diem, suggested a similarly rebellious attitude among the general officers. "During one of the first meetings I had with him," Harkins recalled, "General Don just shook his head and told me, 'We can't do much until we get rid of Diem.' "

Turning a blind eye to political intrigue, Harkins concentrated on helping the Diem government combat the insurgency. In accordance with General Taylor's recommendations, the MACV commander sought to boost ARVN's offensive capabilities and urged government forces to disrupt enemy forces in their base areas. Although publicly extolling the virtues of South Vietnamese fighting men, Harkins had private reservations about their discipline and professionalism: "If they captured an officer of the Viet Cong, they'd leave their post and bring him back to Saigon. They wanted to show Diem [and] get a pat on the back or maybe a promotion."

Like Ambassador Nolting, Harkins tried to build a winning psychology among the South Vietnamese by putting the most optimistic interpretation possible on events. This tendency to accentuate the positive carried over into MACV's command reporting to official Washington. "It wasn't dishonesty, intending to deceive the people back home," reflected George Allen, then a Defense Intelligence Agency analyst who worked on the first MACV Viet Cong order of battle. "It was self-delusion, magnified by the 'can-do' spirit that pervades military organizations, the Boy Scouts, and the Salvation Army."

The civilian agencies in Washington took a more cautious view of the war than General Harkins. In late 1962 the State Department's Bureau of Intelligence and Research had concluded that reports of a turning tide in Vietnam were "pre-

General Paul D. Harkins, commander of U.S. forces in Vietnam, 1962–1964. *(The Library of Congress, U.S. News & World Report Collection, 1952–72)*

mature" in their optimism: "At best, it appears that the rate of deterioration has decelerated. . . ."

The CIA's Office of Current Intelligence warned that the war remained "a slowly escalating stalemate." Agency analysts cautioned that encouraging statistics from Vietnam were a shaky basis for conclusions of a winning trend. While the ratio of captured Viet Cong to lost South Vietnamese weapons had recently taken a favorable turn, many of the Communist weapons had been old French equipment or crude homemade rifles and pistols. South Vietnamese losses, on the other hand, were generally modern U.S. weapons. The casualty figures were also misleading. In 1962, 21,000 Viet Cong had reportedly been killed in action. Despite these estimated losses, their regular forces had increased by about 50 percent to approximately 24,000. Agency analysts concluded, "This suggests either the casualty figures are exaggerated or that the Viet Cong have a remarkable replacement capability—or both."

It would be several years before the U.S. government discovered the extent of the Communists' remarkable replacement capability, a revelation that helped discredit the grinding U.S. attrition strategy in Vietnam. In 1969 MACV estimated that total enemy losses for the previous year were a staggering 291,000, a number equal to military estimates of total Viet Cong main and local forces, guerrillas, and political cadres. Unfortunately, estimates of Viet Cong recruitment and infiltration from North Vietnam totaled 298,000.

CHAPTER FIVE

MORE VIGOR
IS NEEDED

Just after dawn, January 2, 1963, ten lumbering CH-21 "Workhorse" helicopters touched down near Ap Tan Thoi, a small village in the rice-growing delta region south of Saigon. Infantrymen from ARVN's Seventh Division leaped out of the choppers and assembled north of the village. The troopers, among South Vietnam's finest, were the first wave of an operation designed to knock out a COSVN radio transmitter and annihilate the company-sized security force guarding it. According to the plan, infantry would surround Ap Tan Thoi on three sides while a Civil Guard task force, supported by mounted troops in M-113 armored personnel carriers, sealed the trap on the surprised and vastly outnumbered enemy.

The operation went awry almost immediately. Ground fog delayed the second and third waves of infantry, and the Civil Guard task force, which pushed off on schedule, unexpectedly bumped into Viet Cong troops in carefully prepared defensive positions. Obviously tipped off to the operation, the Communist forces were no mere company but a reinforced battalion armed with automatic rifles, heavy machine guns, and 60-mm mortars. Moreover, the enemy troops were not at Ap Tan Thoi but 1,500 meters to the south at Ap Bac—a village whose name would memorialize one of ARVN's most miserable performances.

The first burst of gunfire wounded the Civil Guard task force commander and killed a company commander. The province chief, who exercised independent control over the Civil Guard, unilaterally ordered his forces to halt and assume a blocking position. The Seventh Division commander and his U.S. adviser, Lieutenant Colonel John Paul Vann, sought to regain the initiative by committing their mobile reserves to battle. At

10:20 A.M. fifteen U.S. helicopters descended toward a landing zone west of Ap Bac. Viet Cong gunners, dug in under a nearby tree line, opened up with a withering hail of bullets, hitting all but one of the choppers and downing five of them.

Vann, circling above the battle in a spotter plane, radioed the position of the downed helicopters to the U.S. adviser with the M-113s, diesel-powered "green dragons" armed with .50-caliber machine guns. Initially, the South Vietnamese armored commander refused to move forward. After a furious argument and three hours to negotiate a canal, the first armored personnel carriers inched toward the choppers. Repulsing the uncoordinated advance, the Viet Cong focused their fire on the M-113 gunners, who were exposed from the waist up. Fourteen ARVN gunners died that day in combat.

Despite the operation's horrendous start, the situation did not seem hopeless to Colonel Vann, a wiry, feisty, thirty-eight-year-old who became a minor legend for his knowledge of Vietnam and outspoken perfectionism. The South Vietnamese forces outnumbered the Viet Cong by at least four to one and had them blocked on the north, south, and west. Vann and Colonel Daniel B. Porter, the IV Corps adviser, suggested a parachute drop to the east to slam the door on the Viet Cong's only escape route. At dusk two airborne companies drifted down near Ap Bac—but to the west of the village. After the battle, Vann bitterly complained: "We sat there all day, did not close with the enemy, did not complete an encirclement of him, and that night, of course, he slipped away, as we knew he would."

The militarily incomprehensible decision to let the Viet Cong battalion escape had been made by Brigadier General Huynh Van Cao, the IV Corps commander. A Catholic from central Vietnam who was utterly loyal to Diem, Cao had a good combat record as commander of the Seventh Division until the fall of 1962, when the South Vietnamese president rebuked him for his high rate of casualties. Instantly, the Seventh Division stopped mounting aggressive operations in favor of ineffective "sweeps" through the countryside that seemed designed to minimize contact with the enemy. Cao, who had been promoted to corps commander at the end of the year, now apparently recognized that regardless of the military outcome, an assault on the dug-in Viet Cong battalion at Ap Bac would mean a politically unacceptable number of casualties.

Despite Cao's decision to break off the attack, Ap Bac was still one of the bloodiest battles to date in the second Indochina war. Three Americans, sixty-five government troops, and an estimated 100 Viet Cong died there. The Communists considered the fight a historic triumph over American technology that stiffened morale and undermined confidence in Diem's armed forces. General Harkins and other top U.S. military leaders, however, claimed the battle was a victory for the South Vietnamese, who had inflicted heavier losses and ultimately taken their objective. According to a JCS study, press reports of a defeat at Ap Bac were "contrary to the facts" and "based on ill-considered statements made at a time of high excitement and frustration by a few American officers."

The U.S. military's conventional definition of victory in the guerrilla war appalled many American newsmen, who believed the battle had exposed the ineffectiveness of Diem's politicized armed forces. David Halberstam, the *New York Times* correspondent in Saigon, later wrote, "Ap Bac epitomized all the deficiencies of the system: lack of aggressiveness, hesitancy about taking casualties, lack of battlefield leadership, a nonexistent chain of command."

Despite the debacle at Ap Bac, top U.S. officials in Saigon remained optimistic about the war. American civilian aid programs were finally getting into high gear, and General Harkins was putting the finishing touches on the National Campaign Plan, an accelerating program of decentralized small-unit actions combined with "clear and hold" operations in support of the strategic hamlet program. "I am convinced we have taken the military, psychological, economical, and political initiative from the enemy," Harkins wrote Diem in early 1963.

Roger Hilsman, who was again visiting Vietnam at the request of President Kennedy in early January 1963, took a less sanguine view of the war. There still appeared to be too many counterproductive air attacks and ineffective conventional ground operations. Although still committed to the strategic hamlet concept, he was horrified by the Ngo brothers' implementation of the program. "They were building strategic hamlets right on

Assistant Secretary of State Roger Hilsman. (*U.S. News & World Report*)

the Lao border," Hilsman recalled. "[Nhu] was putting the goddamned things thirty miles from the nearest civilization."

Accompanying Hilsman on this trip was Michael V. Forrestal, who had filled the NSC staff vacancy created by Walt Rostow's transfer to the State Department. Dark-haired and bespectacled, thirty-five-year-old Mike Forrestal was the son of the first secretary of defense, James V. Forrestal. A protégé of Averell Harriman, who virtually adopted him after his father's death, Forrestal had been a partner in a Wall Street law firm when appointed to the White House staff in early 1962.

Although militarily less aggressive than Rostow, Forrestal took a hard line toward Diem's intractability and Ambassador Nolting's empathetic diplomacy. After returning from Vietnam, Forrestal suggested to Kennedy that Nolting be replaced: "More vigor is needed in getting Diem to do what we want."

In their report to the president, Hilsman and Forrestal noted "awesome" problems but still saw many reasons for hope. The CIDG program was in full swing, with camps in all the provinces bordering Laos and teams of Montagnards regularly patrolling the mountain trails. And in both the mountains and lowlands, the areas where one could travel without armed escort had been enlarged. Clearly, the Viet Cong were being hurt: "Our overall judgment, in sum, is that we are probably winning, but certainly more slowly than we had hoped. At the rate it is now going the war will last longer than we would like, cost more in terms of both lives and money than we anticipated, and prolong the period in which a sudden and dramatic event could upset gains already made."

In the annex to their paper for the president's "eyes only," Hilsman and Forrestal reported on the performance of the U.S. mission in Saigon. There seemed to be no overall plan tying together the civilian and military efforts and some confusion over counterguerrilla warfare: "The American military mission must share some of the blame for the excessive emphasis on large-scale operations and air interdiction which have the bad political and useless military effects described in our report."

Hilsman and Forrestal also criticized the lack of coordination among the many U.S. agencies in Vietnam, which had produced a fragmented and duplicative effort. Ideally, authority should be given to a strong executive, either "the right kind of general" or a civilian with sufficient stature to dominate all other departments and agencies: "On balance, our recommendation would be not to make any sudden and dramatic change, but to keep the problem in mind when changes are made in the normal course."

Shortly after Hilsman and Forrestal returned to Washington, Kennedy received a military assessment of the conflict from a JCS team headed by Army Chief of Staff General Earle G. Wheeler. A tall man, low and precise in speech, "Bus" Wheeler, like most military professionals, believed the Kennedy administration placed too much emphasis on the nonmilitary aspects of counterguerrilla warfare. "It is fashionable in some quarters to say that the problems in Southeast Asia are primarily political and economic, rather than military," Wheeler observed in late 1962. "I do not agree. The essence of the problem in Vietnam is military."

Born in Washington, D.C., in January of 1908, Wheeler graduated from West Point and finished first in his class both at the Infantry School at Fort Benning and the Command and General Staff College at Fort Leavenworth. He saw only limited combat during World War II but throughout his career earned high marks for his administrative abilities. After serving as the first director of the Joint Staff and commanding general of the European Command, Wheeler was sworn in as chief of staff in October 1962.

Wheeler and the twelve-man JCS team arrived in Vietnam in mid-January 1963. Their mission: to estimate prospects for successfully concluding the war within "a reasonable period of time." During the eight-day visit, the team traveled the length and breadth of South Vietnam, inspecting corps headquarters, training centers, and strategic hamlets. Wheeler and his colleagues looked favorably upon General Harkins's National Campaign Plan, with its interlocking objectives of destroying Viet Cong strongholds and protecting the population from attacks. And in contrast to Hilsman and Forrestal, the Army chief of staff found adequate coordination among U.S. military, political, and economic programs.

When Wheeler returned to Washington, he immediately presented the team's findings to McNamara and the Joint Chiefs of Staff, then the president. The near desperate situation in Vietnam, the general reported, had been turned around to the point where "victory is now a hopeful prospect." Terming current U.S. support "adequate," he concluded: "[We] are winning slowly on the present thrust, and . . . there is no compelling reason to change."

Wheeler and the JCS team hedged their optimism by noting that political restrictions against attacking Communist sanctuaries in Cambodia and Laos hampered military action and made "victory more remote." Moreover, they recommended making "the North Vietnamese bleed" for directing and supporting the insurgency. In conjunction with the CIA, the military men sought to step up South Vietnam's unconventional warfare capability and to direct "a coordinated program of sabotage, destruction, propaganda, and subversive missions against North Vietnam."

The idea of making Hanoi pay a price for its subversion in Southeast Asia gained ascendancy in the Kennedy administration. In January 1963 National Security Adviser McGeorge Bundy, who chaired the Special Group, passed to Kennedy a "covert operational plan for North Vietnam" prepared by the CIA. In a cover memo Bundy wrote: "There is every reason to think that the execution of this plan will encounter all the difficulties of an operation in a denied area, but there is agreement that it is worth trying."

Despite "considerable effort," clandestine operations against North Vietnam were both modest in size and ineffective in execution during Kennedy's presidency. Planning for a more ambitious program of covert action, however, intensified in May of 1963, when the Joint Chiefs of Staff ordered CINCPAC to prepare "non-attributable" hit-and-run operations against North Vietnam. Conducted by the South Vietnamese, the raids would be supported by "U.S. military materiel, training, and advisory assistance." And just two days before Kennedy's assassination, his senior advisers agreed to develop a twelve-month program of operations against North Vietnam. Designated OPLAN 34A, the program included "commando type coastal raids," which triggered the notorious August 1964 Tonkin Gulf incidents.

Stepped-up planning for *overt* U.S. military action against North Vietnam also began in 1963 during that year's Laotian crisis, by now a hardy perennial that bloomed every spring. The coalition government had failed to integrate the country's three factions, and a split among the neutralists triggered a wave of assassinations and renewed fighting on the Plaine des Jarres. To restore the cease-fire, Kennedy launched a diplomatic effort with the British and the Soviets, the cochairmen of the Geneva conference. To prevent a Pathet Lao victory, he authorized covert shipments of military supplies to the beleaguered neutralists, General Phoumi's troops, and the CIA-trained Hmong tribespeople, who waged guerrilla warfare behind Communist lines.

With the Pathet Lao steadily improving their position, Kennedy met with his top advisers on Saturday, April 20, 1963. They concluded that a failure to respond vigorously would be interpreted as a U.S. decision to abandon Laos. Attributing Pathet Lao aggressiveness and effectiveness to Hanoi, Kennedy ordered a carrier task force and Marine battalion landing team to the waters off South Vietnam, a move that suggested direct military action against North Vietnam. Lest the Communists miss the point of this show of force, the operational orders to the task force were broadcast in clear, uncoded text. Kennedy also instructed the Joint Chiefs of Staff to prepare "plans for possible military action against North Vietnam." The Chiefs selected eight targets, including airfields, bridges, and fuel depots, vulnerable to carrier-based aircraft and U.S. planes in Thailand.

Although the fighting in Laos soon tapered off without U.S. military intervention, the crisis had exposed the inadequacy of keeping the peace through diplomatic means. North Vietnam apparently had no intention of abiding by the Geneva agreements, and Harriman's appeals to Khrushchev fell upon deaf ears. "The Laos accords were a bitter disappointment to Kennedy," recalled Secretary of State Dean Rusk.

No less disappointed was Rusk himself, who viewed the agreements as a test of Communist willingness to honor international commitments. He had all but given up on an effective coalition government in Laos. Keeping the U.S. commitments to neighboring South Vietnam and Thailand within manageable bounds, however, required at least a stabilized de facto partitioning of the country. To prevent further Communist nibbling in Laos, Rusk joined McNamara in proposing a program of covert and overt pressures that culminated in "the initiation of military action against North Vietnam."

Patient and self-effacing, Dean Rusk was temperamentally unsuited to the flash and brilliance of the New Frontier. He respected the ponderous workings of the bureaucracy and disapproved of Kennedy's sometimes freewheeling decision-making process. "President Kennedy had some very informal views about administration," Rusk recalled. "He might read a little squib on page twelve of the morning newspaper and pick up the phone and call the desk officer in the State Department while he was still at home in his bathrobe."

Born in Cherokee County, Georgia, in 1909, Rusk was the son of a Presbyterian minister. He worked his way through Davidson College and earned a Rhodes scholarship to Oxford University. During World War II, he served in the China-Burma-India theater and rose to the rank of colonel. A protégé of General George C. Marshall, Rusk worked in both the Pentagon and the State Department after the war. In 1952 he was appointed president of the Rockefeller Foundation, a position he held until he assumed office as secretary of state in 1961.

Rusk viewed himself as a personal adviser to the president who helped judge, rather than advocate, policy options. Seeking to avoid policy conflicts with the president, he deliberately kept his own position unclear on any issue on which Kennedy did not have a strong conviction. He also refused to debate at meetings attended by subordinates and staff of various government agencies. "When you get to the final decision stage, the room should be cleared of all but those that have formal constitutional responsibility," he had said during the Bay of Pigs inquiry. "People looking down the cannon's mouth should be in a solemn position and make a solemn decision without having large numbers of people in the room."

In June of 1963 Rusk and McNamara proposed their three-phase action program in Southeast Asia, "not as a contingency response to Communist tactics—but as a method of influencing the over-all situation." Kennedy approved the program's modest first steps, which authorized U.S. advisers to encourage right-wing and neutralist offensive military action against the Pathet Lao. Supported by CIA-Special Forces teams based in South Vietnam and Laos, the operations were aimed primarily at controlling the approaches to Thailand and the mountain trails into South Vietnam. The president also sanctioned air strikes by T-28s armed with napalm. According to a State Department directive to the embassy in Vientiane, the "objective is to be able to meet new PL [Pathet Lao] attacks with prompt counterpunches in order to convey message that PL may no longer instigate such actions with impunity."

During Kennedy's presidency, U.S. advisory and covert activ-

Secretary of State Dean Rusk, left, and Kennedy. *(The Library of Congress, U.S. News & World Report Collection, 1952–72)*

ities in the Laotian panhandle never amounted to much. Preparations for larger operations, however, were on the upswing at the time of his assassination. On November 20, 1963, Kennedy's advisers agreed to plan South Vietnamese cross-border operations up to fifty kilometers inside Laos. Whether Kennedy would have authorized Lyndon Johnson's expanded interdiction efforts in 1964 will never be known. As with the covert program directed against North Vietnam, Kennedy provided his successor with both the policy rationale and the military plans for a key step toward a direct U.S. combat role in Vietnam.

In contrast to Laos, South Vietnam enjoyed a relative lull in Communist activity during the spring of 1963. U.S. military authorities cryptically suggested the calm had "both visible and hidden meanings." For top American officials in Saigon, it was a season of great optimism. A MACV Summary of Highlights boldly predicted: "Barring greatly increased resupply and re-

inforcement of the Viet Cong by infiltration, the military phase
of the war can be virtually won in 1963."

Even the more generally pessimistic Washington intelligence
community was taking a less dour view of the war. An April 17
National Intelligence Estimate (NIE), Prospects in South Vietnam, concluded: "We believe that Communist progress has been
blunted and that the situation is improving." The estimate's drafters hedged their conclusions by questioning Diem's ability "to
translate military success into political stability."

Written for top policymakers, NIEs were comprehensive yet
absorbable documents that utilized every overt and clandestine
resource of the U.S. government. The drafters of such estimates sought a consensus paper that neither obscured major
disagreements nor yielded lowest-common-denominator mush.
Prospects in South Vietnam, approved without dissent by intelligence community leaders, had satisified the chiefs but not
all of the Indians. "To my mind," reflected George Carver,
"[the NIE] was not an accurate depiction or analysis of the
situation in Vietnam, and its conclusions were either so atten-
uated as to be virtually meaningless or simply not warranted
by available facts."

Carver, on leave from the CIA's Clandestine Service and
assigned to the Office of National Estimates (ONE), believed
the apparent progress in Vietnam "masked fundamental problems not only still unsolved but, in some cases, steadily wors-
ening." In an earlier draft of Prospects in South Vietnam,
Carver and his ONE colleagues concluded that the gravity of
the Communist threat to South Vietnam was largely attribut-
able to Diem and his style of government. Unwilling to actively
seek popular support, Diem appeared to subordinate the defeat
of the Communists to the preservation and extension of Ngo
family control. The bottom line of ONE's draft estimate: "The
present GVN is not likely to take the political steps necessary
to reduce the VC threat to a point where the U.S. could sig-
nificantly diminish its present involvement in the South Vietnamese struggle."

In other words, the U.S. could not win the war with Diem.

The draft NIE, at marked variance with the officially recorded views of Ambassador Nolting, General Harkins, and

Saigon CIA Station Chief John Richardson, triggered a "py-rotechnic" reaction from the czars of the intelligence com-munity. The director of the Defense Intelligence Agency (DIA), the three service intelligence chiefs, and even some CIA offi-cials heatedly charged that the estimate's drafters had deni-grated political-military progress in South Vietnam and been far too critical of Diem and his family. Central Intelligence Director John McCone, finding the criticism persuasive, for-mally "remanded" the draft estimate with instructions to con-sider fully the views of the U.S. mission in Saigon. After consultations with officials in Vietnam and a complete redraft-ing of the NIE, McCone formally approved the new, more optimistic assessment of the war.

Less than a week after McCone issued Prospects in South Vietnam," events seemed to validate many of the key conclu-sions of the remanded draft estimate. On April 22 the CIA station in Saigon reported the Ngo brothers' increasing concern over U.S. "infringements" on Vietnamese sovereignty. CIA-Special Forces activities among the Montagnards had become particularly irritating to Diem and Nhu. According to CIA sources, Diem planned to demand "a reduction in the number of U.S. personnel in South Vietnam on the basis that the force is too large and unmanageable."

The following month the Ngo brothers publicly aired their grievances. During an interview with Warren Unna of the *Washington Post*, Nhu declared that "at least 50 percent of the U.S. troops in Vietnam are not absolutely necessary." He also suggested there were far too many U.S. intelligence operatives in the country.

The *Post* interview further undermined the Kennedy admin-istration's limited confidence in Nhu, who ominously continued to accumulate power. Although Ambassador Nolting eventu-ally persuaded Diem to endorse the current level of U.S. sup-port, Roger Hilsman feared that Nhu would probably repeat his public outburst "if not brought up sharply." Appointed assistant secretary of state in March of 1963, Hilsman instructed Nolting to impress upon the Ngo brothers the administration's "rough going" in defending its Vietnam program before Con-gress and U.S. public opinion.

But even as the U.S. and South Vietnamese governments haggled over the appropriate level of American aid, the chain of events that would finally destroy Kennedy's confidence in the Ngo brothers was already under way. For Diem and Nhu the consequences would be fatal.

CHAPTER SIX

WHO ARE THESE PEOPLE?

Ironically, the beginning of the end of the Diem regime was neither a military nor political battle, but a religious demonstration in Hue, the former imperial capital of Vietnam and ancestral home of the Ngo family. Five hundred miles north of Saigon, Hue bordered the rugged, jungle-covered Chaine Annamitique to the west and the gently flowing Perfume River to the east. After unifying Vietnam in the early nineteenth century, Emperor Gia Long had selected Hue as the site for his capital, which he modeled after the great walled city of Beijing. Throughout French colonial rule and the struggle for independence, the city remained a repository for the old mandarin traditions.

Hue was also a center of Buddhist learning. Although most Vietnamese were religious eclectics who freely mixed Buddhism with animism, ancestor worship, and Confucian ethical principles, the citizens of Hue were generally more orthodox in their religious beliefs. On May 8, 1963, thousands of Vietnamese gathered in Hue to celebrate the anniversary of Buddha's birth and to protest a government ban on the display of religious flags. The ban was long-standing but largely unenforced. Only a short time before, white and gold Catholic flags had been prominently displayed during an anniversary celebration of the ordination of Ngo Dinh Thuc, Diem's brother and the archbishop of Hue. Two days before the Buddhist holiday, however, the South Vietnamese president had declared that the ban on religious flags would be enforced. American embassy spokesman John Mecklin later compared Diem's politically insensitive declaration to "a presidential proclamation in the United States outlawing carol singing at Christmas."

On the evening of the eighth, protesting Buddhists assembled at the Hue radio station. Demanding the broadcast of a religious speech taped earlier in the day, the demonstrators defied a government order to disperse. Local security troops, under the command of the Catholic deputy province chief, forcibly disbanded the crowd. During the melee, at least seven demonstrators were killed. Government officials claimed a Viet Cong explosive caused the casualties. Citizens of Hue and foreign observers, however, were certain the victims had been killed by the security forces. "The crowd surrounded the armored vehicles and some of the troops, jostling them and shouting," according to John Helble, the American consul in Hue. "There was an immediate reaction on the local ground commander's part bordering on panic, and shots were fired."

The next day more than 10,000 Buddhists gathered in Hue to protest the massacre. Mobilizing quickly, Buddhist leaders drafted a manifesto and transmitted five demands to the Diem government: (1) cancel the ban on religious flags; (2) give Buddhists the same legal rights as Catholics; (3) stop government persecution of Buddhists; (4) allow Buddhists freedom to preach their faith; (5) compensate the families of the Hue victims and punish those responsible for the incident.

The five demands were an expression of the Buddhists' long-smoldering resentment toward the Diem regime. French-educated Catholics, many of whom were refugees from the Communist-controlled north, held a disproportionately high number of official government positions. Moreover, the Diem regime recognized Catholicism as a religion while classifying Buddhism as an "association," a legal distinction that made the acquisition of land for pagodas and permits for rallies completely dependent upon government goodwill.

On May 15, 1963, an eight-member Buddhist delegation officially presented the five demands to Diem in Saigon. Appearing conciliatory at the meeting, the South Vietnamese president agreed in principle with most of the Buddhist demands. He promised an investigation into the Hue incident but refused to compensate the victims' families. In the following weeks Diem took limited steps to redress the Buddhist grievances. He replaced the officials responsible for the Hue incident but delayed appointing a committee to negotiate with Buddhist leaders. According to U.S. intelligence sources, Diem feared that complete satisfaction of the five demands would encourage additional demands by Buddhists and other dissident groups.

Buddhist leaders, unhappy with Diem's limited concessions, vowed to continue demonstrating until all of their grievances were satisfied. On May 30 several hundred Buddhist monks and nuns in Saigon announced a forty-eight-hour hunger strike. Four days later 500 students gathered in Hue to protest religious discrimination. The demonstration turned violent, and sixty-seven students were injured in clashes with government forces.

The Buddhist crisis had caught the U.S. government flat-footed. In modern history Buddhist leaders had not played a significant role in South Vietnamese politics, and Kennedy administration officials quickly discovered that no one in the government really knew anything about Indochinese religions. Initially, the embassy in Saigon considered the demonstrations a local phenomenon peculiar to central Vietnam. But as the protests spread, the U.S. government recognized the magnitude of the threat. "Unless Diem is able to reach a quick reconciliation with the Buddhists," speculated the CIA's Office of Current Intelligence, "the issue could have serious repercussions on government stability."

State Department officials feared the effects of a prolonged religious-political struggle and sought immediate action by Diem to redress the Buddhist grievances. With Ambassador Nolting on home leave, the State Department instructed Deputy Chief of Mission William C. Trueheart to "urge necessary measures in strongest terms." A soft-spoken Virginian, forty-four-year-old Bill Trueheart was a career Foreign Service officer who had arrived in Vietnam nearly two years earlier. On June 4 he met with Nguyen Dinh Thuan, the secretary of state to the presidency. The Buddhist problem required "dramatic action" by the South Vietnamese government, Trueheart warned. In his opinion the United States could not continue to support the Diem government if there were further "bloody repressive action in Hue."

According to Trueheart's report to the State Department, his demarche produced "satisfyingly swift" results. Only hours after the appeal, Thuan had announced Diem's willingness to appoint a committee to resolve the Buddhist problem. The following day Thuan revealed the existence of separate secret negotiations between Buddhist leaders and the Diem government.

The negotiations were conducted in an atmosphere charged with distrust. Both sides ignored the informal propaganda truce and continued to distribute inflammatory tracts and leaflets. On June 7 Madame Nhu enraged Buddhist leaders by issuing a resolution that denounced them as Communist dupes. Trueheart immediately arranged a meeting with Diem to protest Madame Nhu's resolution, nominally a product of her Women's Solidarity Movement, one of the numerous paramilitary groups formed by the Ngo family. Throughout the interview, Diem seemed relaxed and friendly, uncharacteristically allowing his visitor frequent interruptions. "Meetings with Diem were normally occasions to get a long lecture," Trueheart said later. "Two or three hours of talk, usually repetitious of things he had said before and almost never anything worthy of reporting to Washington. They were simply a broken record."

Handing Diem the text of Madame Nhu's resolution, Trueheart said how "profoundly disappointed" he was by it. Speculating that the author sought to undermine the negotiations, Trueheart asked Diem to disavow the paper. The South Vietnamese president reacted calmly to the diplomat's observations but would not repudiate Madame Nhu's tract. Trueheart left the meeting sensing the resolution reflected Diem's own sentiments.

On June 11 Trueheart drafted the embassy's current analysis of the Buddhist problem: Diem's constructive actions had come too slowly to have maximum impact. And despite the South Vietnamese government's allegations, there was no apparent Communist influence on the Buddhist movement. Trueheart also noted that Buddhist actions had not been "above reproach." Their leaders had sought to enlist the foreign press in their cause, and there were reports that some Buddhists hoped to bring down the government. Despite the discouraging prospects for a settlement, the embassy believed "there is still some chance that [the] GVN will come to satisfactory terms with the Buddhists."

But that same day Buddhist leaders staged a dramatic gesture of protest that would virtually end any hope of a peaceful settlement. At about 10 A.M. a gray sedan leading a solemn Buddhist procession apparently stalled in the middle of one of Saigon's busiest intersections. The Venerable Quang Duc, a seventy-three-year-old Buddhist monk, emerged from the car and sat down in the street. Hundreds of curious spectators watched as two other monks drenched Quang Duc with gasoline. Sitting impassively, his head slightly bowed, the elderly monk lit a match and was immediately engulfed in flames. His face contorted in pain, Quang Duc remained silent as he burned alive. After several minutes, his charred body collapsed in the street.

The searing image of Quang Duc's immolation appeared in newspapers and magazines throughout the world. The grisly, visceral photographs fostered the false impression of intense religious persecution in Vietnam. "The [South Vietnamese] government handled the Buddhist crisis fairly badly and allowed it to grow," said William Colby, then chief of the CIA's Far East Division. "But I really don't think there was much they could have done about it once that bonze [Buddhist monk] burned himself."

In the view of State Department officials, the Buddhist problem was now "dangerously near the breaking point." Diem's failure to mollify Buddhist leaders had not only alienated much of the South Vietnamese urban population but also jeopardized American popular support for the war. "You could just see the situation deteriorating," Secretary of State Dean Rusk later recalled. "A large Buddhist majority tyrannized by the Catholic minority. That kind of deterioration in Vietnam would bounce back as a serious problem in this country."

Reacting immediately to Quang Duc's fire-suicide, the State Department cabled new instructions to Trueheart. The American chargé should tell Diem that he "must fully and unequivocally meet Buddhist demands . . . in a public and dramatic fashion." Should Diem not take this action, the U.S. government would "publicly state that it cannot associate itself with the GVN's unwillingness to meet the reasonable demands of the Vietnamese Buddhist leaders."

Intended as "an ominous warning," according to Trueheart, U.S. dissociation from Diem's Buddhist policy would have been an open invitation for a coup d'état. For nine years American support had indirectly shielded the South Vietnamese president from his domestic enemies, who realized that without U.S. goodwill—not to mention financial and military aid—no South Vietnamese government would long survive. Although the U.S. government had internally agonized over Diem's effectiveness, the embassy in Saigon had always discouraged conspiracies against the South Vietnamese president.

Because of Diem's present "precarious" political position, the State Department also suggested to Trueheart that he consider secretly passing a message to South Vietnamese Vice President Nguyen Ngoc Tho: Should Diem be ousted, an action "in which [the] U.S. would play no part," the Kennedy administration would back Tho as the constitutional successor and provide "military support."

Trueheart thought this provocative step, which would give Tho an incentive to conspire against Diem, unwise. Despite misgivings about the South Vietnamese president and his family, the American chargé was "not impressed by the competition." In response to Washington queries about U.S. contacts with Diem's non-Communist opponents, Trueheart reported: "We are receiving just now a surfeit of coup talk and anti-regime comment. It is to be expected in such circumstances that one is never in contact with the people (if any) who really mean business, but we have had all the lines out that we know how to put out and have had for some days. However, everyone is as usual under strict instructions not [repeat] not to encourage coup talk and to meet any that arises with [a] firm statement of U.S. support for GVN."

The private U.S. threat of dissociation momentarily slowed South Vietnam's slide toward political chaos. Trueheart delivered the message to Diem on June 12, and four days later the South Vietnamese president and Buddhist representatives signed a compromise agreement. The government offered to "assist" the families of the Hue incident victims but still refused to "compensate" them. This semantic distinction avoided the admission of government guilt, which Diem steadfastly rejected.

By June 16, however, the Buddhist crisis could no longer be papered over by compromise. The Buddhist movement was becoming increasingly dominated by younger, radical monks, who sought a return to the Buddhists' historic role as advisers of government. During the Ly dynasty (1009–1225), whose armies defeated Kublai Khan, Buddhism had not only achieved unsurpassed official support but had also acquired an aura of nationalism that continued into the twentieth century. By exploiting traditional Vietnamese associations of Buddhism with nationalism and Catholicism with foreign oppression, militant monks aimed to topple the Diem government. In late June Trueheart reported that "leading Buddhist officials" had sanctioned plans for a coup d'état organized by the Dai Viets, a semiclandestine political party opposed to both communism and Diem.

The most influential of the radical Buddhist leaders was Thich Tri Quang. Born about 1922 in northern Vietnam, Tri Quang was well educated and reportedly had been a lawyer before becoming a monk. Organizer of the demonstrations in Hue, he denied deliberately instigating the violence of May 8. He did later admit, however, to exploiting the incident to force a showdown with the Diem government. Eventually, the CIA concluded that Tri Quang was "an ambitious, skillful, ruthless, political manipulator and born demagogue." But during the summer of 1963, the Buddhist monk was a complete enigma to U.S. officials, who could not penetrate the haze of Asian mysticism surrounding his political ambitions. "You'd ask as tactfully and diplomatically as possible the obvious questions about Buddhist intentions and so on," recalled John Helble. "He'd sort of look off to the top of his little room in the pagoda where I'd meet him, and the answer would come out something like, 'The sky is blue, but the clouds drift across it.' And I'm just not very good at interpreting this kind of stuff."

Despite his otherworldly pronouncements and ascetic lifestyle, Tri Quang and his disciples had a secular grasp of public relations, an area in which they outclassed both the Diem government and the U.S. mission in Saigon. Posters at demonstrations were written in both Vietnamese and English to focus U.S. public opinion on the Buddhist cause. Moreover, Buddhist leaders skillfully cultivated Western newsmen, tipping them off to fire-suicides and demonstrations.

As the summer wore on the Ngo family became more intractable, too. On June 25 CIA Chief of Station John Richardson unsuccessfully attempted to persuade Nhu of the need

Buddhist monks at a social gathering with generals Duong Van Minh and Nguyen Khanh in 1964.

for compromise in the crisis. Lashing out at the Buddhist leaders, Diem's brother bitterly observed: "They have never spoken out or taken up the fight against communism."

Nhu regarded the Buddhist demonstrators as outlaws and a dangerous threat to the regime. Deeply resenting American embassy pressure to satisfy the Buddhist demands, Nhu strongly opposed his brother's limited concessions and believed the regime had been weak and ineffective in dealing with the problem. "If a government is incapable of applying the law, it should fall," Nhu declared, "and I am the first to feel so."

Ominously, Diem's brother indicated that in a national emergency, family ties would not prevent him from opposing the government. "Nhu is in a state of emotional shock and is in a dangerous frame of mind," Richardson warned in his report of the meeting. "It is possible that Nhu would lead efforts against Diem should he feel that a point of drastic deterioration had occurred."

With events spinning out of control, Vietnam began to attract Kennedy's daily attention for the first time in his presidency. Sensitive to the appearance of religious persecution, the first Roman Catholic president reacted with extreme shock to the Buddhist crisis. "How could this have happened?" he asked Michael Forrestal. "Who are these people? Why didn't we know about them before?"

On July 4, 1963, senior State Department officials briefed the president on the crisis in South Vietnam. Brother Nhu reportedly intended to sabotage the June 16 agreement with the Buddhists, and the English-language *Times of Vietnam* had contained veiled attacks on the United States. The newspaper, dominated by the Nhus, also suggested that the monk who had burned himself had been drugged. Kennedy interrupted Roger Hilsman's presentation to ask if that were possible. "Religious fervor," replied Hilsman, "was an adequate explanation."

Kennedy, who found Madame Nhu's inflammatory outbursts particularly irritating, next considered the question of removing the Nhus and their malign influence from Saigon. In the past the South Vietnamese president had icily ignored this suggestion. Kennedy and his foreign policy advisers concluded that Diem would still be unwilling to remove his brother and most trusted adviser. Acknowledging that escalating Buddhist demands might threaten Diem's political survival, the assembled officials anticipated coup attempts in the coming months. There was doubt, however, whether any of them would be successful. During a generally optimistic discussion of the likely consequences of a successful coup d'état, Hilsman declared: "The chances of chaos in the wake of a coup are considerably less than they were a year ago."

The U.S. intelligence community also believed a coup was likely. On the same day as Kennedy's meeting with the State Department officials, the CIA station in Saigon received its first reliable report of active plotting among ARVN general officers. One week later Central Intelligence Director McCone issued a Special National Intelligence Estimate (SNIE) examining the political crisis. Guardedly optimistic about the prospects of a successor government, the SNIE concluded: "A non-Communist successor regime might be initially less effective against the Viet Cong, but, given continued support from the U.S., could provide reasonably effective leadership for the government and the war effort."

Not all American officials, however, shared such hopeful estimates of the effects of a coup d'état. Ambassador Frederick Nolting believed that "the most likely result of a coup attempt that succeeded in killing Diem was civil war." His European vacation over, the embittered diplomat stopped off in Washington before returning to Saigon. During the previous six weeks, his patient, often frustrating two-year attempt to build up Diem's confidence in the U.S. government had been almost completely destroyed. Critical of the tough U.S. policy toward the South Vietnamese government, Nolting resented the vigor with which Bill Trueheart, his friend and hand-picked deputy, had executed the instructions from Washington. Years later Nolting admitted it had been a mistake to take a vacation during such a crucial period but berated the embassy and State Department for failing to keep him informed. "Nobody let me know one word of what was happening," he charged. "It seems obvious to me that those who wanted to let Diem hang himself didn't want me back in Saigon."

Washington officials had also neglected to inform Nolting that he would be replaced as ambassador by Henry Cabot

Lodge, whose appointment the vacationing diplomat had learned of by commercial radio broadcast. Before returning to Vietnam, the lame-duck ambassador defended the South Vietnamese government to doubting Kennedy administration officials. He also criticized the State Department's tactics with Diem. The more he was prodded, Nolting warned, the slower Diem would go. Furthermore, if Lodge were built up as a strongman, his job would be that much tougher.

In Saigon, Nolting made a last-ditch effort to persuade Diem to take the steps necessary to resolve the Buddhist problem. On July 18 the ambassador reported: "Day spent urging, encouraging, warning, [and] trying to get President Diem to move in [a] constructive manner." For all his effort, Nolting succeeded only in wringing a terse nationwide radio broadcast out of Diem that instructed government negotiators to "closely cooperate" with the Buddhist representatives.

During the final days of the ambassador's term, Vietnam's political fabric continued to disintegrate. The civil disturbances increased in frequency and intensity, and there was a second Buddhist fire-suicide. Madame Nhu, exhibiting her unerring flair for venomous pronouncements, publicly denounced Buddhist leaders: "All they have done is barbecue a bonze."

Nolting bid farewell to Diem on August 14. During, in his own words, a "strenuous goodbye," the ambassador made a final plea for a public statement by Diem that would restore faith in his stated policy of conciliation with the Buddhists. If Diem refused to repudiate Madame Nhu's remarks and clearly demonstrate who was running the government, warned Nolting, "it would be impossible for the U.S. government to continue our present relationship."

Diem responded with his standard rebuttals: Americans understood neither the Buddhist problem nor his family's selfless contributions to Vietnam. Finally, perhaps as a parting gesture of friendship to Nolting, Diem promised to issue a statement. In an interview the next day the South Vietnamese president solemnly declared: "My policy of reconciliation with the Buddhists is irreversible."

During the interregnum between Nolting's departure and Lodge's arrival, the Diem regime took a desperate gamble to suppress the Buddhist problem once and for all. If successful,

Henry Cabot Lodge, left, replaced Frederick E. Nolting, Jr., as American ambassador to South Vietnam in August 1963. *(John F. Kennedy Library)*

the plan would present the new ambassador with a fait accompli. The Americans would undoubtedly protest, perhaps even dissociate themselves from the government, but they might also eventually acquiesce. Predictably, the plan was Ngo Dinh Nhu's.

He began by attempting to blunt the impact of a possible U.S. declaration of dissociation. On August 15, the day Nolting left Saigon, Nhu warned ARVN's general officers of a possible change in U.S. policy toward South Vietnam. He cited the recently concluded nuclear test ban treaty with the Soviet Union as evidence of an emerging U.S. policy of appeasement toward communism. South Vietnam, he said, must be prepared to stand independently of the United States.

Nhu's announcement was part of a deadly game of cat and mouse that he played with senior ARVN commanders. Aware of conspiracies among the generals, he constantly sought to confuse and divide them. One month earlier Diem's brother had informed several general officers that he knew of their plans to move against the government. He observed that there were two ways for dealing with a coup d'état—either break it like an egg before the chicken has hatched, or, if it cannot be prevented join in and exploit it.

Many of the generals had interpreted Nhu's statement as a bid for support to oust Diem. Although he was universally hated by the military, some officers viewed the president's brother as a vehicle to power. After the July confrontation with Nhu, one general had observed conspiratorially: There are "many methods of attacking a target in a military operation."

On August 20 the army unwittingly furthered Nhu's plan to suppress the Buddhists by asking the government to impose martial law. Some officers sought to prevent the civil disturbances from undermining the war effort; others intended to advance their plot. The proposed martial law decree would rearrange army command relationships to the plotters' advantage.

Nhu unhesitatingly supported the generals' request. With martial law in effect, the army would be held responsible for his planned operation against the Buddhists. Discredited by the crackdown, the military would become much less attractive alternative leadership to both the Vietnamese population and the American government. With his brother's endorsement, Diem agreed to impose martial law immediately.

Then Nhu sprang the trap.

Shortly after midnight on August 21, 1963, only minutes after the martial law decree went into effect, Combat Police and Special Forces units launched a series of nationwide attacks against Buddhist pagodas. Nhu's shock troops, who took their orders directly from the palace rather than the regular military chain of command, stormed pagodas in Saigon, Hue, Quang Tri, and Nha Trang. They arrested more than 1,400 Buddhist monks and nuns, stripping the movement of most of its leadership.

The violent repudiation of Diem's avowed policy of conciliation stunned Americans in Saigon and Washington. Ambassador Nolting, who was conferring with Lodge and other senior officials in Honolulu, sent Diem a personal telegram: "This is the first time you have ever gone back on your word to me."

Nolting's reproach would be among the mildest American reactions to the pagoda raids. Their patience exhausted, Kennedy administration officials soon turned to an instrument of policy more pointed than a note of diplomatic protest but less visible than a battalion of Marines: the covert action capability of the CIA.

CHAPTER SEVEN

THE POINT OF
NO RETURN

The aging, propeller-driven Lockheed Constellation touched down at Saigon's Tan Son Nhut Airport at 9:30 P.M., August 22, 1963. A small group of American officials, a South Vietnamese protocol officer, and about forty newspaper reporters waited as the plane taxied up to the VIP terminal. With flashbulbs popping in the evening drizzle, Henry Cabot Lodge, the new U.S. ambassador to South Vietnam, stepped out of the plane. After uttering a greeting in Vietnamese, Lodge made a brief statement to the press. Although declining comment on the martial law decree, the pagoda raids, or other substantive issues, Lodge spoke of the importance of the news media in a democracy and welcomed the chance to assist the newsmen in their work.

Lodge's friendly chat with the reporters contrasted sharply with his predecessor's frequently bitter press relations and demonstrated the new ambassador's deft political touch. Earlier that day in Tokyo Lodge had similarly pacified a Buddhist delegation, one of whom, a tearful, agitated nun, had threatened to starve herself to death should the situation in Vietnam not improve. Lodge made no direct attempt to dissuade the nun, but he did stress President Kennedy's personal concern for Vietnamese Buddhists. After the forty-minute meeting, the nun solemnly promised not to commit suicide.

Born to a distinguished New England family, Henry Cabot Lodge was a nationally known Republican who had been a U.S. senator, a delegate to the United Nations, and his party's 1960 vice presidential candidate. During his career in government, Lodge had acquired a reputation for being aloof, independent, and imperious. The similarity between his and Diem's

108

patrician bearing and the assumption that Lodge's appointment signaled a tougher U.S. policy prompted American newsmen to joke with Vietnamese that "our old mandarin can lick your old mandarin."

Lodge had originally volunteered for the Vietnam assignment in 1961, when Kennedy considered introducing U.S. combat troops into the country. Although a defeated political rival of the president, Lodge had earned Kennedy's respect for his strength and toughness. Shortly after the first Buddhist fire-suicide, the president finally accepted Lodge's offer of service. Initially, some White House staffers objected to the appointment of an opposition politician. President Kennedy, however, viewed Lodge's party affiliation as an asset. Should the situation in Vietnam collapse, the presence of a prominent Republican might help to prevent the bitter partisan recriminations that followed the 1949 Communist revolution in China.

Lodge arrived in Saigon thirty minutes after the curfew prescribed by martial law. As his motorcade sped from the airport through the empty Saigon streets, the only people he saw were armed soldiers posted at every intersection. The sight of South Vietnamese troops occupying their own capital strengthened Lodge's belief that Diem had lost the support of his own people. One of the ambassador's first official tasks was to sort out the tangled power relationships in Saigon. Had the military taken over the government? Had Diem strengthened his position by using the army to crush the Buddhists? Or was Ngo Dinh Nhu now calling the shots? After briefings by senior mission officials, Lodge reported to Washington: "We feel reasonably sure that no military coup has taken place and that the palace is in control. Exact roles of Diem, Nhu and Madame Nhu are not clear but weight of evidence is that the influence of Nhus has not diminished."

One day after Lodge's arrival Major General Tran Van Don invited Lieutenant Colonel Lucien Conein to Joint General Staff headquarters. General Don, commander of the South Vietnamese armed forces under the martial law decree, had a very important and confidential message for Conein to deliver to the new American ambassador: The army had not been responsible for the crackdown on the Buddhists.

Conein accepted Don's invitation. The Vietnamese general,

like many of ARVN's leading officers, was a long-standing friend of the irreverent, leather-lunged raconteur who never old the same story twice about how he had lost the last joints of the forefinger and middle finger of his right hand. Yet it was not merely friendship that drew Conein to this meeting. Nominally a military adviser in the Ministry of Interior, Lou Conein worked for the CIA.

A Foreign Legionnaire until the fall of France in 1940, Conein had enlisted in the U.S. Army and volunteered for the Office of Strategic Services. Like many OSS officers, he learned his trade from the British Secret Intelligence Service and Special Operations Executive. One of the first Americans to parachute into Vietnam near the end of World War II, he had helped organize resistance to the Japanese. Conein returned to Vietnam on July 1, 1954, two months after the French defeat at Dien Bien Phu. Headquartered in Hanoi, he was a member of Colonel Edward G. Lansdale's Saigon Military Mission. Throughout the summer and early fall of 1954, Conein conducted sabotage operations and organized a network of Vietnamese agents. Before leaving Hanoi on October 9, 1954, the date by which all foreign troops had to leave North Vietnam, he prepared a surprise for the Communists. He had been living in the mansion of the Vietnamese governor and assumed that a high-ranking party official would inherit the house. Conein filled the refrigerator with C-3 plastic explosive and armed the huge bomb with an electrical detonator. If the refrigerator were plugged in, the explosives would destroy the house and most of the surrounding neighborhood. The American consul in Hanoi, unimpressed by Conein's initiative, ordered the bomb dismantled.

Conein left Vietnam in 1956 and, after a hitch in Iran, returned in December 1961. Drawing on established friendships within the South Vietnamese military, Conein provided the embassy with timely intelligence about conspiracies brewing in the army. "He had a relationship with these generals that nobody else could match," recalled Trueheart. "He had known them since he was a lieutenant and they were corporals and sergeants."

Despite his long friendship with General Don, the CIA operative was apprehensive about their planned meeting. In the wake of the pagoda raids, Saigon seethed with intrigue and treachery. Taking no chances, Conein went to JGS headquarters armed. During a rambling and sometimes cryptic conversation, Don denied prior knowledge of the pagoda raids and protested recent Voice of America broadcasts blaming the army for the attacks. Conein probed to discover if there were plans for a coup, but Don was evasive. The martial law decree was "the first step," said the Vietnamese general, "and the secret of what is going to happen [next] is not mine to give."

General Don's conversation with Conein was the first of several reports by senior South Vietnamese officials identifying Ngo Dinh Nhu as the éminence grise behind the pagoda raids. Later that same day Brigadier General Le Van Kim, Don's deputy and brother-in-law, warned that the public impression of army responsibility for the attacks would hamper the war effort against the Communists. The key question, declared Kim, was the attitude of the United States. If the U.S. government were to take a clear position against the Nhus and support "an army action to remove them from the government," the military would carry it out.

Civilian government officials added their voices to the growing chorus seeking Nhu's ouster and a clear expression of U.S. support. Even Diem's personal secretary, Vo Van Hai, pleaded with a Foreign Service officer to "save the boss by getting rid of Nhu." Ambassador Lodge reported these meetings to Washington but refrained from endorsing any army action to remove Nhu. Noting that several important military commanders in Saigon were still presumed loyal to the regime, Lodge cabled that at this time U.S. support for any such plan would be a "shot in the dark."

The telegrams reporting the ground swell of Vietnamese support for Ngo Dinh Nhu's expulsion landed on the desk of Assistant Secretary of State Roger Hilsman, who had been outraged by the pagoda raids. He believed that "if Nhu continued in power the regime would continue to follow the suicidal policies that were not only dragging Vietnam down to ignominy and disaster but the United States as well." While Hilsman recognized the potential for political chaos in South Vietnam if the army moved against the government, he was convinced "there would be even more political instability if the Diem-Nhu regime continued as it was."

Averell Harriman, then under secretary of state for political affairs, agreed that the United States could no longer support a Diem-Nhu government. With Harriman providing the prestige and Hilsman the energy, the two State Department officials drafted one of the most controversial telegrams of the entire Vietnam conflict. The message would not only initiate official U.S. involvement in the overthrow of Diem but would also bitterly divide Kennedy's top foreign policy advisers.

Known as the August 24 cable, the telegram informed Lodge that the "U.S. government cannot tolerate [a] situation in which power lies in Nhu's hands" and instructed the new ambassador to demand his removal. Realizing that Diem might not comply with the U.S. ultimatum, Harriman and Hilsman ominously warned: "We must face the possibility that Diem himself cannot be preserved."

The cable ordered Lodge to "tell key military leaders that [the] U.S. would find it impossible to continue to support [the] GVN militarily and economically" unless the Buddhist grievances were redressed and the Nhus removed from power. The telegram also instructed the U.S. mission to "make detailed plans as to how we might bring about Diem's replacement if this should become necessary." Although refusing to give "detailed instructions as to how this operation should proceed," the State Department assured Lodge: "We will back you to the hilt on actions you take to achieve our objectives."

Hilsman sent an early draft of the cable to Secretary of State Rusk, who was spending the weekend in New York at the United Nations. According to Hilsman, Rusk strengthened the telegram by adding a sentence offering South Vietnamese military leaders "direct support in any interim period of breakdown [of the] central government." Dean Rusk, however, is "absolutely certain" that he did not add this sentence to the cable.

Throughout the drafting process, Harriman and Hilsman maintained continuous contact with Michael Forrestal, who participated in drafting the cable and kept the president informed. The State Department officials wanted to send out the telegram immediately to take advantage of the political chaos

Department of State

INDICATE: ☐ COLLECT
☐ CHARGE TO

TOP SECRET
───────────────────────
Classification

Origin

ACTION: AmEmbassy SAIGON - OPERATIONAL IMMEDIATE, Aug 24 8 36 PM '63

243

Info:

EYES ONLY - AMBASSADOR LODGE
FOR CINCPAC/POLAD EXCLUSIVE FOR ADMIRAL FELT
NO FURTHER DISTRIBUTION

~~XROMXHARRIMANXXANEXHIESMAN~~

Re CAS Saigon 0265 reporting General Don's views; Saigon
320, ~~and~~ Saigon 316, and Saigon 329.

It is now clear that whether military proposed martial
law or whether Nhu tricked them into it, Nhu took advantage of
its imposition to smash pagodas with police and Tung's Special
Forces loyal to him, thus placing onus on military in eyes of
world and Vietnamese people. Also clear that Nhu has maneuvered
himself into commanding position.

US Government cannot tolerate situation in which power
lies in Nhu's hands. Diem must be given chance to rid himself
of Nhu x and his coterie and replace them with best military
and political personalities available.

If, in spite of all of your efforts, Diem remains obdurate
and refuses, then we must face the possibility that Diem himself
cannot be preserved.

Drafted by:
FE:RHilsman:ml   8/24/63

Telegraphic transmissions and
classification approved by: M - W. Averell Harriman

Clearances:
FE - Mr. Hilsman
WH - Mr. Forrestal
U - Mr. Ball   S/S-O - Mr. ~~Collingwood~~ Getsinger

TOP SECRET

FORM
8-61 DS-322

Classification

Facsimile of page 1 of the August 24 cable.

in Saigon and to prevent Nhu from consolidating his position. With White House muscle behind the cable, Harriman and Hilsman hoped to shortcut the time-consuming deliberations that would normally be involved in such an important policy decision.

On Saturday afternoon Forrestal called the president, who was spending the weekend in Hyannis Port, Massachusetts, and read him the telegram. "I told him that at this time the only people who had functioned on it were with the Department of State," recalled Forrestal.

"Can't we wait until Monday, when everybody is back?" Kennedy asked.

Averell and Roger, replied Forrestal, "really want to get this thing out right away."

"Well," said the president, "go and see what you can do to get it cleared."

Forrestal immediately began seeking concurrence with the telegram from government agencies with an interest in Vietnam. This task was complicated by the absence from Washington of virtually all of the administration's senior officials. McNamara was climbing Grand Teton Mountain in Wyoming, McCone was on a brief holiday at his home in California, and McGeorge Bundy, the president's national security adviser, was also away on a short vacation. Forrestal managed to track down Marine Major General Victor H. Krulak at the Chevy Chase Club in suburban Maryland, where he had just finished a round of golf. Krulak, the Joint Chiefs' special assistant for counterinsurgency, agreed to meet the presidential aide at the White House Situation Room. "I read the cable," Krulak recalled, "and realized it was a very important one that I wouldn't touch."

Throughout the summer, Krulak's chiefs at the Pentagon had warned that no real alternative leadership to Diem existed and that his overthrow would damage the war effort against the Communists. Speaking for the military years later, General Maxwell D. Taylor remembered: "Our position was that Diem is certainly not ideal; he is a terrible pain in the neck in many ways. But he is an honest man; he is devoted to his country, and we are for him until we can find someone better—looking under the bushes for George Washington, as I used to call it."

After informing Forrestal that the message would require the judgment of the "heavies" in the Pentagon, Krulak set out to find General Taylor. While the White House aide tried to reach the Pentagon's civilian leaders, Harriman and Hilsman located Under Secretary of State George Ball, who also happened to be playing golf at the Chevy Chase Club. As acting secretary of state in Rusk's absence, Ball would have to sign the cable. The State Department officials went to Ball's home, where Harriman showed the under secretary the proposed telegram. Refusing to initial the cable until he had spoken with the president, Ball telephoned Kennedy in Hyannis Port and read him the key passages. According to Ball, "The president on the whole seemed favorable to our proposed message, although he recognized the risk that, if a coup occurred, we might not like Diem's successor any better than Diem himself. But finally he said, 'If Rusk and [Deputy Secretary of Defense Roswell] Gilpatric agree, George, then go ahead.' "

Ball then called Secretary of State Rusk in New York and told him about the cable and his discussion with the president. Rusk "was cautious," wrote Ball in his memoirs, "but made it clear that, if the president understood the implications, he would give a green light." Years later Rusk explained his concurrence with the telegram: "If Ball, Harriman, and President Kennedy were going to send it out, I wasn't going to raise any questions."

Late Saturday afternoon Forrestal telephoned Gilpatric at his farm in Maryland. After learning that the president, Rusk, and Ball favored the cable, Gilpatric cleared it for the civilian side of the Defense Department. Although "somewhat unhappy about the thrust of the cable," Gilpatric regarded the message as a political decision and, therefore, a State Department matter. Richard Helms, the CIA's deputy director of plans and the agency's watch officer that day, shared Gilpatric's view that the telegram was a policy decision. Without informing McCone, Helms cleared the cable for the CIA, bluntly expressing his personal agreement with the message: "It's about time we bit this bullet."

By dusk on Saturday every interested agency in the government, with the exception of the Joint Chiefs, had approved the August 24 cable. Finally, according to Forrestal, Krulak reported in by telephone: Although General Taylor had not liked the telegram, he would raise no objections. But Krulak, years later, did not recall making any such phone call. By his account, the Marine general found Taylor late in the day and told him about the telegram: "I described to him [Taylor] the situation, and he took it from there."

Complicating the matter further is General Taylor's claim that he first learned of the cable when Roswell Gilpatric phoned him Saturday evening. Although Gilpatric had not called McNamara, he was sufficiently disturbed by the message to inform Taylor, who requested that a copy of the telegram be brought to his quarters at Fort Myer, Virginia. While Taylor waited for the text of the message, Forrestal called the president, who now had a copy of the cable in front of him. The White House aide reported to Kennedy that his government had concurred with the telegram; everybody was on board. Without comment, the president replied: "Send it out." And at 9:36 P.M., EDT, August 24, the State Department transmitted DEPTEL (State Department telegram) 243 to Saigon.

The hurried and irregular fashion in which the August 24 cable had been drafted, cleared, and sent triggered a furious backlash among the president's senior advisers. Although the Defense Department and CIA had concurred with the cable, neither McNamara nor McCone had been personally informed of it. And when General Taylor finally received a copy of the telegram—sometime between 10:00 and 11:00 P.M. that Saturday night—he was enraged, believing that "the anti-Diem group centered in State had taken advantage of the absence of the principal officials to get out instructions which would never have been approved as written under normal circumstances."

Ambassador Lodge received the State Department cable on Sunday, August 25. Accepting the message as a policy decision from Washington, he convened a meeting of top mission officials to determine how best to execute the instructions. They agreed that Diem would never remove Nhu from power. Even to deliver such an ultimatum might alert the palace to the army's plans, giving Nhu the chance to block the generals' action. Lodge believed this risk was not worth taking. After the meeting, he asked the State Department to modify his instructions: "Propose we go straight to generals with our demands, without informing Diem. Would tell them we [are] prepared [to] have

Diem without Nhus but it is in effect up to them whether to keep him."

The State Department replied that same day: "Agree to modification proposed."

Yet before Lodge had a chance to communicate with any of the South Vietnamese generals, the Voice of America (VOA) inadvertently jeopardized the budding conspiracy. On Monday morning, August 26, the VOA broadcast a statement authorized by the State Department absolving the army of responsibility for the pagoda raids: "High American officials blame police, headed by President Diem's brother Ngo Dinh Nhu, for anti-Buddhist actions in the Vietnam Republic. The officials say Vietnam military leaders are not, repeat not, responsible for last week's attacks against pagodas and the mass arrest of monks and students."

The 8:00 A.M. broadcast also contained American press speculation echoing the State Department ultimatum to remove Nhu: "The U.S. may sharply reduce its aid to Vietnam unless President Diem gets rid of secret police officials responsible for the attacks."

Embassy officials were horrified by the broadcast. By publicly exonerating the military, the U.S. government had, in effect, declared itself with the army and against the government. "We thought the VOA broadcast was very ill-advised," Trueheart later said. "It didn't make much sense to me to telegraph your intentions."

Lodge fired off an angry telegram to Washington. The VOA broadcast, he charged, had "complicated our already difficult problem" by eliminating "the possibility of the generals' effort achieving surprise." Dean Rusk cabled an apology to Lodge, and the VOA promptly broadcast a denial that the U.S. was considering cutting off aid to South Vietnam—thereby intensifying Vietnamese speculation about U.S. intentions.

Lodge and Trueheart believed the VOA broadcast had endangered the U.S. mission. The ambassador was scheduled to present his diplomatic credentials to Diem at 11:00 A.M., and they feared that Lodge and the party accompanying him might be taken hostage. Deciding it would be unwise for all senior mission personnel to attend the ceremony, Lodge instructed General Harkins and CIA Station Chief Richardson to remain behind. To the Americans' relief, the ten-minute diplomatic ceremony went smoothly.

Despite the exposed American position, Lodge ordered the CIA to canvass its ARVN contacts and to help the generals develop a plan for a coup d'état. To encourage the generals to move, CIA operatives should warn them that unless the Nhus were removed from power and the Buddhist grievances redressed, the U.S. government would no longer support South Vietnam militarily and economically. Although prepared to offer direct support during an interim period of central government breakdown, the U.S. would not help in the initial act of assuming power. Win or lose, the coup would be a Vietnamese affair, and the generals should not expect to be "bailed out."

Later in the day Lou Conein conveyed these points to Brigadier General Tran Thien Khiem, ARVN chief of staff. General Khiem, thirty-seven, had been one of Diem's staunchest supporters. He had commanded the loyalist forces that rescued Diem during the unsuccessful 1960 paratroopers' coup d'état. Promoted and favored by the South Vietnamese president, Khiem remarked to Conein: "I am one of the people who has profited most by my relationship with Diem." But like many ARVN commanders, General Khiem had become disaffected by Diem's military meddling, the Buddhist crisis, and Nhu's increasing influence. Khiem agreed with the American points and suggested that Conein meet with Major General Duong Van "Big" Minh, President Diem's military adviser and the leader of the generals' coup committee.

While Conein met with Khiem, CIA operative Al Spera flew to the Central Highlands headquarters of Brigadier General Nguyen Khanh. Spera, nominally an embassy political adviser to the ARVN Joint General Staff, had worked with Khanh for years, and the two men had developed a mutual trust. Only the day before the general had come to Spera's home in Saigon, where he had revealed the plan to move against the government. Khanh had refused to identify the other officers in the conspiracy, but when asked about General Khiem's loyalties, he had clasped his hands together and replied: "We are like this."

Now, twenty-four hours later, the CIA operative reported

that the United States government supported the generals' coup. Following instructions, Spera informed the Vietnamese general that the embassy was simultaneously approaching Khiem, a decision based on Khanh's remark the day before. Khanh, feeling compromised and convinced that the Americans could not keep a secret, threw his hands up in despair. "The U.S. government is endangering the entire plan," he said.

Khanh decided to fly to Saigon immediately to assess the damage caused by the American security breach. From this point on, said the general upon leaving, he would have nothing further to do with anyone from the U.S. embassy.

When President Kennedy returned to Washington on Monday, August 26, he was surprised to find Robert McNamara and John McCone angrily raising objections to the August 24 cable, which supposedly had the concurrence of the entire government. General Taylor, after conferring with the Joint Chiefs, also voiced his misgivings about the telegram. "Great indignation was felt by McCone, McNamara, and myself," General Taylor later said, "particularly when we saw the last line of the cable: 'knowledge of this telegram [has been restricted] to minimum essential people.' "

Central Intelligence Director John McCone, sixty-one, was particularly distressed about the lack of consultation. A conservative Republican, he had served in the Defense Department during Truman's presidency and had assisted in the establishment of the CIA. Like senior military officials, McCone believed Diem was the best available leader in South Vietnam. Furthermore, the CIA would be heavily involved in executing the telegram's instructions. "McCone made no bones about the fact that he felt he had a responsibility to give advice on the intelligence aspects of things," recalled William Colby.

Kennedy had specifically sought McCone's endorsement of the August 24 cable and was furious with Michael Forrestal for not holding up the telegram until Monday. Forrestal offered his resignation, but the president refused it, snapping: "You're not worth firing. You owe me something, so you stick around."

At a stormy noon White House meeting, Kennedy's advisers battled among themselves to determine whether the instructions in the August 24 cable should or could be reversed. State

Department officials argued for reaffirming the message. "I held my ground that the telegram was essential in view of the evil influence of the Nhus," George Ball wrote in his memoirs.

Despite their objections, neither the military nor McCone recommended rescinding the cable. "I wasn't for calling it back," Taylor recalled. "You can't change American policy in twenty-four hours and expect anyone to ever believe you again."

To avoid any possible misunderstanding, the president, who seemed to Ball "annoyed by the waffling of his top command," went around the table, asking each of his advisers if he favored backing off from the cable: "John, do you want to cancel it? Bob, do you want to cancel it? Dean, do you want to cancel it?" None of them did. The August 24 cable stood as written.

During the meeting, General Taylor asked the State Department officials about the telegram's reference to "direct support" to the generals. Hilsman explained that the United States could bypass the port of Saigon and the Diem government by resupplying the army through Hue. General Taylor, the man ultimately responsible for such a logistical feat, considered Hilsman's answer "cock-eyed" and requested time to study the feasibility of such a plan.

As the meeting adjourned, General Taylor suggested that Ambassador Nolting, who was now back in Washington, be invited to the next meeting. Harriman opposed this, saying that Nolting's view was "colored."

"Maybe properly colored," mused the president.

On Tuesday, August 27, Kennedy met again with his advisers to assess the prospects and progress of the anticipated coup d'état. Nolting doubted that the operation would succeed. "The Vietnamese generals haven't the guts of Diem or Nhu," he said. "They will not be a unified group, but will be badly split. They do not have real leadership, and they do not control the predominant military force in the country."

The president questioned Nolting about Diem: Why hasn't he kept his promises to us? Why had the South Vietnamese government used force against the Buddhists? What was Madame Nhu's authority? Reading from handwritten notes, Ambassador Nolting defended the South Vietnamese president and recommended that the U.S. government "try once again to persuade Diem to limit the authority of Nhu and to force the political liquidation of Madame Nhu."

According to the meeting minutes, Nolting told the president that Diem and Nhu were "Siamese twins who could not be forced apart." He reminded Kennedy that three years earlier Ambassador Durbrow had asked Diem to post Nhu abroad. The South Vietnamese president had refused, and it was Durbrow who left Vietnam. Smiling at the irony of the situation, Kennedy remarked, "If you're right, Lodge's tour will be the shortest round trip in history."

The doubts raised at this meeting prompted Washington to cable the embassy for more information about the planned coup and its leaders. Despite the policymakers' misgivings, Secretary of State Rusk concluded the meeting by saying: "We should make clear to our officials in Saigon that we [are] not changing their existing directive [the August 24 cable] on which they [have] already proceeded to take numerous actions."

In Saigon, Vietnamese and Americans braced for the seemingly inevitable collision between Diem and his army. The government had closed the schools, and Nhu had ordered civilian opponents of the regime arrested. As coup rumors swirled through the streets of the city, the conspiring generals quietly moved another airborne battalion into Saigon, bringing the number under their direct command to four. Two additional battalions could be deployed to the capital within eight hours.

Diem and Nhu were also making military preparations for a showdown. They had already deliberately split the South Vietnamese military forces around Saigon into three separate commands. By dealing with each of the three commanders separately, the regime hoped to prevent any single officer from controlling the troops necessary for a successful coup.

The cornerstone of the Ngo brothers' defenses was Brigadier General Ton That Dinh, the mercurial military governor of Saigon. "An aggressive, arrogant officer frequently erratic in personal behavior," according to the CIA, Dinh was a "rice-bowl" Catholic, whose conversion had been prompted by the belief that it would advance his career. The thirty-six-year-old general had 2,500 paratroopers, 1,500 marines, and 700 military police at his disposal. His command also included the Fifth

Infantry Division, which had helped lift the siege of the presidential palace during the unsuccessful 1960 coup.

The Diem regime's other bulwark was Colonel Le Quang Tung. A devout Catholic from central Vietnam, the bespectacled Tung commanded the Ngo family's Praetorian Guard: 900 Special Forces, 1,700 Presidential Guards, and 750 Combat Police. One week earlier, the Special Forces, funded and trained by the CIA for covert operations in North Vietnam and Laos, and the Combat Police had conducted the pagoda raids. Hated by the military, Tung was the leader of the military Can Lao, a network of spies within the army that reported to Nhu.

On Wednesday, August 28, John Richardson warned: "Situation here has reached [the] point of no return. Saigon is [an] armed camp. Current indications are that [the] Ngo family have dug in for a last ditch battle." Richardson believed the conspiring generals could not retreat now. He predicted they would act and win, but unless the generals "neutralized" General Dinh and Colonel Tung at the outset, there might be "widespread fighting in Saigon and serious loss of life."

Ostensibly an embassy first secretary, forty-nine-year-old John Hammond Richardson had served in Greece and the Philippines, two countries that had successfully resisted Communist insurgencies in the 1950s. Because he maintained a close relationship with Nhu, who supervised all of the government's intelligence activities, the conspiring generals mistrusted Richardson. In fact, he was sympathetic to the regime. Like his predecessor in Saigon, William Colby, he had not been particularly disturbed by Diem's authoritarian and heavy-handed style of government. The United States, Richardson believed, was in Vietnam to fight communism, not democratize the government.

But the CIA station chief also thought the situation had "changed drastically" since the pagoda raids. In his August 28 telegram to McCone, he predicted: "If the Ngo family wins now, they and Vietnam will stagger on to final defeat at the hands of their own people and the VC. . . . If this attempt by the generals does not take place or if it fails, we believe it no exaggeration to say that [Vietnam] runs serious risk of being lost over the course of time."

That same day, Ambassador Lodge responded to State Department queries about the planned coup and its leaders. The prospects for a coup were favorable, wired Lodge, and the "chances of success would be diminished by delay." In contrast to Richardson and Lodge, General Harkins was skeptical of the generals' operation. The balance of forces, he cabled, did not seem to give the rebels a clear-cut advantage: "I don't believe there is sufficient reason for a crash approval on our part at this time."

General Harkins's uncharacteristic pessimism surprised Kennedy and his civilian advisers. Suspicious, the president requested a copy of the Pentagon telegram soliciting Harkins's advice. Drafted by General Taylor, the Pentagon message urgently requested Harkins's views on the overall feasibility of the generals' planned coup. The last paragraph of Taylor's cable, however, seemed to suggest how General Harkins should answer the inquiry: "FYI State to Saigon 243 [the August 24 cable] was prepared without DOD or JCS participation. Authorities are now having second thoughts."

Taylor's telegram angered the president. The cable not only tainted Harkins's assessment but also implied that Kennedy was running a government incapable of making up its mind. The dissension within the Kennedy administration grew sharper at the noon August 28 NSC meeting. The State Department officials promoting the coup argued that the U.S. "must decide now to go through to a successful overthrow." Ambassador Nolting disagreed. By abandoning Diem and Nhu, said Nolting, the U.S. would be reneging on past commitments. At that, Harriman, known as "the crocodile," sharply denounced Nolting's political judgment and advice, charging that he had not adequately represented U.S. interests during his term as ambassador. Deputy Secretary of Defense Gilpatric could not recall when anyone in the presence of the president "took the tongue-lashing that Nolting did from Harriman."

"The president was appalled at the emotions this problem had stirred up and the basic lack of information about Vietnam," remembered Michael Forrestal. "He just couldn't understand how so many Americans could divide almost down the middle in their opinions of what was going on in the country and what should be done about it."

The growing rift among the president's advisers and General

Taylor's "second thoughts" cable prompted Kennedy to seek new and independent advice from Ambassador Lodge and General Harkins. In his instructions of the twenty-eighth to Lodge, the president reaffirmed his pro-coup policy, "but this judgment in turn is heavily dependent on your on-the-spot advice, and I trust you will not hesitate to recommend delay or change in plans if at any time you think it wise."

At about 5:00 A.M., Thursday, August 29, CIA Station Chief John Richardson and Lou Conein received phone calls asking them to report to the MACV war room. There they were shown General Taylor's "second thoughts" cable. Conein was scheduled to meet with Major General Duong Van Minh, the leader of the conspiring generals, at 10:00 A.M. But now, with Washington apparently backing off from the coup, Richardson instructed Conein to give no further encouragement to the generals. He was only to listen and to report whatever Minh said.

Like the other conspiring officers, "Big" Minh had been surprised by the abrupt reversal of U.S. support for Diem. Aware of the divided opinion within the U.S. mission, the general feared betrayal by the Americans. At his meeting with Conein, Minh questioned the American commitment to the coup. He told the CIA officer that the generals must be cautious until they had clear evidence the United States would not betray them. As a sign of American support, Minh wanted the U.S. government to suspend economic aid to the Diem regime. Conein, following Richardson's instructions, remained noncommittal—allowing the general to interpret as he would.

Returning to the embassy, Conein reported his meeting to Richardson. Ambassador Lodge, anxious to hear the generals' latest plans, also went to the station chief's second-floor office. Lodge became infuriated when he learned of the change in Conein's instructions and demanded an explanation.

Because of the "second thoughts" cable, answered Richardson.

"Why wasn't I informed of this cable?" Lodge roared. From this point on, he ordered, Conein would report first to the ambassador and then to the station chief. In a cable to Secretary of State Rusk that same day, Lodge declared it was too late for second thoughts: "We are launched on a course from which there is no respectable turning back: the overthrow of the Diem government. . . .

"[The] U.S. is already publicly committed to this end," reasoned Lodge, "[and] there is no possibility, in my view, that the war can be won under a Diem administration." Urging an "all-out effort to get [the] generals to move promptly," Lodge requested authorization for Harkins to approach the coup leaders. The ambassador also sought permission to suspend economic aid to the Diem government should the generals continue to insist on a public expression of U.S. support.

General Harkins concurred with Ambassador Lodge's assessment. Their evaluations differed only over a final ultimatum to Diem demanding Nhu's removal. The MACV commander believed there was still time for such an approach without endangering the conspiracy. Lodge adamantly opposed this course: "Such a step has no chance of getting the desired result and would [be] regarded by the generals as a sign of American indecision and delay. I believe this is a risk we should not run. The generals distrust us too much already."

The White House replied to Lodge the same day, authorizing Harkins to approach the coup leaders and permitting the ambassador to suspend economic aid at his discretion. The question of an ultimatum to Diem was left undecided. In a personal message to Lodge, Kennedy emphasized his "full support" for these steps but rejected the ambassador's assertion that there was no turning back. Gently reminding Lodge of the commander-in-chief's prerogatives, Kennedy tried to temper the ambassador's unconditional commitment to a coup by making a veiled reference to the Bay of Pigs fiasco: "I know from experience that failure is more destructive than an appearance of indecision. . . . When we go, we must go to win, but it will be better to change our minds than fail."

By Friday, August 30, John Kennedy's government had planned for the worst. Anticipating a bloodbath in Saigon, CINCPAC prepared to evacuate the nearly 5,000 American noncombatants in Vietnam. An attack carrier task group, complete with helicopter assault ships, attack transports, and destroyers, cruised off the coast of Vietnam. In Okinawa two reinforced Marine battalions, totaling 3,000 men, were on twenty-four-hour alert.

At the State Department, Roger Hilsman submitted a memo requested by Rusk listing possible moves by the Ngo brothers to maintain power and a wide range of potential U.S. countermoves. In response to prolonged fighting between rebel and loyalist forces, the memo suggested: "If necessary, we should bring in U.S. combat forces to assist the coup group to achieve victory."

For the fifth straight day, Kennedy's top advisers convened secretly to review Ambassador Lodge's latest reports. "The days come and go and nothing happens," brooded Lodge in one cable. "There is not yet enough to show for the hours which we have all put in." Administration officials also sifted through CIA reports of the Ngo brothers' desperate attempts to thwart a coup. Nhu apparently intended to arrest all of the conspiring generals within the next twenty-four hours and had threatened to raze Saigon should there be a coup.

After the meeting, Rusk cabled Lodge, expressing the administration's "uneasiness at the absence of bone and muscle" in the generals' conspiracy. Although changing none of the ambassador's instructions, Rusk raised the subject of direct U.S. intervention: "Possibility therefore increasingly that if there is to be a change, it can only be brought about by [an] American rather than Vietnamese effort. Obviously, an abortive effort inspired by or attributed to the United States will be disastrous."

Rusk concluded his message by admitting the government faced hard choices in the near future: "The distinction between what is desirable and what is possible is one which we may have to face in the next few days. . . . Can assure you that highest levels in Washington are giving this problem almost full-time attention."

On Saturday, August 31, Harkins attempted to reassure the generals of U.S. support for their coup. He invited General Khiem to stop by MACV headquarters. "I told him what the proposition was," Harkins recalled. "If the generals were ready to remove Diem, the United States government would back them."

Khiem passed the message to "Big" Minh and returned to see Harkins later in the day. The ARVN chief of staff then shattered U.S. hopes for a Vietnamese overthrow of the Diem-Nhu government: General Minh had stopped planning a coup, and the other generals were following his lead. Khiem claimed the conspiring officers had insufficient forces for a decisive victory over Diem's loyal units. The army did not want to start anything it could not finish, he said.

During the meeting, Khiem reported an abrupt about-face by Nhu. The day before Diem's brother had told several generals that he now agreed with everything the U.S. wanted the Diem regime to do. The government, Nhu had said, now has the backing of President Kennedy. Unsure whether Nhu's statement was true, the general wondered aloud to Harkins whether Diem's brother "was again trying to flush out the generals." Khiem's mistrust of the Americans was transparent. Like his fellow conspirators, he suspected that John Richardson kept the palace informed of the generals' plans and worried that the Nhus might be on the CIA payroll.

One week to the day after the August 24 cable Lodge, Harkins, and Richardson independently informed Washington the plot was dead. Lodge bitterly observed: "There is neither the will nor the organization among the generals to accomplish anything. . . . [If] at some [i]ndeterminate date in the future some other group with the necessary strength and lust for office comes forward, we can contemplate another effort."

Richardson warned: "There is little doubt that GVN [is] aware [of] U.S. role and may have considerable detail."

And General Harkins, echoing the mutual doubts and mistrust that had doomed the coup, reported: "So we see we have an 'organisation de confusion' with everyone suspicious of everyone else and none desiring to take any positive action right now. You can't hurry the east."

CHAPTER EIGHT

WE MUST ALL SIGN ON

The South Vietnamese generals' failure to overthrow Diem disgusted President Kennedy and his foreign policy advisers. "Pushing a piece of spaghetti" was the metaphor used to describe the administration's futile effort to motivate the generals. State Department officials felt particularly frustrated. The United States could neither force Diem to remove Nhu nor induce the South Vietnamese military to oust the Ngo brothers. At 11:00 A.M., August 31, 1963, Kennedy's advisers gathered at the State Department for a where-do-we-go-from-here meeting. Roger Hilsman and Paul Kattenburg, director of the interdepartmental Vietnam task force, quarreled wth Defense Secretary McNamara and General Taylor over the extent of South Vietnamese political support for Diem. The State Department officials argued there was none; the Pentagon officials demanded evidence.

Kattenburg, an Indochina analyst and Vietnam desk officer in the fifties, had just returned from Vietnam. He was dismayed by the administration's ignorance of Vietnam, its recent history, and the personalities and forces in contention there. The forty-year-old Foreign Service officer reported Ambassador Lodge's warning that if the U.S. continued to support "this repressive regime, with its bayonets at every street corner and its transparent negotiations with puppet bonzes, we are going to be thrown out of the country in six months." Believing that Kennedy's advisers "were leading themselves down a garden path to tragedy," Kattenburg then blurted out the unthinkable: "At this juncture, it would be better for us to make the decision to get out honorably."

Kattenburg's suggestion to withdraw from Vietnam had absolutely no support among top administration officials. The government had not yet divided into "hawks" and "doves," and Kennedy's senior advisers unanimously assumed that the consequences of a Communist victory would be catastrophic. General Taylor, reflecting the administration's confidence in its ability to shape events in a developing Southeast Asian nation, asked Kattenburg what he meant by being forced out of Vietnam. The civilian explained, "In from six months to a year, as the [South Vietnamese] people see we are losing the war, they will gradually go to the other side, and we will be obliged to leave."

Rusk, dismissing Kattenburg's remarks as "largely speculative," declared: "We will not pull out of Vietnam until the war is won, and . . . we will not run a coup."

The secretary of state then turned to a man whose views on Vietnam were seldom sought by Kennedy: Vice President Lyndon B. Johnson. Appalled by the previous week's plot to overthrow Diem, Johnson believed there was no real alternative leadership to the South Vietnamese president. When asked by Rusk if he had any contribution to make, the vice president replied, "We should stop playing cops and robbers" and "get back to talking straight" with Diem. The U.S., said Johnson, "should once again go about winning the war."

While the president's advisers groped for viable policy recommendations, Kennedy publicly stated his own views on Vietnam. Interviewed in Hyannisport, Massachusetts, he appeared on the September 2 CBS Evening News, the inaugural broadcast of the program's expanded thirty-minute format. Omitting any mention of the previous week's attempt to overthrow Diem, Kennedy candidly assessed the prospects in Vietnam: "I don't think that unless a greater effort is made by the government to win popular support that the war can be won out there."

CBS correspondent Walter Cronkite asked the president whether Diem's government still had time to regain the support of the South Vietnamese people. In an understated, but unmistakable, message to Diem, Kennedy implied that this would depend on whether the South Vietnamese president reformed politically and banished Nhu from the government: "With changes in policy, and perhaps with personnel, I think it can. If it doesn't make those changes, I would think that the chances of winning it would not be very good."

During the interview, the president reaffirmed the predominant themes of his Vietnam policy. "In the final analysis, it is their war," he said. "They are the ones who have to win it or lose it. We can help them, we can give them equipment, we can send our men out there as advisers, but they have to win it, the people of Vietnam, against the Communists."

Kennedy also underscored his view that Vietnam played an important part in American national security. "I don't agree with those who say we should withdraw," he said. "That would be a great mistake. I know people don't like Americans to be engaged in this kind of an effort. Forty-seven Americans have been killed in combat with the enemy, but this is a very important struggle even though it is far away.

"We . . . made this effort to defend Europe. Now Europe is quite secure. We also have to participate—we may not like it—in the defense of Asia."

On the same day as Kennedy's televised criticism of the South Vietnamese government, Diem and his family launched a campaign of public confrontation with the U.S. mission in Saigon. The *Times of Vietnam* ran a front-page article charging the CIA with attempting to organize a coup d'état. "I think it showed the degree to which the Nhus and Diem felt themselves trapped," William Colby said later. "It was an indirect way of saying, 'Keep your hands off.' "

Madame Nhu privately claimed to have written the anti-American article. Although correctly inferring CIA involvement in the attempted coup, Vietnam's volatile first lady appeared to be losing her tenuous grasp on reality. She not only considered herself the savior of South Vietnam but also thought an international conspiracy involving both Americans and Communists controlled the Buddhist movement. According to a CIA report, Madame Nhu believed Ambassador Lodge intended to have her murdered.

In an apparent act of retaliation, Madame Nhu's brother, Tran Van Khiem (no relation to ARVN Chief of Staff Tran Thien Khiem), drew up a "hit list" of Americans marked for assassination. During a conversation with Australian journalist Denis Warner, Khiem scribbled the names of doomed U.S. officials. Legible names included John Richardson, Lou Conein, and embassy spokesman John Mecklin. Warner warned Khiem that any attacks on Americans would immediately bring the U.S. Marines into Saigon. A correspondent in the Pacific during World War II, Warner told Madame Nhu's brother that the U.S. Marines were the world's fiercest fighters. The journalist estimated it would take them "no more than three hours to wipe out every Vietnamese soldier in the city."

Warner's prediction perceptibly deflated Khiem's self-confidence.

While relations between Washington and Saigon deteriorated, the internal political chaos in South Vietnam continued unabated. Protesting students filled the void left by Buddhist monks arrested during the pagoda raids. In a single day in early September, 800 high-school students were jailed for antigovernment activity. Many of them were children of military and civilian officials upon whom Diem depended for support. Student arrests soon spread to junior high schools and even elementary schools.

Perhaps nothing better symbolized the South Vietnamese government's desperate effort to retain power than the attempt to kill "the miraculous fish" of Quang Nam Province. According to Buddhist sources, the giant fish first appeared in a pond some thirty miles west of Da Nang about July 1. The fish, apparently an enormous carp, was believed to be a "disciple of Buddha." Soon peasants in the area began making pilgrimages to the pond.

The local district chief, a Catholic, became concerned that the pilgrimages were acts of opposition to the government. He ordered the fish destroyed. Troops from Colonel Tung's dreaded Special Forces were summoned from Saigon. They sprayed the pond with automatic weapons but failed to kill the fish. Next, they mined the pond but were still unsuccessful. Finally, in desperation, the soldiers lured the fish to the surface with bread crumbs and threw hand grenades at it. "They blew up and killed everything in that pond except the fish," according to one observer. "The fish kept swimming."

The fish's apparent indestructibility convinced the pilgrims that it was indeed a miraculous fish. South Vietnamese peasants flocked to the pond by the thousands, carrying water away with them. Even ARVN soldiers traveled to the pond to fill their canteens. Fearing violent protests, the district chief abandoned the effort to kill the fish. As a last resort, the government planted a newspaper story claiming the water in the pond was poisonous and that many people had died from drinking it.

Ten thousand miles away from the pond in Quang Nam Province (and perhaps an even greater distance culturally), officials in Washington sought to assess the impact of South Vietnam's political turmoil on the war against the Viet Cong. Before the pagoda raids and the aborted coup, the war had seemed to be going well. In the past two weeks, however, many South Vietnamese military and civilian officials had voiced grave doubts about the future of the struggle.

At 10:30 A.M., September 6, President Kennedy's foreign policy advisers met at the White House. Attorney General Robert Kennedy, who had taken a more active interest in Vietnam since the uproar over the August 24 cable, asked probing questions on his brother's behalf: Can we win the war with Diem and Nhu? Will the Nhus ever change? What should be done if the war cannot be won with Diem? "I think the president used Bobby to ask those unpleasant questions and, no doubt, stoked him up to do it," Michael Forrestal said later. "And Bobby liked that role and did it fairly well."

Robert Kennedy urged a hard line with Diem, according to the minutes of the meeting. "We have to be tough," he said. "Ambassador Lodge has to do more than say our president is unhappy. We have to tell Diem that he must do the things we demand or we will have to cut down our effort as forced by the U.S. public."

The attorney general then suggested that the U.S. apply unnamed but presumably drastic sanctions against Diem: "If we have concluded that we are going to lose with Diem, why do we not grasp the nettle now?"

The president's advisers generally avoided direct answers to Kennedy's questions. "We have insufficient information in Washington," explained McNamara. When the attorney general asked the Pentagon officials whether they could get the

Attorney General Robert F. Kennedy. (*The Library of Congress, U.S. News & World Report Collection, 1952–72*)

views of American military advisers in the field, General Taylor recommended sending Major General Victor Krulak to Vietnam that day. Roger Hilsman, bothered that the problem in Vietnam had too often been defined in purely military terms, suggested sending a State Department representative as well to check on political developments. He chose Joseph A. Mendenhall, a senior Foreign Service officer who had worked on the department's Vietnam desk and served as political counsellor in the Saigon embassy.

Within hours Krulak and Mendenhall boarded a small White House jet at Andrews Air Force Base to begin the grueling 10,000-mile trip to Vietnam. They arrived in Vietnam at 6:00 A.M., September 8. Parting company almost immediately, they agreed to meet at the airport thirty-six hours later. General Krulak, nicknamed "Brute" for his short stature, went "up country" and spoke with more than eighty American military advisers, including enlisted men and senior officers. Relentlessly, he asked the same questions again and again: How is the war going? What are your South Vietnamese counterpart's feeling about the Buddhist crisis? How does your counterpart feel about the political leadership? Have there been any changes in the past few weeks? On the basis of these discussions, Krulak concluded that the South Vietnamese army was fighting the war against the Communists and fighting it well.

Mendenhall, on the other hand, spent most of the trip speaking with Vietnamese and American civilian officials in the central coastal provinces, where the Buddhist problem was most acute. He also met with Vietnamese sources from his Saigon days whom he regarded as knowledgeable and objective. Struck by the fear that pervaded Saigon, Hue, and Da Nang, Mendenhall described them as "cities of hate . . . living under [a] reign of terror." He concluded that the population's hatred of the Nhus was now spilling over onto Diem.

Krulak and Mendenhall left Saigon for the return trip to Washington on September 9. They were joined by embassy public affairs officer John Mecklin. A former correspondent who had covered the French-Viet Minh War in the fifties, Mecklin had been summoned back to Washington to report his views on Diem and the war. The three officials, the only passengers on the windowless, 135-foot tanker and a microcosm of the split within Kennedy's government, prepared their reports in an atmosphere of smoldering hostility. According to Mecklin, the Foreign Service officer and the Marine general apparently disliked each other, speaking "only when it was unavoidable."

The friction between Krulak and Mecklin was even worse. During the flight, Krulak noticed the embassy spokesman had brought aboard several cans of television film that the Diem government had tried to censor. Krulak protested: South Vietnam is a sovereign nation; its laws must be respected. "It's wrong for us to smuggle," he said. After a long argument, the general ordered Mecklin to remove the film from the plane when it landed for refueling at Elmendorf Air Force Base in Alaska. Krulak further suggested that Mecklin needn't leave the film unattended—he could always remain with it in Alaska.

At 10:30 A.M., September 10, the president and his advisers convened at the White House to hear the findings of the travelers returning from Vietnam. General Krulak submitted his report, crisply and confidently reading his conclusions: "The shooting war is still going ahead at an impressive pace. It has been affected adversely by the political crisis, but the impact is not great. . . . The Viet Cong war will be won if the current U.S. military and sociological programs are pursued, irrespective of the grave defects in the ruling regime."

Joe Mendenhall, however, painted a completely different picture of Vietnam, citing "the breakdown of civilian government in Saigon . . . [and the] civilian fear and hate of the Nhus." The Foreign Service officer foresaw "the possibility of a religious war or a large-scale movement to the Viet Cong" and concluded: "Nhu must go if the war is to be won."

The president, looking from one to the other, asked wryly, "Did you two gentlemen visit the same country?"

After a brief silence punctuated by a muffled chuckle, General Krulak replied, "I think I can answer your question, sir." Years later Krulak could still remember General Taylor glaring at him as if to ask, "What in the world are you going to say now?"

"Mr. Mendenhall went to the urban part of Vietnam," said Krulak, "and I went to the rural part of Vietnam. And that is where the war is." Krulak then expressed his strong conviction that the U.S. could "stagger through to win the war with Nhu remaining in control."

The conflicting reports from Mendenhall and Krulak ignited yet another debate between Diem's supporters and detractors. Ambassador Nolting pointed out that the South Vietnamese government had weathered fear and hatred in 1961 but had survived and made gains in the war. Nolting anticipated a similar improvement in the current situation. National Security Adviser McGeorge Bundy, the former Harvard dean, objected to the analogy: "In 1961, the hatred and fear [were] directed against the Viet Cong. It is now directed against the Diem government."

During a pause in the argument, Michael Forrestal introduced Rufus Phillips to the president and his advisers. A former CIA officer, Phillips had been a member of Ed Lansdale's Saigon Military Mission. After a tour in Laos, Phillips left the CIA and returned to Vietnam in 1962. As the Agency for International Development's assistant director for rural affairs, he was responsible for all economic assistance to the strategic hamlet program. Phillips began by saying that he had been involved with Vietnam since 1954 and had developed close personal relations with both Diem and Nhu. It appeared to Phillips that Nhu had lost the respect of most Vietnamese officials and that a coup was inevitable. He suggested sending Ed Lansdale back to Vietnam. If Lansdale could not persuade Diem to remove Nhu, said Phillips, no one would be more qualified to help put together a new government.

What would you do specifically? asked Kennedy.

"[I] would cut off U.S. aid to Colonel Tung, commander of the Special Forces," replied Phillips. "The Vietnamese generals say that they can't move as long as we support Colonel Tung."

Phillips told the president that this sanction would be a "psychological squeeze." In addition to demonstrating dramatically U.S. displeasure with Nhu's presence in the government, selective cuts in aid would also be an unmistakable sign to the generals of U.S. support for a coup d'état. In a memorandum written later in the week, Phillips explained that the absence of such action had derailed the aborted August coup: "The key missing item was confidence in the U.S.—without some tangible evidence of U.S. support it was extremely difficult if not impossible to rally the subordinate unit commanders required."

At the White House meeting, the president then asked Phillips what he thought of the military situation.

"I'm sorry to differ with General Krulak," replied Phillips, "but I don't believe we're winning the war, particularly in the Delta." While he admitted the war was going "OK" in much of the country, Phillips declared that the war "in the Delta south of Saigon was going to pieces . . . [and] the strategic hamlet program there was collapsing."

Krulak interrupted Phillips, saying this was not the view of General Harkins. The Marine general commented that while U.S. military advisers were not competent to report on palace intrigue, they were able to report on whether the war was being won or lost. "The battle," declared Krulak insistently, "is not being lost from a military point of view."

Embassy spokesman John Mecklin was the last of the returning officials to speak. He agreed with Phillips's pessimistic conclusions about the South Vietnamese government and its deleterious effect on the war effort. But suspension of aid would be inadequate, said Mecklin. He recommended the introduction of U.S. combat troops to Vietnam, "both to promote unseating of the regime and against the VC."

This suggestion threw the meeting into an uproar. President Kennedy closed the disorganized meeting by instructing his advisers to study the feasibility of cutting off economic aid to the South Vietnamese government. Although he had responded humorously to the opposite appraisals of Krulak and Mendenhall, Kennedy was alarmed and irritated by the split in his government. "This is impossible," he said angrily after the meeting. "We can't run a policy when there are such divergent views on the same set of facts."

Despite the Kennedy administration's intense debate over Diem and the war, the president and his advisers had once again avoided the larger questions of U.S. involvement in Vietnam. While some officials argued that the war could not be won with Diem and others countered that it could not be won without him, none of Kennedy's senior advisers suggested these two points of view were not mutually exclusive. In other words, with or without Diem the war might be a loser.

The president's men in Saigon were no less divided than officials in Washington. Ambassador Lodge and General Harkins clouded the muddle further with their comments on the September 10 White House meeting. The MACV commander believed Krulak's report was an "authentic appraisal" of the situation. Lodge, however, in a separate cable to the secretary of state, doubted "the value of the answers which are given by young officers to direct questions by generals—or, for that matter, by ambassadors. The urge to give an optimistic and favorable answer is quite understandable."

Although Harkins refrained from commenting on the political scene, the ambassador was thoroughly pessimistic: "The [South Vietnamese] government is obviously cut off from reality." Concluding that "the ship of state here is slowly sinking," Lodge advocated another attempt to stimulate a coup d'état: "The time has arrived for the U.S. to use what effective sanctions it has to bring about the fall of the existing government and the installation of another." Lodge believed the most effective sanction would be selective cuts in U.S. aid, the sign of support the generals had requested in August.

But President Kennedy quickly discovered there were serious risks associated with the suspension of economic aid. Most cuts would not only affect the war adversely but would also back the Ngo family into a corner, where its only options would be complete surrender to U.S. demands or loss of all political power. "Faced with such extreme alternatives," speculated a CIA analysis, "they [Diem and Nhu] might well be moved to cast about for some sort of agreement with Hanoi."

Throughout the summer of 1963, Nhu had privately acknowledged his contacts with Hanoi and expressed a willingness to seek a negotiated settlement of the war. His motivation for seeking a rapprochement with the north baffled the Kennedy administration. Nhu had frequently expressed his ideological and personal hatred of the Communists, who had tortured and killed one of his brothers. Was Nhu seriously seeking a settlement? Or was he attempting to blackmail the U.S. into greater support for Diem's government?

Seeking to avoid a fiasco similar to the August 24 cable, Kennedy was determined to act deliberately and prudently. On September 11 he ordered that no immediate decision would be

made on the suspension of economic aid. Since it seemed unlikely that the South Vietnamese army would soon move against
the government, the president and his advisers considered a
series of gradually escalating pressures that would force Diem
to remove Nhu and reform politically. Although later phases
of this program included dissociation from the Diem-Nhu regime and the suspension of all U.S. aid, the first phase relied
exclusively on persuasion. In a September 17 telegram to Lodge,
the White House described the new program as "obviously an
interim plan," intended to achieve modest improvements in
the performance of the South Vietnamese government. Should
it be unsuccessful, this low-risk course would still be "consistent
with more drastic effort as and when means become available."

Lodge was unenthusiastic about the new tactics. In the past
Diem had proved to be resistant to jawboning of any kind: "I
believe that for me to press Diem on things which are *not* in
the cards and to repeat what we have said several times already
would be a little shrill and would make us look weak."

Instead, Lodge wanted to maintain an attitude of inscrutable
silence toward the regime and force Diem to come to him.
Should the South Vietnamese president seek an audience, Lodge
intended to turn the tables on Diem and "launch into a long
statement on something that interests me, to wit, how urgent
it is for him to take action so that it will appear in America
that there has been some real improvement in GVN."

Although he reluctantly agreed a coup d'état seemed unlikely
in the near future, the ambassador remained convinced Diem's
overthrow was ultimately the only workable solution. He recommended that any economic sanctions "should be directly
tied to a promising coup d'état. . . . In this connection, I believe
we should pursue contact with Big Minh and urge him along
if he looks like acting."

In mid-September 1963 John Kennedy's government was more
deeply divided than at any time during his thousand-day presidency. His advisers could not agree on whether to continue
supporting Diem, or even if the war in Vietnam was being won
or lost. With his Vietnam policy drifting, the president turned
to his two ranking officials in the Pentagon: Robert McNamara
and General Maxwell D. Taylor. Kennedy wanted them to visit

Vietnam, evaluate the progress of the war, and estimate its future course. If the prognosis was not hopeful, the president wanted their views on what should be done. Additional responsibilities included evaluating the prospects of a coup d'état and investigating why there were such conflicting reports from U.S. officials in Vietnam.

The choice of McNamara to lead this mission was inevitable. If anyone could get behind the conflicting data it would be Bob McNamara, master of the statistical indexes that measured the war's progress. Described as an "agnostic" on the debate over Diem, he had little tolerance for the qualitative State Department reports. "I think it was largely a matter of perspective," said William Sullivan, Harriman's special assistant for Southeast Asia. "Those who were doing the military analysis were not entirely bean counters, but to some degree they were. Each of their immediate goals was being realized in terms of numbers of people, weapons, and so forth."

The McNamara-Taylor mission included representatives from every interested government agency. William Colby represented the CIA, and Michael Forrestal the White House. The military made it clear that it did not want Roger Hilsman to represent the State Department; his bridges with top Pentagon officials had been completely burned. Instead, Harriman selected William Sullivan to represent the State Department. Secretary McNamara also invited Deputy Assistant Secretary of Defense William P. Bundy to accompany him. A former CIA official and the older brother of the president's national security adviser, Bundy was in charge of coordinating U.S. military aid programs. One reason McNamara picked Bundy for the trip was because he had been out of the country for the previous month. "You're not emotionally engaged in this thing as everybody else in town seems to be," said McNamara.

"We just desperately needed a balanced proposal and, if possible, an agreed one," recalled William Bundy. "McNamara pulled us all in and said, 'We're all going to be just as honest as we know how to be . . . but we are going to do our damnedest to see if we can arrive at some sort of coherent and consensus appraisal on key points.' "

During their intensive ten-day visit, McNamara and General Taylor toured virtually every operational area in Vietnam. The chairman of the Joint Chiefs concurred with Krulak's optimistic findings two weeks earlier. To Taylor, the war appeared to be going so well that if Diem stabilized the political front, "the Viet Cong threat could be reduced to a state approximating low order banditry by the end of 1965." Furthermore, the apparent military progress justified adhering to a scheduled withdrawal of 1,000 U.S. advisers by the end of 1963, a reduction conceived before the eruption of the Buddhist crisis.

The Pentagon civilians, however, were more skeptical. "I became aware for the first time how immensely diverse the war was in itself—how different from one province to another, and above all how dependent on local leadership and teamwork," Bundy later reflected. "I was left, as I think McNamara was, with a lasting skepticism of the ability of any man, however honest, to interpret accurately what was going on. It was just too diffuse and too much that was critical took place below the surface."

Although the Pentagon civilians had their doubts about the war's progress, they were unwilling to refute their uniformed colleagues' optimistic assessments. "The U.S. military family under General Harkins was honestly convinced that the war was going well," Bundy later explained, "and their judgment could not lightly be rejected, nor certainly in a week could one confidently come to an opposite conclusion."

William Sullivan, the State Department representative, was less reticent about contradicting the military conclusions. Although more diplomatic than Hilsman, Sullivan argued that with Diem in such serious political trouble it would be "patently deceitful" to pretend the U.S. could soon disengage from Vietnam. "I felt that it would be misleading to suggest that the job could be done by 1965 and that we could start withdrawing people by the end of 1963," Sullivan recalled. "It looked to me as though it was going to be just the opposite: We were going to be putting in more people by the end of 1963."

Although Taylor's view would ultimately prevail in the trip report, the pessimism of Sullivan and others would be validated by the end of the year. Diem's overthrow would reveal a thoroughly corrupt South Vietnamese reporting system and shatter the myth of military progress. "It is abundantly clear," reported Central Intelligence Director John McCone in December of

1963, "that statistics received over the past year or more from GVN officials and reported by the U.S. mission on which we gauged the trend of the war were grossly in error."

On that same day in December, one month after the assassination of John Kennedy, McNamara himself would ruefully observe to President Lyndon B. Johnson: "Viet Cong progress has been great since the coup, with my best guess being that the situation has in fact been deteriorating since July."

Before returning to Washington, McNamara and Taylor, together with Ambassador Lodge and General Harkins, met with the South Vietnamese president at Gia Long Palace. Diem began the meeting with one of his characteristic monologues. Chain-smoking and frequently leaping up and referring to maps, Diem made a rambling speech about the wisdom of his policies and the progress of the war. During a pause some two hours later, Secretary McNamara deliberately and forcefully conveyed U.S. concern about South Vietnamese political unrest. While agreeing with Diem that the progress of the war was "reasonably satisfactory," McNamara warned of "the disturbing probability that the war effort would be damaged by the government's political deficiencies."

Diem flatly rejected McNamara's assertion. Vicious attacks by the press, said Diem, were responsible for the U.S. misunderstanding about the real situation in Vietnam.

Although some press accounts may have been in error, replied the defense secretary, there was no escaping the serious crisis of confidence in the Diem government both in Vietnam and in the United States. The South Vietnamese president again disagreed with McNamara. The students, Diem said serenely, "were most immature, untrained, and irresponsible." The government had no choice but to arrest them. The South Vietnamese president acknowledged, however, that he bore a certain responsibility for the Buddhists' unrest: He had been "too kind to the Buddhists."

Diem then made a fleeting reference to Americans engaged in antigovernment plotting and muttered that he was "preparing a dossier." Acting on Kennedy's explicit instructions, none of the Americans pursued this topic. Secretary McNamara also raised the subject of Madame Nhu. No small part of the Vietnamese government's public relations difficulties had come from her ill-advised and unfortunate declarations, said McNamara. He then took from his pocket a newspaper clipping quoting Madame Nhu's remark that "American junior officers in Vietnam were behaving like little soldiers of fortune." Such outbursts, said the defense secretary, were deeply offensive to U.S. public opinion. One of the Americans present bluntly asked Diem if there were not something the government could do "to shut her up."

Diem's manner and glances seemed to indicate that for the first time he understood what the Americans were talking about. Ambassador Lodge reminded the South Vietnamese president that Madame Chiang Kai-shek had played a decisive role in losing China to communism. Regaining his composure, Diem defended Madame Nhu: She was a member of Parliament and had the right to speak her mind. The Americans must consider the "merciless and scurrilous press attack" she had been under.

"This [is] not satisfactory," said McNamara. The problems discussed that day were real and serious. They would have to be solved before the war could be won, he said. General Taylor later recalled Diem's lack of comprehension of McNamara's remarks: "You could just see it bouncing off him."

The U.S. officials returned to Washington on the morning of October 2. Their report to the president melded Pentagon optimism about the war with State Department pessimism about the political situation. "The military campaign has made great progress and continues to progress . . ." the report concluded. "[But] further repressive actions by Diem and Nhu could change the present favorable military trends."

Although its conclusions echoed the military view of the conflict, the paper's recommendations tilted toward the tough State Department stance. McNamara and Taylor suggested a series of economic and psychological pressures against the South Vietnamese government. Seeking maximum pressure on Diem with minimal effect on the war, the Pentagon officials recommended suspension of the Commodity Import Program, an economic aid program providing Vietnam with approximately 40 percent of the country's commercial imports and substantial revenues for the spiraling military budget. Although a short-

After a visit to Vietnam in September of 1963, General Maxwell D. Taylor, left, and Robert McNamara, right, reported their conclusions to the president. *(John F. Kennedy Library)*

term cut in the program would have little economic impact, a permanent suspension would seriously affect both the Vietnamese economy and the war effort.

A key element of the pressures on Diem would be the "cryptic posture" assumed by the U.S. government. There would be no public or private announcement of the aid suspension, since neither seemed to have any discernible effect on Diem or the conspiring generals. As the aid cuts became known, all elements of Vietnamese society could draw their own conclusions. To Kennedy administration officials, it seemed likely that the symbolism would be apparent to both Diem and his enemies. "The program outlined in [the] report," predicted McNamara, "will [either] push us toward a reconciliation with Diem or toward a coup to overthrow Diem."

Secretary McNamara and General Taylor had delivered to President Kennedy a Vietnam policy that most of his government could accept. No one knew for certain where it would lead, but at least everyone would be on board. Kennedy went to great pains to declare his administration's unity at the 6:00 P.M. October 2 NSC meeting:

> Most of the officials involved are in agreement [with the McNamara-Taylor Report]. We are not papering over our differences. . . . Reports of disagreements do not help the war effort in Vietnam and do no good to the government as a whole. We must all sign on and with good heart set out to implement the actions decided upon. . . . Because we are agreed, we should convey our agreement to our subordinates. There are no differences between Washington and Ambassador Lodge or among the State and Defense Departments and the CIA.

The new policy and the agreement among the president's advisers would last for three days. The South Vietnamese generals were now ready to move.

CHAPTER NINE

PLAUSIBLE DENIAL

On October 2, 1963, the same day McNamara and Taylor returned to Washington, Major General Tran Van Don encountered his old friend Lou Conein at Saigon's Tan Son Nhut Airport. After an exchange of pleasantries, Don said he had been trying to reach the CIA operative for some time. The chief of ARVN's Joint General Staff asked if they could meet later that night at his quarters in Nha Trang, a central coastal port 200 miles northeast of Saigon.

Conein reported his encounter with Don to the American embassy. Although the general had avoided mentioning the topic of the proposed meeting, U.S. officials assumed ARVN's senior officers were again planning a coup d'état. Deputy Chief of Mission William Trueheart instructed Conein to neither encourage nor discourage a coup—just get information.

At Nha Trang, General Don announced the army's readiness to move against the government. A key element of the plan was the participation of Brigadier General Ton That Dinh, whose troops were Diem's primary countercoup force. Loyal to Diem during the August plot, Dinh boasted that he had saved the regime from Buddhists, Communists, and "foreign adventurers." As his reward, the ARVN general had brashly asked Diem to appoint him minister of interior, a request the South Vietnamese president flatly refused. Throughout September, General Don had exploited Dinh's wounded pride and converted him to the conspiracy.

During his meeting with Conein, Don asked the American to meet privately with "Big" Minh, the leader of the generals' coup committee. With Lodge's approval, the CIA operative met General Minh at his Saigon headquarters on Saturday,

October 5. Alone and conversing entirely in French, Minh came straight to the point: "[I] must know [the] American government's position with respect to a change in [the] government of Vietnam within the very near future." While neither expecting nor requesting support for a coup, the South Vietnamese general did want assurance that the U.S. would not thwart the operation. Furthermore, the new government would require continued American military and economic assistance.

Minh outlined three possible plans to Conein. The first called for the assassination of Nhu and Ngo Dinh Can, Diem's youngest brother. Although he had no formal title, Can ruled central Vietnam with an iron hand and had directed the anti-Buddhist crackdown in Hue. A reclusive xenophobe, he detested the West and refused to see foreigners. Among his own countrymen, Can had the distinction of being the most unpopular member of the Ngo family. "He was even more anathema than Nhu to [the generals]," remembered William Trueheart. "He had the worst reputation of any of the brothers."

General Minh's second plan called for the encirclement of Saigon by rebel military units. The third plan outlined a direct confrontation between coup and loyalist forces in Saigon. Conein, who had been instructed by Lodge to be noncommittal and to refuse to speculate on U.S. policy, said he was unable to give assurances of noninterference or to advise the general on any of his plans. Minh appeared to understand and said he would contact the CIA officer in the near future.

Almost simultaneously with the transmission of Conein's cable reporting his meeting with Minh, Ambassador Lodge received the policy instructions arising from the McNamara-Taylor mission. While authorizing economic pressure against Diem, Kennedy had decided: "No initiative should now be taken to give any active covert encouragement to a coup." To the president and his advisers, the risks of explicitly encouraging Diem's ouster seemed prohibitive. They lacked a clear picture of the kind of government that might emerge from a coup d'état, and exposure of the U.S. hand would not only damage American prestige but would also identify the successor government as a U.S. "puppet."

Although he had decided against engineering a coup, Kennedy did order Lodge to undertake an "urgent covert effort

. . . to identify and build contacts with possible alternative leadership as and when it appears." In an apparent effort to restrain his coup-minded ambassador, the president emphasized: "We repeat that this effort is not repeat not to be aimed at active promotion of [a] coup but only at surveillance and readiness."

The White House instructions stressed that "this effort be totally secure and fully deniable." Information about coup plotting would be separated from routine embassy reporting and transmitted on the CIA channel rather than the less secure State Department communications. Furthermore, Lodge alone was to issue orders to the CIA, and these orders were to be issued orally. "Ambassador Lodge made it very clear to me," Conein later recalled, "that if something went wrong . . . he would have to be able to have deniability that I even existed."

After learning of "Big" Minh's plans to move against Diem, President Kennedy nudged U.S. policy away from his clearly defined position of "no active encouragement" of a coup. In a contradictory October 9 telegram, the White House both reaffirmed the earlier directive and authorized encouragement of a coup d'état: "While we do not wish to stimulate a coup, we also do not wish to leave [the] impression that [the] U.S. would thwart a change in government or deny economic and military assistance to a new regime if it appeared capable of increasing [the] effectiveness of [the] military effort, ensuring popular support to win [the] war, and improving working relations with [the] U.S."

The distinction between stimulating a coup d'état and not thwarting one was a tortuous semantic exercise that ignored American influence in South Vietnam. The promise of U.S. military and economic support would encourage a coup in the same way threats of denying aid had discouraged conspiracies in the past. "There's this nice theory that keeps coming through [the cables]: that it's really the generals who are going to decide, and not us, about the removal of Diem," William Colby said later. "There's an unreality to it when you think of the enormous importance of the American position."

In addition to partial suspension of economic aid to Diem and a pledge of assistance to a successor regime, the U.S. government sent another powerful signal of encouragement to the conspiring generals: John Richardson's recall to Washington. Enjoying the Saigon station chief's traditionally close relationship with Nhu, Richardson was perceived by most Vietnamese as a Ngo family sympathizer who would inform the palace of any conspiracies within the army. "Rightly or wrongly, a lot of the people who plotted against Diem were concerned that Richardson would eventually know about the coup," recalled Bui Diem, a civilian opponent of the regime and later South Vietnamese ambassador to the United States. "What kind of assurances could you give them that Richardson wouldn't talk to Nhu?"

According to Kennedy administration officials, Richardson's recall was not an intentional effort to promote a coup d'état. Ambassador Lodge, who had requested Richardson's removal, believed the station chief's independent channel to Nhu undercut his own negotiating posture with Diem. "Richardson's recall was the result of a general lack of confidence in him by Lodge," according to Roger Hilsman. "I have often thought that I should have realized how the Vietnamese would interpret it. But the truth is that I didn't."

Lodge's latest instructions from Washington regarding coup plotting made no mention of "Big" Minh's suggestion of assassinating Diem's younger brothers, Nhu and Can. In an apparent effort to deny that the president had even considered such a repugnant option, Minh's assassination plan was handled as an internal CIA matter.

After Conein's October 5 meeting with "Big" Minh, acting CIA Chief of Station David Smith recommended to Ambassador Lodge and Central Intelligence Director John McCone that "we do not set ourselves irrevocably against the assassination plot, since the other two alternatives mean either a bloodbath in Saigon or a protracted struggle which could rip the army and the country asunder."

McCone's initial response to the Saigon station echoed the studied ambiguity of Lodge's instructions. Recommending a "hands off" approach, McCone declared: "[W]e certainly cannot be in the position of stimulating, approving, or supporting assassination, but on the other hand, we are in no way responsible for stopping every threat of which we might receive even partial knowledge." The CIA chief explicitly stated that

Central Intelligence Director John McCone. *U.S. News & World Report*

the U.S. "certainly would not favor [the] assassination of Diem." The absence of any specific mention of Nhu and Can, the targets of Minh's plan, left unanswered whether the U.S. might "favor" the assassination of Diem's troublesome brothers.

Seeking policy guidance, McCone met privately with the president and Robert Kennedy. According to his 1975 testimony before a Senate committee investigating U.S. involvement in assassination plots, McCone did not directly mention Minh's plan to the president. Instead, he discussed the role of the CIA in Vietnam and whether the U.S. should influence a coup d'état. Repeating his view that there was no alternative leadership to Diem, McCone advised: "Mr. President, if I was manager of a baseball team, and I had one pitcher, I'd keep him in the box whether he was a good pitcher or not."

McCone's stated reluctance to mention assassination explicitly typified an agency tradition of speaking in "circumlocutious" terms when discussing highly sensitive intelligence operations with the president. Such indirect expression was designed to insulate the president from potentially embarrassing clandestine activities yet provide him with sufficient information to terminate them. "Such an approach to the president," explained the CIA's Richard Bissell, who evidence and a Congressional Committee Report indicate either authorized or at least was well aware of assassination plots against Patrice Lumumba and Fidel Castro, "would have had as its purpose to leave him in the position to deny knowledge of the operation if it should surface."

At the 1975 assassination hearings, Richard Helms, McCone's deputy director of plans and later director of Central Intelligence, offered a plausible—if not completely convincing—explanation of why top CIA officials might speak in riddles to the president: "I think that any of us would have found it very difficult to discuss assassinations with a president of the United States. I just think we all had the feeling that we were hired out to keep those things out of the Oval Office."

Despite the stated indirection of his conversation with the president, McCone left the meeting with the impression that Kennedy agreed with his "hands off" suggestion. On October 6 the CIA chief formally and unambiguously ordered David Smith to withdraw his recommendation to consider Minh's assassination plan: "We cannot be in [a] position of actively condoning such [a] course of action and thereby engaging our responsibility."

With Smith's recommendation withdrawn, the record clearly demonstrated unanimous U.S. opposition to political assassination. Later in the month Conein informed General Don of American antipathy toward any such plan and of his orders forbidding even the discussion of assassination. "All right," said Don deferentially, "[if] you don't like it, we won't talk about it anymore."

But unfortunately for Diem and Nhu, the U.S. condemnation included no sanctions to deter the South Vietnamese generals from assassination. Alert to the danger in which the Ngo family might find itself, the U.S. government never made its acquiescence in the coup plot and pledge of continued support conditional upon sparing the lives of Diem or his brothers. To have made such a demand would have dropped the fig leaf of plausibly deniable U.S. involvement in the coup. This cynical posture would yield a bitter irony: Although no American official desired Diem's death—much less conspired to kill him—the U.S. government's attempt to distance itself from the plotting contributed to his assassination.

Although the Kennedy administration had forsworn political assassination, it remained unclear whether the Ngo brothers felt similarly constrained. On October 10 the Saigon CIA station reported rumors of a government-orchestrated riot to burn the U.S. chancery and assassinate the ambassador. Since Lodge's arrival, there had been such a rumor every ten days or so. But now there were reports that Nhu smoked opium, and he was said to have been pleased with the pagoda raids and annoyed by the ambassador's recommendation that he leave the country. "For all these reasons," cabled Lodge, "my associates here, whose experience antedates mine, consider assassination to be a real possibility."

In addition to developing contingency plans to protect the embassy and himself, Lodge secretly passed the word to the Diem government that should it "mount such an operation, American retaliation will be prompt and awful beyond description." Alluding to the combat record of the U.S. Marines during World War II, Lodge invited the Ngo brothers to consider whether they wished "to have such a horrible and crushing blow descend on them."

By the middle of October 1963 it seemed as if Saigon's poisonous atmosphere of intrigue had infected the top level of the U.S. mission. The relationship between Ambassador Lodge and General Harkins had deteriorated to the point where they were barely speaking to each other. Taking the "eyes only" instructions on his telegrams quite literally, Lodge had neglected to inform the MACV commander of Conein's latest contacts with the plotting generals. Further aggravating their relationship was Lodge's practice of reporting on the war without consulting Harkins, the senior military man in the country. "He was a maverick, a loner," Harkins bitterly recalled. "He wanted to do everything by himself."

General Harkins was not alone in this estimate of Lodge. A

back-channel CIA cable to McCone, presumably sent by David Smith, reported that the ambassador was "running very much a vest pocket operation and not a country team or total American effort." Characterizing the recall of John Richardson as "the overture to the opera," the message speculated that Lodge wanted Harkins replaced.

The poor relations between Lodge and Harkins complicated the execution of Washington's ambiguous policy directives. The ambassador, a forceful proponent of a coup, emphasized the "not thwarting" instructions, whereas General Harkins, who personally opposed such an operation, stressed the "not stimulating" orders. Because of his interpretation of Washington's instructions, the MACV commander inadvertently derailed a coup d'état planned for late October. On two occasions an ARVN colonel approached U.S. advisers to ask whether the U.S. would back a coup. When informed of the plotting, Harkins instructed his subordinates to inform the colonel that the U.S. military was in Vietnam to advise and support the government in its fight against communism. Furthermore, the ARVN conspirator would do well to "bend his efforts along that line." On October 23 Harkins reported the incidents to Don, informing the Vietnamese general of his opposition to a coup d'état.

General Don, feigning surprise at news of the conspiracy, interpreted Harkins's remarks as official U.S. discouragement of a coup. He immediately summoned Conein to JGS headquarters. Visibly upset, Don asked if there had been any change in U.S. policy. Conein reassured the anxious general that the U.S. government would not thwart their operation and would support a successor government likely to win the war against the Communists. Only then did General Don admit to the CIA operative that a coup planned for October 26 had been scrubbed because the palace had moved vital military units away from Saigon. Flashing his distrust of Harkins, Don implied that the MACV commander had leaked the plan to the palace.

On the following morning, October 24, Conein and General Don met again at the VIP lounge at Tan Son Nhut Airport. Don reported that everything was ready. All the plans had been checked and rechecked. Although he did not name a specific date, the ARVN general informed Conein that the coup would occur no later than November 2. Later on the twenty-fourth, Conein and Don rendezvoused at the office of the general's dentist. Don reported the coup committee's refusal to release the political plan for the new government. He did, however, reassure Conein on the points that most concerned the Americans: The successor government would be religiously and politically tolerant and work with the U.S. mission to defeat the Viet Cong. To ensure close communication between the generals and the embassy during the coup, Conein and Don agreed that the CIA operative would be present at rebel headquarters during the operation. "Lou," said Don, "don't leave town within the next week."

In Washington the reports of the planned coup d'état were greeted with a mixture of skepticism and anxiety. To officials who followed the Byzantine machinations of Diem's disloyal military, it seemed that every other day some obscure officer was preparing to move against the government. At 3:00 A.M., October 24, watch officers in the White House, State Department, Pentagon, and CIA rousted top officials out of bed with reports of an imminent coup d'état led by Lieutenant Colonel Pham Ngoc Thao. According to a CRITIC, or critical intelligence message, from the Saigon CIA station, Thao planned to move against Diem with troops from ARVN's Eighth Regiment.

A former Viet Minh officer, Thao had defected to the Diem government in 1956. Rising through the ranks, he was appointed chief of Kien Hoa Province, where he launched an unusually successful pacification campaign. There were allegations, but no concrete evidence, that Thao was a Communist agent. After falling out of favor with Diem, he began plotting in early 1963 and was ready to move by that summer. Both the palace and conspiring generals had managed to thwart Thao's efforts by moving crucial military forces away from Saigon. His coup d'état planned for October 24 sputtered to a halt when he was unable to arrange transportation for his troops. After the debacle, the generals convinced him to join their plot.

The false alarm from Saigon undermined official Washington's faith in its men in the field and aggravated concerns about General Don's reliability. What was the extent of his backing? Why had he not provided more detailed information about the generals' plan? Was he acting as an agent for Nhu? The dossier on Don at CIA headquarters was hardly comforting: "Real loyalty uncertain and probably [an] opportunist. Seems to be in all camps: reported close to French, to Nhu, impressive to many Americans, and close to chief military critics of GVN but not fully trusted by them."

Don's CIA contact, Lou Conein, did not inspire confidence either. Although the embassy considered him "absolutely reliable," Conein's notorious reputation created fears in Washington that perhaps he was an erratic adventurer who had been in Asia too long. The White House suggested finding a replacement for him, but General Don was adamant. He would deal with no one but Conein.

Ambassador Lodge tried to steady the jittery nerves of the president and his advisers by explaining that Don's unwillingness to provide more detailed plans stemmed from his fear of security breaches by the Americans. The ambassador also assured the president that Conein had been "punctilious in carrying out my instructions." And even if the coup aborted or turned out to be one of Nhu's schemes, reasoned Lodge, "our involvement to date through Conein is still within the realm of plausible denial."

Lodge's certitude did little to allay President Kennedy's persistent fear that an unsuccessful coup attempt would tear Vietnam apart, allowing the Viet Cong to exploit the chaos. On October 25 McGeorge Bundy drafted the president's reply: "While sharing your view that we should not be in [a] position of thwarting [a] coup, we would like to have option of judging and warning on any plan with poor prospects of success. We recognize that this is a large order, but [the] president wants you to know of our concern."

In the past the cool, dispassionate, forty-four-year-old national security adviser had delegated Southeast Asian affairs first to Rostow, then Forrestal. Since the August 24 cable, however, "Mac" Bundy had taken a more active role in Vietnam decision making, orchestrating the flow of paper in and out of the Oval Office. His ability to analyze and summarize ideas made him invaluable to Kennedy. Intolerant of ambiguity, uncertainty, and those less mentally agile than himself, Bundy had a wry awareness of the president's paradoxical position toward the generals' plotting. In draft instructions to

CIA operative Lucien E. Conein, the American liaison with the conspiring generals.

Lodge he wrote: "The difficulty is of course that we want to be able to judge these plans without accepting responsibility for them; the impossible takes a little longer."

Despite the apparent nearness of the coup, Lodge continued to assess whether the economic and psychological pressures recommended by McNamara and Taylor were having any effect on Diem. Only days after the Pentagon officials' return to Washington, news of the aid suspension had leaked to the *Times of Vietnam*. Intensifying its virulent anti-American campaign, the newspaper had charged the U.S. with subverting the war effort. On October 23 the ambassador had reported: "Diem/Nhu give every appearance of sitting tight and reacting to U.S. pressure with counterpressure and implying through public statements that they can go it alone."

In late October Diem took a first tentative step toward compromise with the U.S. government. Swallowing his pride, he reestablished a dialogue with the aloof American ambassador by inviting Lodge and his wife to spend October 27 at the presidential villa in Dalat, a cool, lush retreat in the Central Highlands. There Lodge pressed Diem about the release of Buddhist and student prisoners and complained of the public opinion pressures his repressive policies placed on President Kennedy. But the South Vietnamese president was intransigent. "When it was evident that the conversation was practically over," Lodge reported to Washington, "I said: 'Mr. President, every single specific suggestion which I have made, you have rejected. Isn't there some one thing you may think of that is within your capabilities to do and that would favorably impress U.S. opinion?' As on other previous occasions when I asked him similar questions, he gave me a blank look and changed the subject."

As Diem and Lodge prepared to leave Dalat, General Don discreetly approached the American at the airport. Concerned that Conein might be acting independently, Don asked if the CIA operative were authorized to speak on the ambassador's behalf. Confirming this, Lodge repeated the U.S. pledge of noninterference in the planned coup d'état. Assured of Conein's good faith, General Don met with him that night, Monday, October 28. A coup was imminent, Don announced, and the command post would be at Joint General Staff headquarters at Tan Son Nhut. Although again refusing to divulge the exact date of the operation, Don told the CIA officer to remain at home from October 30 until further notice. The ARVN general promised the U.S. government four hours' notice before the start of the coup.

Conein asked Don for more details about the planned coup and its leaders. Naming several of the participating units, Don revealed that "Big" Minh was in charge of military operations, Brigadier General Le Van Kim was responsible for political planning, and he himself was the liaison with the Americans. When asked about Ton That Dinh, Don replied that the generals were not completely certain of his new loyalties and were prepared "to eliminate Dinh if he showed any signs of compromising the coup."

On October 29 Lodge warned Washington of an "imminent" coup attempt. From the ambassador's perspective, it seemed neither desirable nor possible to halt the operation: "No positive action by the [U.S. government] can prevent a coup attempt short of informing Diem and Nhu with all the opprobrium that such an action would entail."

Although Lodge's report persuaded the president of the coup's likelihood, Kennedy was unwilling to let events unfold naturally. An October 30 cable drafted by McGeorge Bundy expressed the president's conviction that the U.S. could still effectively orchestrate a coup d'état: "Believe our attitude to coup group can still have decisive effect on its decisions."

"One of the problems in all this was that people in Washington always thought they could manage things much more precisely than was really practical," William Trueheart said later, echoing the complaint of a generation of U.S. civilian and military officials who served in Vietnam. "They never wanted to turn loose. They wanted to give an order and then lean over your shoulder as you carried it out and never give up the right to stop you at any point."

Kennedy might have been less reluctant to "turn loose" if the prospects for a successful coup were more encouraging. To the president, the balance of forces seemed unfavorable, General Don's intentions remained inscrutable, and the chances of prolonged fighting or even defeat appeared possible. Abandoning any pretense of U.S. noninvolvement, Kennedy ordered Lodge to intervene in the plotting if the operation appeared too risky: "We reiterate burden of proof must be on coup group to show a substantial possibility of quick success; otherwise, we should discourage them from proceeding since a miscalculation could result in jeopardizing [the] U.S. position in Southeast Asia."

Lodge, appalled by the thought of a U.S. attempt to thwart a coup, replied with a strident variation on the theme of his earlier cables: "Do not think we have the power to delay or discourage a coup. . . . It is theoretically possible for us to turn over the information which has been given to us in confidence to Diem and this would undoubtedly stop the coup and would make traitors out of us."

The ambassador also responded with evident exasperation to the assertion that the burden of proof rested with the generals: "I do not know what more proof can be offered than the fact these men are obviously prepared to risk their lives and that they want nothing for themselves."

In a masterpiece of understatement, Lodge concluded his message: "General Harkins has read this and does not concur."

The MACV commander had learned of the coup's imminence only after CINCPAC alerted him to the movement of a Marine battalion landing team off the coast of Vietnam. Firing off an angry cable to General Taylor, Harkins complained about being cut out of the embassy cable traffic and stated his opposition to a coup: "I am not opposed to a change in government, no indeed, but I am inclined to feel that at this time the change should be in methods of governing rather than [a] complete change of personnel. . . . After all, rightly or wrongly, we have backed Diem for eight long, hard years. To me it seems incongruous now to get him down, kick him around, and get rid of him."

Explaining his nonconcurrence with the ambassador's assessment, Harkins cabled: "[We] should have more information. Even though Don says his effort is purely Vietnamese, [the] U.S. will soon be involved whether we like it or not. I feel we should go along with only a sure thing. This or continue to go along with Diem until we have exhausted all pressures. The prestige of the U.S. is really involved one way or the other and it must be upheld at all costs."

In Washington the president and his advisers were alarmed both by Lodge's contrariness and the apparent communication breakdown between the ambassador and the MACV commander. On October 30 McGeorge Bundy upbraided Lodge on behalf of the president: "We do not accept as a basis for U.S. policy that we have no power to delay or discourage a coup." In a more moderate tone, Kennedy's national security adviser politely suggested to Lodge that he keep the MACV commander and the acting CIA station chief apprised of his plans: "We are sure it will help to have Harkins fully informed at all stages and to use advice from him and Smith in framing guidance for coup contacts and assessment."

This White House telegram, the last instructions Lodge would receive before the coup, outlined the U.S. posture toward the struggle. These guidelines included rejection of appeals for intervention from either side, U.S. willingness to mediate an indecisive contest, and an offer of asylum to coup leaders if their attempt should fail: "But once a coup under responsible leadership has begun, and within these restrictions, it is in the interest of the U.S. government that it should succeed."

CHAPTER TEN

NINE, NINE . . . NINE, NINE

After a sleepless night, Major General Tran Van Don arrived at Joint General Staff (JGS) headquarters at 7:30 A.M., November 1, 1963. With H hour only six hours away, he ordered extra rations for the rebel command post and increased his personal security detail. While nervously attending to the coup's final details, Don prepared for a 9:15 A.M. meeting with General Harkins and Admiral Harry D. Felt, commander of all U.S. forces in the Pacific. The admiral had unexpectedly arrived in Vietnam the day before. As a courtesy to the JGS chief, Felt had requested a meeting with General Don for the morning of November 1. The visiting American had offered to drop by JGS; but to Felt's surprise, Don had insisted they meet at MACV headquarters.

Determined to conceal the coup's imminence, General Don maintained a business-as-usual attitude toward the American military men. He made small talk and declared that winning the population's confidence was the key to defeating the Viet Cong. During the meeting, General Harkins pointed to his wall map of Vietnam and asked Don about two uncommitted airborne battalions. The Vietnamese general assured Harkins these units were en route to Tay Ninh Province, northwest of Saigon. In fact, these battalions were bearing down on the capital and would play a key role in the coup d'état.

At 9:45 A.M. Admiral Felt left MACV headquarters for an audience with President Diem. This meeting had not been part of Felt's original itinerary, but General Don, afraid that Diem might leave Saigon on November 1, had persuaded Felt to call on the South Vietnamese president. Ambassador Lodge had arranged the appointment, deciding to attend as well. At the palace Diem treated the Americans to a replay of his meeting with McNamara and Taylor six weeks earlier: a monologue celebrating the success of the war against the Viet Cong. During the conversation, Diem voiced his apprehension about a coup d'état. "I know there is going to be a coup, but I don't know who is going to do it," he said. "Usually, I have better sources, but they have really concealed this one."

According to Felt, Lodge replied that he did not think there was anything to worry about. Although he would later offer to help secure Diem's physical safety, Lodge had no intention of revealing what he knew about the coup. At about 11:45 A.M. Felt bid farewell to Diem and left the palace for his return flight to CINCPAC headquarters. Accompanied by Generals Harkins and Don, Felt held a brief press conference at Tan Son Nhut Airport. After his departure, General Harkins invited Don to lunch. The Vietnamese general, nervously chewing gum, declined, explaining that he had "to attend to some other business."

At Gia Long Palace, Diem sat alone with Lodge and his embassy interpreter. The South Vietnamese president charged the Americans with "intoxicating" the Buddhists and spreading false rumors of a coup d'état. Lodge, in his courtly, patrician manner, replied: Mr. President, you can "be sure if any American [has] committed an impropriety, I [will] send him out of the country."

Diem then made one last attempt to explain himself and his policies to the U.S. government. Defending his brother, the South Vietnamese president asked Lodge to speak with Ambassador Nolting and CIA Far Eastern Chief William Colby, who would explain how much he needed Nhu's counsel. As Lodge got up to leave, Diem made a remark that the ambassador interpreted as a reference to a coup: "Please tell President Kennedy that I am a good and frank ally [and] that I would rather be frank and settle questions now than talk about them after we have lost everything."

Lodge's report of this meeting, delayed by the priority messages that would soon flood the channels between Saigon and Washington, did not reach the State Department until after the coup was in progress.

While President Diem met with Lodge, Lou Conein received

the promised advance notice of the coup. An aide to General Don arrived at the CIA operative's home and told him to report to JGS headquarters immediately. Expecting a coded telephone message, Conein suspiciously questioned the ARVN captain, who was not an authorized "cut out" between Don and himself. Minutes later the general's dentist arrived at Conein's house to confirm the start of the coup.

Instructed to "bring all available money" to the rebel command post, Conein packed a bag with 3,000,000 piasters ($42,000), which he had earlier withdrawn from the station's operational funds. According to Conein, the money paid for food for the rebel troops and death benefits to the families of those killed in the coup. A few days before the coup, however, Lodge had suggested to Washington another use for CIA money: "buy[ing] off potential opposition." In addition to the cash, Conein packed a pistol, several hand grenades, and a special radio to relay information about the coup to the station and other CIA officers cut into his net. Before leaving for JGS, he broadcast the code indicating the coup was on: "nine, nine . . . nine, nine . . . nine, nine."

The ARVN generals had already linked a direct telephone line between the rebel command post and the American embassy; another telephone line connected JGS with Conein's home. This enabled him to keep in continuous contact with the twelve-man Special Forces "A" team protecting his wife and children. Should the coup fail, the U.S. soldiers would whisk his family out of the country. Conein arrived in uniform at rebel headquarters between 12:15 and 12:30 P.M. His contact, General Don, had not yet returned from escorting Admiral Felt to the airport. Seeing the American, "Big" Minh belligerently asked, "What are you doing here?"

"I was told to report here," replied Conein.

Threatening Conein with abduction to an unspecified location, Minh warned, "In case we fail, you're going with us."

Despite General Minh's chilly greeting, Conein radioed the code indicating his safe arrival at JGS: "I need a bottle of whiskey."

Conein's entrance had undoubtedly reminded Minh of the disastrous 1960 paratroopers' coup, when CIA officers had arrived at rebel headquarters and persuaded the coup's military and civilian leaders to negotiate with Diem. But "Big" Minh needn't have worried about Conein. A successful coup d'état was now a matter of U.S. policy. Although he has repeatedly claimed that his job at JGS was merely to report, Conein has probably understated his role in the coup. Considering the minimal U.S. confidence in the ARVN generals, it seems likely the veteran covert operator had been instructed to discreetly help the rebels in any way he could. In a word—and in the spirit of the U.S.–South Vietnamese relationship—it appears that Conein served as an adviser to the generals' operation.

By midday on November 1 most of the army's senior officers, both loyalist and rebel, had gathered at the JGS Officers' Club to attend a luncheon hosted by ARVN Chief of Staff Tran Thien Khiem. When all of the officers had been seated, "Big" Minh rose from his chair and announced the coup d'état. The general's declaration was punctuated by the arrival of military police. Armed with submachine guns, they burst into the officers' club and spread throughout the hall.

Minh asked his guests to stand if they supported the coup. They would be free to move around JGS but could not leave the command post. The officers who remained seated were immediately arrested and placed under armed guard. Minh next ordered a tape recorder brought to the officers' club. He read a proclamation that justified the insurrection, denounced Diem's "family dictatorship," and pledged a "more effectively commanded" army. The ARVN general then asked every officer present to sign the proclamation and to pledge his support for the rebellion into the tape recorder. Several copies of this tape were made for broadcast later in the day. Should the coup fail, no one would be able to say that he had not voluntarily participated.

With all of ARVN's general officers either present or accounted for, rebel military operations began in earnest at 1:30 P.M. Wearing red neckerchiefs—the traditional attire for coup forces in South Vietnam—and transported in armored personnel carriers, two marine battalions poured into Saigon from Bien Hoa, twenty miles north of the capital. The first attacks had been planned to coincide with the post-lunch siesta. By striking during daylight hours, the rebels would achieve tactical

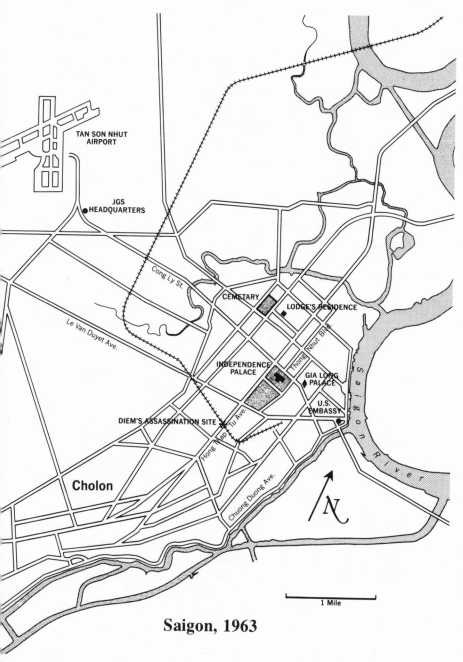

TAN SON NHUT
AIRPORT

JGS
HEADQUARTERS

Cong Ly St.

CEMETARY

LODGE'S RESIDENCE

Le Van Duyet Ave.

Thong Nhut Blvd.

INDEPENDENCE
PALACE

GIA LONG
PALACE

U.S.
EMBASSY

DIEM'S ASSASSINATION SITE

Hong Thap Tu Ave.

Saigon River

Cholon

Chuong Duong Ave.

N

1 Mile

Saigon, 1963

Map of Saigon. (Map by Mark Seidler)

surprise. Moreover, the clear Saigon streets would facilitate troop movements.

The coup forces enjoyed numerical superiority over Diem's troops and included virtually all the combat units adjacent to Saigon: one airborne and one infantry battalion from Vung Tau, two airborne battalions from Binh Duong Province, combat elements of the Fifth Infantry Division, and instructors and student cadets from nearby training camps. Despite this advantage, the rebel plan relied on surprise and speed rather than overwhelming military power. The leaders of the coup hoped to avoid bloody combat between forces who would eventually have to fight side by side against the Viet Cong.

With little or no resistance, the coup forces captured Tan Son Nhut Airport, naval headquarters, and the Ministry of National Defense. Approximately 500 marines surrounded the national police headquarters, preventing Diem supporters from reaching the huge cache of arms stored there. The rebels also quickly seized the Central Post Office, the source of Saigon's telegraphic communications. Loyal government troops put up some opposition at Radio Saigon, the other major communications facility, which went off the air abruptly between 2:00 and 2:15 P.M. But by 3:30 P.M. the coup forces controlled the radio station.

The heaviest fighting of the afternoon occurred at the Cong Hoa Barracks of the presidential guard brigade, only 1,000 meters from Gia Long Palace. Thundering loyalist tank fire rocked buildings and shattered windows in the area, sending Saigon residents diving to the ground from their bicycles and motor scooters. Inveterate coup spectators, the citizens of Saigon watched the fighting from what Westerners would consider imprudently close range.

After word of this stubborn resistance at the Cong Hoa Barracks reached the rebel command post, General Khiem phoned Lieutenant Colonel Nguyen Cao Ky at South Vietnamese Air Force headquarters. "Ky," said Khiem, "Diem's bodyguards are holding us up and time is running out. It's now or never. Are you ready to help?"

"Of course," replied Ky, "right away."

The flamboyant, mustachioed Ky, who customarily sported a bright purple scarf and an ivory-handled pistol, had already arrested the commander of the air force by bursting into his office with a submachine gun in hand. Responding to Khiem's request, Colonel Ky ordered two pilots to scramble to their planes. At approximately 4:00 P.M. the two T-28s appeared in the sky over Saigon, the first planes to do so since the 1962 bombing of Independence Palace. Flying through black and white shellbursts of antiaircraft fire, the planes made a pass at Cong Hoa Barracks, strafing the camp and firing one rocket each. Both rockets missed their intended target. One struck an unoccupied U.S. Marines barracks a few blocks beyond Gia Long Palace. Despite the demonstration of rebel air power, the fighting at Cong Hoa continued into the evening.

When the first reports of unusual military activity reached Gia Long Palace, Nhu was intially unconcerned. He believed the attacks were part of his bizarre two-part scheme to identify and destroy enemies of the regime. The first part of the plan, code-named Bravo I, was a fake coup. With several units of proven loyalty deployed outside Saigon, forces allied with the real conspiracy would be ordered to attack selected targets in the capital. Once the attacks had begun, Diem and Nhu would escape to Vung Tau, a seaside resort fifty miles southeast of Saigon. After several days of lawlessness and chaos, the government's enemies would come out into the open. Loyalist units would then move into Saigon and crush the rebels in a countercoup, code-named Bravo II. "By this plan," Nhu had predicted, "we shall trap the friends of the Americans in a dead shell of a capital city."

Unfortunately for the Ngo brothers, Nhu had entrusted the execution of the plan to rebel general Ton That Dinh. On the afternoon of November 1 Nhu tried to contact Dinh but was unable to reach him. Diem's brother also tried to raise other officers presumed loyal to the regime. When none of them could be reached, Nhu realized that this coup was real. Shortly after 4:00 P.M., Diem tried to telephone General Khiem, who had rescued the South Vietnamese president during the 1960 coup attempt. Instead, Diem reached Tran Van Don. "What are you generals doing?" Diem asked.

"Sir," replied Don, "the time has come when the army must respond to the wishes of the people."

Diem chastised the rebel general for not expressing his "wishes . . . in a sincere discussion." Belatedly, Diem announced his willingness to implement reforms suggested by the South Vietnamese military in early September. He invited Don and the other generals to Gia Long Palace to discuss their grievances. Like Conein's arrival at JGS, Diem's invitation must have been a chilling reminder of the 1960 paratroopers' coup, when the South Vietnamese president had stalled for time until rescued by loyalist troops. General Don politely declined Diem's gambit.

At 4:30 P.M. Diem called Ambassador Lodge, who was at home when the coup broke out. According to Lodge's report to the State Department, the following conversation ensued:

Diem: Some units have made a rebellion and I want to know what is the attitude of the U.S.?

Lodge: I do not feel well enough informed to be able to tell you. I have heard the shooting, but am not acquainted with all the facts. Also it is 4:30 a.m. in Washington and the U.S. government cannot possibly have a view.

Diem: But you must have some general ideas. After all, I am a chief of state. I have tried to do my duty. I want to do now what duty and good sense require. I believe in duty above all.

Lodge: You have certainly done your duty. As I told you only this morning, I admire your courage and your great contributions to your country. No one can take away from you the credit for all you have done. Now I am worried about your physical safety. I have a report that those in charge of the current activity offer you and your brother safe conduct out of the country if you resign. Had you heard this?

Diem: No. (And then after a pause) You have my telephone number.

Lodge: Yes. If I can do anything for your physical safety, please call me.

Diem: I am trying to reestablish order.

During the late afternoon and early evening of November 1, the rebel generals kept in constant telephone contact with the palace and repeatedly ordered Diem and Nhu to surrender. At 4:45 P.M. "Big" Minh announced to Nhu that if he and his brother did not resign, the palace would receive massive artillery and air bombardment. To convince Nhu of the strength of the coup forces and of the futility of resistance, other rebel generals got on the phone and demanded the surrender of the Ngo brothers.

The leaders of the coup also brought Colonel Le Quang Tung, the loyalist Special Forces commander, to the phone at gunpoint. Terrified, Tung reported the capture of all key military and civilian installations and the participation of Generals Khiem and Dinh in the rebellion. The Special Forces commander urged immediate surrender, but Nhu refused.

Colonel Tung, hated by all the rebel officers for his spying among the military, had now outlived his usefulness to the generals. Later that evening, Tung and his brother, the deputy commander of the Special Forces, were turned over to "Big" Minh's bodyguard. Their hands bound tightly behind their backs, Tung and his brother were pushed into a jeep and driven to a spot within the JGS compound where two holes had been freshly dug. Here they were shot and buried.

At 5:15 P.M. "Big" Minh phoned Diem to demand his surrender. The South Vietnamese president refused to speak to the rebel leader and contemptuously hung up on him. Enraged by Diem's transparent effort to make him lose face in front of the other generals, Minh called the palace again two hours later. If the Ngo brothers did not surrender immediately, threatened Minh, the palace would be "blasted off the face of the earth."

Diem still refused to speak with the rebel leader, much less discuss surrender.

For all his fury and violent threats, General Minh vetoed an immediate all-out assault on the palace. One reason for his restraint was a sincere desire to keep bloodshed between rebel and loyalist forces to a minimum. More importantly, General Minh and his confederates had simply not planned for an assault on Gia Long Palace. They had erroneously assumed that after a clear display of rebel military superiority, Diem would capitulate. His stubborn refusal to choose the "honorable" solution of surrendering left the generals both surprised and appalled. Minh's decision to delay an assault on the palace alarmed some of the rebel officers, who feared a repetition of the dawdling that had doomed the 1960 coup. Lou Conein also advised against delay: "If you hesitate, you will be lost."

None of the rebel officers was eager to lead the assault on Gia Long Palace. Ngo Dinh Diem was still a figure of considerable respect, and no one wanted to endure the shame of a direct attack on him. The generals selected Colonel Nguyen Van Thieu to lead the assault. Commander of the Fifth Infantry Division and presumed to have been a Diem loyalist throughout the Buddhist crisis, Thieu could unconditionally prove his loyalty to the rebels by commanding the siege of the palace. The selection of Thieu, a Catholic, was also religiously motivated. Let one Catholic destroy another, reasoned the Buddhist generals.

Shortly after 3:00 A.M., November 2, Colonel Thieu launched a series of increasingly heavy attacks against the palace, complete with mortar, tank, and artillery fire. Fierce loyalist resistance from within the palace repulsed each of the probes. Although it was only a matter of time before the rebels wore down the beleaguered defenders, who were outnumbered, exhausted from a day and night of fighting, and demoralized by lack of reinforcement, Diem still refused to capitulate. During a 6:00 A.M. phone conversation with General Dinh, Diem brazenly demanded the surrender of the rebel officer. Around dawn, the defensive perimeter around Gia Long Palace began to crumble. Rebel troops, advancing through the burning wreckage of destroyed tanks, entered the palace and began to search for Diem and Nhu. To their astonishment and alarm, the rebels discovered that the Ngo brothers were gone.

Diem and Nhu had escaped from Gia Long Palace around 8:00 P.M. the previous evening, before the rebel forces had completely sealed off the area. Leaving through the palace's back gate, Diem and Nhu slipped into an inconspicuous black sedan and rode to Cholon, the Chinese section of Saigon. After a circuitous journey, they arrived at the home of a wealthy Chinese businessman at 9:00 P.M. The house was equipped with a special telephone connection to the palace switchboard, which enabled Diem and Nhu to conceal their whereabouts.

The Ngo brothers initially planned to travel to either the Central Highlands or the southern delta. There, they would personally rally loyal troops for a countercoup. Diem and Nhu, however, quickly recognized the hopelessness of their situation. All of the country's top military commanders had declared their support for the junta; there were no loyal troops left to rally. The Ngo brothers, apparently distrusting the Americans, sought asylum in the Nationalist Chinese embassy but failed.

At 6:20 A.M., November 2, Diem—still refusing to speak with "Big" Minh—called General Don and offered to surrender "with honor." The South Vietnamese president sought safe conduct to the airport and a flight out of the country. Minh, furious at the repeated insults, refused to accept Diem's surrender "until Vietnamese have stopped killing Vietnamese," a reference to the continuing fighting at Gia Long Palace. Thirty minutes later, Diem again phoned the rebel command post. He reported his cease-fire order to the presidential guards and announced his unconditional surrender. This time the generals accepted.

During the surrender negotiations, the rebel leaders asked Conein to secure an American aircraft to fly the Ngo brothers out of the country. The CIA operative telephoned the request to Acting Station Chief David Smith. After a ten-minute delay, Smith replied that it would take twenty-four hours to procure a plane. The U.S. government intended to fly Diem to the first country willing to offer him asylum, preferably a European nation where his opportunities for a countercoup would be limited. The flight had to be direct—no stops for refueling—and the only aircraft with sufficient range were in Guam.

Conein repeated Smith's declaration to an uncomprehending Minh, who ominously replied, "We can't hold them that long."

Once again it appears that the doctrine of plausible denial placed the lives of the Ngo brothers at risk. Although American officials in Washington and Saigon had advance knowledge of the coup and the danger in which Diem might find himself, no arrangements had been made to fly him out of the country. To have done so would have tacitly admitted U.S. involvement in the conspiracy. Plausible denial, however, does not explain why on the morning of November 2, seventeen hours after the start of the coup, there had still been no attempt to arrange for a plane to fly Diem out of the country.

Accepting Diem's surrender, "Big" Minh dispatched an M-113 armored personnel carrier and four armed jeeps to pick up the Ngo brothers. After the armored column had left JGS, a rebel officer reported that the brothers had fled the palace. Minh immediately ordered a search of known Ngo family villas and houses in the Saigon area. Apparently tipped off by an informant, the rebel leaders discovered that Diem and Nhu were at a Catholic church in Cholon, where they had gone to pray before surrendering to the junta. The armored convoy, diverted from the palace, lumbered toward the Chinese section of Saigon.

At 8:10 A.M. Diem and Nhu, both wearing gray suits, were captured at the Don Thanh Catholic Church. According to one ARVN officer, "Diem had acted with his customary dignity, but Nhu had been sardonic to the last." Nhu reportedly objected to his brother being transported in an armored personnel carrier: "You use such a vehicle to drive the president?"

Their hands bound, Diem and Nhu were hustled into the M-113. On the return trip to the rebel command post, the convoy stopped at a train crossing for about five minutes. Here, according to most accounts, "Big" Minh's aide-de-camp and personal bodyguard, Captain Nguyen Van Nhung, shot and stabbed the Ngo brothers. Other accounts of the assassination also implicate Major Duong Hieu Nghia, who rode in the turret of the armored personnel carrier. According to Brigadier General Nguyen Khanh, who investigated the death of Diem after his own coup d'état in January of 1964, Nhung was a professional assassin: "He killed forty people. Every time he killed a person, he put one mark on his revolver."

Nhung was arrested by General Khanh in early 1964 but did not live long enough to reveal on whose orders he was acting. Diem's presumed assassin was found dead in his jail cell, apparently a suicide victim by hanging.

Shrouded in mystery, the details surrounding the decision to murder the Ngo brothers have been obscured by the conflicting

An M-113 armored personnel carrier similar to the vehicle in which Diem and Nhu were murdered. *(U.S. Army)*

testimony of the rebel generals, who either have been implicated in the assassination or have axes to grind with one another. General Don, for example, claimed in his memoirs that Minh was responsible for ordering the assassinations: "I can state without equivocation that this was done by General 'Big' Minh, and by him alone." Other officers, however, have implicated most, if not all, of the rebel leadership. According to Major Nhgia, "the fate of President Diem was decided by the majority of the members of the Revolutionary Committee."

Informed American sources have been no more illuminating on this decision than the finger-pointing and posterior-covering ARVN generals. To William Colby, "It's pretty clear . . . that the decision to kill Diem and Nhu was taken by Duong Van Minh himself." George Carver, however, has remained unconvinced: "I doubt if 'Big' Minh did this completely on his own, since doing so would have been quite out of character. He liked the comfort of company and shared responsibility on major decisions to hedge against future blame."

Lou Conein, the one Westerner who could shed light on the

decision to assassinate Diem, has been Delphic on the subject. Admitting there were "heated arguments" over Diem's fate, Conein has adamantly denied reports of a vote among the generals to assassinate the South Vietnamese president. In an interview years after the coup, the usually direct CIA operative ducked the question of responsibility for Diem's murder by cryptically observing, "My co-conspirators let me down."

According to Conein, he left JGS at about the same time the convoy departed to pick up Diem and Nhu. The press had been invited to the rebel command post, and it seemed imprudent for the CIA officer to remain there. At home he received orders from David Smith to report to the embassy. There Conein learned of instructions from the "highest authority," a government euphemism for the president, to find Diem.

At about 10:30 A.M. Conein returned to the rebel command post. Several of the generals claimed that Diem and Nhu had committed suicide at a church in Cholon. Informed of the improbability of the Roman Catholic Ngo brothers committing suicide, the leaders of the coup later amended the cause of death to "accidental suicide." The junta's explanation of Diem's death appeared preposterous to most Westerners. But to many Vietnamese, the term "accidental suicide" was both apt and accurate, according to Carver: "By being perfidious to the end, by causing needless ARVN casualties on both sides, and by attempting to humiliate Minh in his colleagues' eyes, Diem and Nhu metaphorically signed their own death warrants."

Conein declined an invitation by "Big" Minh to view the bodies. The CIA officer assumed he could easily tell whether the Ngo brothers had committed suicide, knowledge that could be very dangerous. If in the unlikely event the public accepted the generals' explanation, Conein was quite sure that his old friends would contrive a "VC incident" to eliminate the only Westerner who knew the truth. Later that day the bodies of Diem and Nhu were taken to Saigon's St. Paul's Hospital for legal identification. The brothers were then buried in an unmarked grave at the municipal cemetery, which, ironically, was only one block from Ambassador Lodge's official residence.

In Washington top officials had been following the battle since 1:30 A.M., November 1, when the first CRITIC announced that a coup d'état was in progress. Because of Colonel

Thao's phantom coup one week earlier, the initial reports were greeted with some skepticism. After establishing a direct telephone hookup with the embassy, Michael Forrestal spoke to Deputy Chief of Mission William Trueheart, who reported Conein's presence at the rebel command post. "This coup is real," said Trueheart. "It is not more of our scare reporting." Only then did Forrestal awaken Kennedy, who came to the Situation Room and followed the coup throughout the day.

The report of Ngo Dinh Diem's brutal murder deeply shocked the president. General Maxwell Taylor, who was with the president when he received the news, wrote in his memoirs: "Kennedy leaped to his feet and rushed from the room with such a look of shock and dismay on his face which I had never seen before."

"It shook him personally . . . bothered him as a moral and religious matter," said Forrestal. "It shook his confidence, I think, in the kind of advice he was getting about South Vietnam."

Although President Kennedy was shocked by Diem's assassination, many other American officials were not. Military and CIA officers had always appreciated the inherent violence of a coup d'état. "The execution of a coup is not like organizing a tea party," General Taylor observed later. "It's a very dangerous business."

To State Department officials, the limited solidarity among the generals had seemed to preclude Diem's safe conduct out of Vietnam. In exile Diem would always have the potential to lead one faction of the army against another. In a back-channel telegram to the State Department before the coup, Deputy Chief of Mission William Trueheart had warned: "There was a real risk Diem and Nhu would be executed . . . [because] the generals feared that [they] might somehow get back in power."

Trueheart, who considered his conclusion fairly obvious, later remarked: "I didn't think it was a particularly penetrating analysis."

Perhaps least surprised of all by Diem's death was Assistant Secretary of State Roger Hilsman, coauthor of the August 24 cable. When asked by journalist Marguerite Higgins how it felt to have "blood on your hands," Hilsman responded with a callousness that seemed to typify the administration's minimal concern for Diem's life: "Oh, come on now, Maggie. Revolutions are rough. People get hurt."

Diem and Nhu were not the only members of the Ngo family "hurt" by the coup. Archbishop Thuc and Madame Nhu, out of the country when the rebellion occurred, were beyond the grasp of the generals. And a few days later the Saigon embassy made arrangements to fly Madame Nhu's three children to safety in Europe. But Ngo Dinh Can, Diem's youngest brother and the dreaded ruler of central Vietnam, was not so lucky.

On November 2 rebel forces encircled Can's residence in Hue with barbed wire and armored personnel carriers, ostensibly for his own protection. Like his brothers in Saigon, Can initially escaped from his would-be captors. He reportedly took refuge in a nearby Catholic seminary. That same day priests from the seminary went to the U.S. consulate in Hue and inquired about political asylum for Can. American Consul John Helble passed the request to Saigon and the State Department, advising against it. According to international law, only an embassy can grant asylum. Moreover, Can was a hated figure in Hue, the popular mood of which had become very ugly since the discovery of mass graves on the grounds of his residence. "Sheltering this fellow . . . was going to be a risk to the American citizens [in Hue] and the U.S. facility," Helble later observed.

Despite the consulate's objections, the State Department ordered Helble to grant asylum to Can to protect him from both the population and the junta. Kennedy administration officials, still reeling from Diem's assassination, feared that "further violence would harm [the] international reputation [of the] new regime."

At 10:45 A.M., November 5, Diem's brother arrived alone at the Hue consulate. Minutes later Brigadier General Do Cao Tri, commander of the First Division and the military governor of Hue, appeared at the consulate and demanded Can's release. The general made a veiled threat that he could not guarantee the consulate's security if the population learned of Can's presence there. Without acknowledging Can's whereabouts, Helble reminded Tri of his responsibility to protect the consulate. That same day the American consul urged the embassy to remove Can from Hue at the earliest opportunity. "I was told that he would be sent out of the country," Helble recalled, "and, indeed, I was told to ask him where he would like to go."

Accompanied by a U.S. military officer, Can boarded an American plane bound for Tan Son Nhut Airport. He was met not by embassy officials, as promised, but by the ubiquitous CIA operative Lou Conein, who immediately turned the Vietnamese over to security representatives of the generals. According to Conein, he had received his instructions from the ambassador: "[Lodge] told me that he was going to make special arrangements for landing this airplane at a certain place at Tan Son Nhut, and that the person on board was to be turned over to the Vietnamese authorities."

Lodge had made this decision without consulting Washington. While Can's plane was en route to Saigon, the ambassador had informed the State Department: "I have received assurances from General Don personally that Can's physical safety is guaranteed, and that he will be dealt with 'legally and juridically.' On the basis of this assurance, Can will be turned over to Vietnamese authorities at the airport."

In this telegram Lodge rationalized Can's betrayal: "Giving him asylum, as I understand it, was to protect him from being lynched and to provide him with physical safety. As [the] government gives assurances [of] his personal safety and that he will be dealt with by legal process, it seems to me that our reason for giving him asylum therefore no longer exists. I also consider that we would be subject to justifiable criticism if we attempted to obstruct the course of justice here, particularly as Can is undoubtedly a reprehensible figure who deserves all the loathing which he now receives."

Lodge, undoubtedly, had few illusions as to Can's fate in the hands of the generals. The previous month General Minh had proposed assassinating him. Three days earlier his two older brothers had been murdered in the rear of an armored personnel carrier. And in a report written after the coup but *before* Can was turned over to the junta, Saigon CIA officials observed: "As to Ngo Dinh Nhu and Ngo Dinh Can, there was never dissension [among the generals]. The attitude was that their deaths, along with Madame Ngo Dinh Nhu, would be welcomed."

In the spring of 1964 Can was tried and found guilty of murder, attempted murder, extortion, illegal arrests, and damaging the national economy. Despite a plea for clemency by Ambassador Lodge, Diem's brother was executed before a firing squad on May 9—one year and one day after the outbreak of the Buddhist crisis in Hue.

A VERY DISTURBING SITUATION

In the immediate aftermath of Diem's overthrow, many U.S. officials succumbed, in McNamara's words, to "a certain euphoria" about prospects in Vietnam, where worst-case predictions of the coup's consequences had not materialized. The Viet Cong, hampered by a primitive command and communications system, had not yet effectively reacted to the coup. Despite the junta's acknowledged fragility, it appeared that the new regime might successfully prosecute the war against the Communists.

Although Kennedy's government was hopeful, the president had come to doubt Vietnam's manageability. He had learned painfully from Diem's assassination that the U.S. could influence events there but not necessarily control them. Two days before his trip to Dallas—and a rendezvous with his own assassin—Kennedy questioned Michael Forrestal about South Vietnam's viability. "It was the first time that he ever got really philosophical and reflective about Vietnam with me," said Forrestal.

Kennedy's assassination on November 22, 1963, ended whatever possibility existed of a fresh look at U.S. policy in Vietnam. Lyndon B. Johnson, whose commitment to containing communism was at least as great as the slain president's, sought continuity in Kennedy administration programs and personnel. On November 26, 1963, President Johnson issued his first Vietnam directive, which emphatically declared his determination to stay the course: "It remains the central objective of the United States in South Vietnam to assist the people and government of that country to win their contest against the externally directed and supported Communist conspiracy."

During Johnson's first weeks in office, reports of rapid military deterioration began pouring into the White House. Diem's overthrow had not only triggered increased Viet Cong activity but had also exposed the corrupt Vietnamese reporting system upon which official American assessments of the war had been made. In December of 1963 McNamara grimly reported Viet Cong control of key provinces around Saigon and in the Mekong River Delta. Political developments were even more discouraging. "Big" Minh was an indolent and inept political leader, and factionalism split the twelve-man Military Revolutionary Council. "The situation is very disturbing," McNamara concluded. "Current trends unless reversed in the next 2–3 months, will lead to neutralization at best and more likely to a Communist-controlled state."

As U.S. officials began facing up to Vietnam's harsh realities, Communist leaders in Hanoi secretly agreed to escalate the conflict in the south, a momentous decision influenced by Diem's overthrow. Although "Big" Minh and the ruling junta enjoyed tremendous popular support immediately after the coup, Lao Dong party leaders believed a military government would eventually become unpopular and unstable. After a ten-day meeting in December, the Central Committee resolved "to rapidly strengthen our military forces in order to create a basic change in the balance of forces between the enemy and us in South Vietnam."

The Communist prediction of South Vietnamese political instability was quickly fulfilled. On January 30, 1964, Major General Nguyen Khanh staged a bloodless coup deposing the top generals. The new regime was the third South Vietnamese government in three months. Despite Khanh's naive belief that he was "absolutely totally protected against another coup," weak South Vietnamese regimes succeeded each other until the relatively durable team of Nguyen Cao Ky and Nguyen Van Thieu assumed power in June of 1965.

While South Vietnam slowly disintegrated militarily and politically, President Johnson and his advisers plunged America deeper into war. Controlling neither Communists nor coup plotters in the south, the Johnson administration moved northward, seeking to punish Hanoi for its participation in the war. Initial operations against North Vietnam were covert and conducted by the South Vietnamese and mercenaries. In February of 1965, however, President Johnson crossed the advisory threshold and authorized a gradually intensifying program of overt U.S. air operations against North Vietnam. Later in the year massive numbers of U.S. combat forces were deployed to South Vietnam. At last American leaders had become fully engaged in a war they had hoped to avoid—a bitterly divisive conflict that would send 2.6 million U.S. servicemen to Vietnam and cost the lives of 58,000 GIs.

But the question still lingers. What would President John F. Kennedy have done about Vietnam had he lived? The absence of a clear direction to Kennedy's policy and the contradictory speculation of his former advisers preclude a confident answer. My guess is that he would not have crossed the covert action-advisory threshold, would not have bombed North Vietnam, and would not have committed U.S. ground troops to South Vietnam. Undoubtedly, Kennedy would have put off the really hard choices in Vietnam until after the 1964 election. Like Lyndon B. Johnson, he would have campaigned as a man of restraint and moderation—a sharp and reassuring contrast to the trigger-happy image of his opponent, Senator Barry Goldwater.

The crunch would have come in January of 1965, when McGeorge Bundy and Robert McNamara jointly declared that time had run out on fifteen years of limited involvement in Vietnam. Characterizing U.S. policy as "first aid to squabbling politicos and passive reaction to events we do not try to control," Bundy and McNamara suggested either direct U.S. military operations or negotiations without further escalation. "Bob and I tend to favor the first course," wrote Bundy, "but we believe that both sides should be carefully studied."

At this point Kennedy might well have chosen the negotiations route, realizing full well that it would eventually mean Communist domination of Vietnam, Laos, and Cambodia and a divisive search for scapegoats at home. Such bitter consequences, however, could have appeared preferable to becoming a co-belligerent in a war where virtually every U.S. military and political initiative had failed. Indeed, Kennedy's own failures in Vietnam might have created an unshakeable skepticism about the efficacy of bombing the north and of sending ground troops into the south

It seems possible that Kennedy would have been strongly attracted to the proposed option in which the U.S. assumed the role of a "good doctor" who has done everything within reason to keep a terminally ill patient alive. This scenario, advanced in late 1964, called for highlighting the unique combination of factors that prevented the Vietnamese from saving themselves: a bad colonial heritage, totally inadequate preparation for self-government, and a nationalist movement coopted by the Communists. In assuming such a posture, Kennedy would have taken his lumps both at home and abroad for reneging on past commitments and "losing" South Vietnam to communism. On the other hand, pulling out of Vietnam would have enabled Kennedy to demonstrate the kind of political courage he so greatly admired in others yet so infrequently exhibited during his presidency.

SOURCE NOTES

Page

INTRODUCTION: **Socratic Questions**

ix "He talked about some personal things . . ." Michael V. Forrestal, interview with the author, Sept. 2, 1981.

ix 'You go out there and tell . . ." *Ibid.*

ix "Wait a minute. When you . . ." *Ibid.*

x "He didn't say, 'It's not . . ." *Ibid.*

x "I had hundreds of talks . . ." Dean Rusk, U.S. News Books
interview, Sept. 22, 1980.

x "Well, we'd have faced that . . ." Robert F. Kennedy, recorded
interview by John Bartlow Martin, April 30, 1964, p. 379. John
F. Kennedy Library Oral History Program.

x "Our security and strength . . ." *Public Papers of the Presidents
of the United States: John F. Kennedy, 1963* (Washington: GPO,
1964), p. 477.

xi "In the final analysis . . ." *Ibid.*, p. 340.

xiii "Frankly, we have no solution . . ." Telegram, State to Paris,
Feb. 3, 1947, *Foreign Relations of the United States* (Washington: GPO).

xiii "all practicable measures be taken . . ." NSC 64, "The Position
of the United States with Respect to Indochina," NSC—custody
of the National Archives, Modern Military Branch.

xv   "We have allied ourselves . . ." John F. Kennedy, "The War in Indochina," *A Compilation of Statements and Speeches Made During His Service in the United States Senate and House of Representatives* (Washington: Legislative Reference Service, 1964), p. 287.

xv   "I am frankly of the belief . . ." *Ibid.*

xv   "united action"; "realizing full well . . ." *Ibid.*, p. 285.

xvi   "This is our offspring . . ." John F. Kennedy, "America's Stake in Vietnam," *Anatomy of a Conflict* (Itasca, Illinois: 1968), Wesley R. Fishel, editor, p. 144.

xvii   "It was a firebell warning . . ." George A. Carver, Jr., "An Unheeded Firebell: The November 1960 Coup Attempt," unpublished contract monograph for U.S. News Books.

CHAPTER 1: **Kill All the Paratroopers!**

1   Assault on Independence Palace. Airgram G-219, Saigon to State, Nov. 21, 1960, declassified by the Department of State, March 10, 1982; *Times of Vietnam*, Nov. 12, 1960; "The Coup That Failed," *Times of Vietnam*, Nov. 19, 1960; Carver, "An Unheeded Firebell."

2   "opportunist and a man . . ." CIA Office of Central Reference Biographic Register, Box 28, International Meetings and Trips, National Security Files, Lyndon B. Johnson Library.

2   "tough, unscrupulous, and fearless . . ." *Ibid.*

2   "The military coup planners . . ." Carver, "An Unheeded Firebell."

3   "feudal totalitarianism." *Times of Vietnam*, Nov. 12, 1960, p. 2.

3   "Diem showed a curious . . ." Telegram 48, Saigon to State, July 4, 1954, *Foreign Relations of the United States, 1952–54* (Washington: GPO, 1982), XIII, p. 1783.

5   "nothing but an instrument . . ." Bernard B. Fall, *The Two Viet-Nams* (New York: Frederick A. Praeger, 1967), p. 239.

5   "weak, venal, infused with a sense . . ." National Intelligence Estimate 63–7–54, "Probable Developments in South Vietnam,

Laos, and Cambodia Through July, 1956," Nov. 23, 1954, *Foreign Relations*, p. 2291.

6 "suave, Europeanized, money-seeking . . ." Telegram 4542, Paris to State, May 26, 1954, *ibid.*, p. 1618.

6 "He impresses one as a mystic . . ." Telegram 4521, Paris to State, May 24, 1954, *ibid.*, p. 1609.

6 "U.S. support most probably would stop." Report, Saigon Military Mission. Printed in Neil Sheehan et al., *The Pentagon Papers as Published by The New York Times* (New York: Bantam Books, 1971), p. 59.

6 "marked inability to understand . . ." Memorandum for the assistant secretary of defense (ISA), April 25, 1955, "Debriefing of General Collins," *United States–Vietnam Relations, 1945–1967* (Washington: GPO, 1971), X, p. 937.

6 "Diem must be replaced . . ." Memorandum for the assistant secretary of state (FE), April 30, 1955, "Report on Collins Visit and Vietnam Situation," *ibid.*, p. 945.

7 "oppressions against the population"; "liberalize the regime." *The Pentagon Papers* (Boston: Beacon Press, 1971), I, p. 318.

7 "It's funny when civilians . . ." Nguyen Khanh, interview with the author, April 12, 1982.

7 "the generals all sat calmly . . ." George Carver, interview with the author, Oct. 29, 1981.

8 "I ducked behind tree after . . ." John Helble, interview with the author, Aug. 10, 1982.

8 "A report was cabled to Washington . . ." Carver, "An Unheeded Firebell."

9 "I hadn't prompted the coup . . ." Carver interview.

9 "Where is your command group?" Russell F. Miller, interview with the author, Sept. 8, 1982.

10 "of course, not in a position . . ." Telegram 1022, Saigon to State, Nov. 11, 1960, declassified by the Department of State, May 17, 1982.

10 "a 100-percent containment . . ." Elbridge Durbrow, interview with the author, Oct. 28, 1981.

10 "best available Vietnamese leader"; "It may become necessary . . ." Telegram 624, Saigon to State, Sept. 16, 1960, *United States–Vietnam Relations*, p. 1316.

11 "a most sensitive and delicate matter." Telegram 802, Saigon to State, Oct. 15, 1960, *ibid.*, p. 1324.

11 "These rumors about the Nhus . . ." *United States–Vietnam Relations*, X, p. 1324.

11 "It was pretty damn tough . . ." Durbrow interview.

11 "I was convinced that my orders . . ." Carver interview.

12 "Every fiber of my being . . ." *Ibid.*

12 "Don't worry, we have already . . ." Khanh interview.

12 "If you want to get in . . ." *Ibid.*

13 "All right, I will meet . . ." *Ibid.*

13 "The first thing . . ." *Ibid.*

14 "It is the will . . ." *Ibid.*

17 "must speak firmly"; "After all these efforts . . ." Telegram 1049, Saigon to State, Nov. 12, 1960, declassified by the Department of State, May 17, 1982.

17 "must negotiate immediately." *Ibid.*

17 "flagrant violation." *Times of Vietnam*, Nov. 12, 1960, p. 2.

18 "the howitzers ought not . . ." Miller interview.

18 "If you couldn't succeed . . ." *Ibid.*

18 "touch and go." *Ibid.*

19 "I think President Diem interpreted . . ." William Colby, interview with the author, Oct. 28, 1981.

19 "All nations conduct espionage . . ." William Colby, *Honorable Men* (New York: Simon & Schuster, 1978), p. 164.

19 "betrayal of the rebel cause." Carver, "An Unheeded Firebell."

19 "The death threat looked like . . ." Colby interview.

19 "vengeful attitude"; "quite serious undercurrent . . ." Telegram 1151, Saigon to State, Dec. 4, 1960, *United States–Vietnam Relations*, X, p. 1334.

20 "We should help encourage . . ." *Ibid.*

CHAPTER 2: **We Must Change Our Course**

21 "Get down here right away." Edward G. Lansdale, interview with the author, April 23, 1982.

22 "Each night we sat up . . ." Edward G. Lansdale, *In the Midst of Wars* (New York: Harper & Row, 1972), p. 37.

23 "I was convinced he was not . . ." Roswell L. Gilpatric, recorded interview by Dennis J. O'Brien, May 5, 1970, p. 9, John F. Kennedy Library Oral History Program.

23 "Diem cannot help but . . ." *United States–Vietnam Relations*, X, p. 1330.

23 "I took a dim view . . ." Lansdale interview.

23 "shambles"; "He obviously thought . . ." William Colby, *Honorable Men*, p. 172.

24 "In our first meeting . . ." Memorandum, Lansdale to the secretary of defense, Jan. 17, 1961, *United States-Vietnam Relations*, XI, p. 1.

24 "He showed me where . . ." Lansdale interview.

24 "combat area of the cold war . . ." Lansdale to the secretary of defense.

25 "It did not take much . . ." William Bundy, unpublished manuscript.

25 "keen interest." Memorandum, McGeorge Bundy to McNamara, Rusk, and Dulles, Jan. 27, 1961, National Security Files, John F. Kennedy Library.

25 "a sense of the danger . . ." Memorandum, Rostow to Bundy, Jan. 30, 1961, Box 193, National Security Files, John F. Kennedy Library.

25 "I found myself trying . . ." J. Graham Parsons, recorded interview by Dennis J. O'Brien, Aug. 22, 1969, p. 22, John F. Kennedy Library Oral History Program.

26 "would really permit a shift . . ." Rostow to Bundy.

26 "Why so little?" Durbrow interview.

26 "The Communists regard 1961 . . ." Rostow to Bundy.

26 "very close to those . . ." *Ibid.*

27   "Did Dean tell you I . . ." Lansdale interview.

27   "We must change our course . . ." Rostow to Bundy.

27   "[Do you] realize the implications . . ." Parsons, oral history interview, p. 23.

27   "He was in the doghouse . . ." Gilpatric, oral history interview.

28   "We will begin with . . ." Lansdale interview.

28   "It was a fight . . ." *Ibid.*

28   "It is this new dimension . . ." *Public Papers of the Presidents of the United States: John F. Kennedy, 1961* (Washington: GPO, 1962), p. 213.

28   "If these attacks do not stop . . ." *Ibid.*

29   "I remember one report of the two . . ." Rusk interview.

29   "immoral." John Lewis Gaddis, *Strategies of Containment* (New York: Oxford University Press, 1982), p. 154.

30   "key to Southeast Asia"; "if Laos should fall . . ." Memorandum, conference between Eisenhower and Kennedy, Jan. 19, 1961, *United States-Vietnam Relations*, X, p. 1362.

30   "We came to the conclusion . . ." Rusk interview.

31   "As we have feared . . ." Memorandum, Rostow to the president, March 7, 1961, Box 194, National Security Files, John F. Kennedy Library.

31   "new phase." Walt W. Rostow, *The Diffusion of Power* (New York: Macmillan Co., 1972), p. 266.

31   "prospect of [a] large-scale . . ." Telegram 1567, Rusk to Moscow, March 23, 1961, Box 193, National Security Files, John F. Kennedy Library.

31   "In the short run . . ." Rostow, p. 267.

31   "Communism is best understood . . ." Walt W. Rostow, "Guerrilla Warfare in the Underdeveloped Areas," *Department of State Bulletin*, Aug. 7, 1961.

31   "It is somehow wrong . . ." Memorandum, Rostow to the president, March 29, 1961, Box 194, National Security Files, John F. Kennedy Library.

32   "too difficult to read." Memorandum, Rostow to the president,

July 21, 1961, Box 231, National Security Files, John F. Kennedy Library.

32   "[Kennedy's] most typical response . . ." Rostow, *The Diffusion of Power*, p. 126.

32   "Never thereafter would civilian leaders . . ." Bundy, unpublished manuscript.

33   "We cannot win a conventional war . . ." Memorandum, "Meeting on Laos," April 29, 1961, *United States–Vietnam Relations*, XI, p. 64.

33   "We would have to throw in . . ." *Ibid.*

33   "I never saw the American military . . ." Rostow, *The Diffusion of Power*, pp. 664–665.

33   "contained bluff with real . . ." Theodore Sorensen, *Kennedy* (New York: Harper & Row, 1965), p. 646.

34   "Where would be the best . . ." *United States–Vietnam Relations*, XI, p. 64.

34   "[President] Kennedy had decided . . ." Walt W. Rostow, Conference on the Presidency of John Fitzgerald Kennedy, Los Angeles, Nov. 14, 1980.

34   "to join with you in an intensified . . ." Letter, Kennedy to Diem, May 8, 1961, Box 242, National Security Files, John F. Kennedy Library.

34   "President Diem be encouraged." JCS memorandum 320-61, May 10, 1961, *United States–Vietnam Relations*, XI, p. 43.

35   "If these men I saw at your request . . ." Memorandum, Johnson to Kennedy, May 23, 1961, Box 242, National Security Files, John F. Kennedy Library.

35   "to prevent Communist domination . . ." National Security Action Memorandum 52, May 11, 1961, Box 330, National Security Files, John F. Kennedy Library.

36   "the size and composition of forces . . ." *Ibid.*

36   "I was most deeply gratified by this . . ." Letter, Diem to Kennedy, May 15, 1961, Box 193, National Security Files, John F. Kennedy Library.

36   "threat from Southern Laos"; "considerable expansion of the

. . ." Letter, Diem to Kennedy, June 9, 1961, Box 193, National Security Files, John F. Kennedy Library.

36   "[T]he Department of Defense is urgently . . ." Letter, Kennedy to Diem, July 3, 1961, Box 193, National Security Files, John F. Kennedy Library.

36   "[W]e must find out . . ." Memorandum, Rostow to the president, Box 193, National Security Files, John F. Kennedy Library.

CHAPTER 3: **A Certain Dilemma**

37   "intended to ambush the guerrillas . . ." *Time*, Sept. 29, 1961, p. 33.

38   "on the anvil and under . . ." R. Michael Pearce, *The Insurgent Environment* (Santa Monica, California: Rand, 1969), p. 103.

38   "[The Viet Cong] bumped off . . ." Charles Maechling, Jr., interview with the author, April 1981.

38   "We are yellow, surrounded . . ." Lucien E. Conein, interview with the author, Nov. 3, 1982.

39   "to avoid going down the road . . ." Resolution of an Enlarged Conference of the Central Office for South Vietnam, October 1961, *Vietnam: The Definitive Documentation of Human Decisions* (Stanfordville, New York: Coleman, 1979), II, p. 121.

40   "[T]he ability of U.S. imperialism . . ." *Ibid.*

40   "It is probable that the . . ." SNIE 53-2-61, "Bloc Support of the Communist Effort against the Government of Vietnam," Oct. 5, 1961, Box 194, National Security Files, John F. Kennedy Library.

40   "[W]e must move quite radically . . ." Memorandum, Rostow to the president, Oct. 5, 1961, Box 231, National Security Files, John F. Kennedy Library.

40   "If we go in now . . ." *Ibid.*

41   "not feasible"; "militarily unsound." JCS memorandum 716–61, Oct. 9, 1961, Box 194, National Security Files, John F. Kennedy Library.

42   "there is no assurance that . . ." Report, "Concept for Inter-

vention," Oct. 10, 1961, Box 194, National Security Files, John F. Kennedy Library.

42 "He talked with an elegance . . ." George Ball, *The Past Has Another Pattern* (New York: W. W. Norton & Co., 1982), p. 365.

43 "for coping with anything . . ." Maxwell D. Taylor, *The Uncertain Trumpet* (New York: Harper & Brothers, Publishers, 1960), p. 6.

43 "While I never particularly . . ." Maxwell D. Taylor, *Swords and Plowshares* (New York: W. W. Norton, 1972), p. 170.

43 "most persuasive"; "shap[ing] my own thinking." *Ibid.*, p. 180.

44 "bear in mind that the initial . . ." *Ibid.*, p. 225.

44 "two professors going over . . ." Rostow, *The Diffusion of Power*, p. 274.

45 "human defoliation." Taylor Report, "Unconventional Warfare Appendix," Box 203, National Security Files, John F. Kennedy Library.

45 "They might very well have . . ." Edward G. Lansdale, interview with the author, April 23, 1982.

45 "Lansdale was an idea man . . ." Maxwell D. Taylor, interview with the author, June 9, 1982.

45 "Well, I'm an old friend . . ." Lansdale interview.

46 "What do you want U.S. troops for?" *Ibid.*

46 "It got obnoxious after a time . . ." *Ibid.*

46 "Because of [the] Laos situation." *United States–Vietnam Relations*, II, p. 90.

46 "He avoided the subject . . ." Taylor, *Swords and Plowshares*, p. 232.

47 "I was somewhat startled . . ." Taylor, *Ibid.*, p. 234.

48 "The strength of the force . . ." Telegram 537, Taylor to the president October 25, 1961, Box 74, National Security Files, Lyndon B. Johnson Library.

48 "expressed satisfaction." *United States–Vietnam Relations*, II, p. 90.

48   "double crisis in confidence." Telegram 537, Taylor to the pres-
      ident, Nov. 1, 1961, *United States–Vietnam Relations*, XI, p.
      332.

48   "a massive joint effort." *Ibid.*, p. 333.

48   "limited partnership." Taylor Report, "Evaluations and Con-
      clusions," Box 203, National Security Files, John F. Kennedy
      Library.

48   "this force is not proposed . . ." *United States–Vietnam Rela-
      tions*, XI, p. 339.

49   "Drop everything else you're . . ." Lansdale interview.

49   "When are you going to . . ." Letter, Lansdale to the author,
      Oct. 16, 1982.

49   "relative handful"; "losing horse." Telegram 6, Rusk to State,
      Nov. 1, 1961, Box 194, National Security Files, John F. Ken-
      nedy Library.

50   "great help"; "we mean business." Memorandum, McNamara
      to the president, Nov. 8, 1961, *United States–Vietnam Relations*,
      XI, p. 343.

50   "If we commit 6–8,000 troops . . ." Memorandum, Johnson to
      Bundy, Oct. 31, 1961, Box 194, National Security Files, John
      F. Kennedy Library.

50   "They want a force of American . . ." Arthur M. Schlesinger,
      Jr., *A Thousand Days* (New York: Fawcett Premier, 1965), p.
      505.

50   "George, you're crazier than hell." George Ball, *The Past Has
      Another Pattern*, p. 366.

51   "move to complete accommodation with . . ." Memorandum,
      Rusk and McNamara to the president, Nov. 11, 1961, Box 128,
      Presidential Office Files, John F. Kennedy Library.

52   "drawn up to the president's specifications." *United States–Viet-
      nam Relations*, II, p. 124.

52   "the fall of South Vietnam to communism." Rusk and Mc-
      Namara to the president.

52   "sharply increased joint effort." Telegram 619, State to Saigon,
      Nov. 15, 1961, Box 195, National Security Files, John F. Ken-
      nedy Library.

52 "show [the South Vietnamese] how the job . . ." Taylor Report, "Evaluations and Conclusions."

52 "a certain dilemma." Rusk and McNamara to the president.

52 "recognized as having real . . ." Telegram 619, State to Saigon.

53 "as handing over." Telegram 608, Saigon to State, Nov. 7, 1961, National Security Files, Box 194, John F. Kennedy Library.

53 "Fritz was considered at that time . . ." William H. Sullivan, recorded interview by Dennis J. O'Brien, June 16, 1970, p. 36, John F. Kennedy Library Oral History Program.

53 "a man dedicated to high principles . . ." Telegram 70, Saigon to State, July 14, 1961, Box 193, National Security Files, John F. Kennedy Library.

53 "It seems clear to me . . ." *Ibid.*

53 "far-reaching and difficult measures . . ." Telegram 678, Saigon to State, Nov. 18, 1961, Box 195, National Security Files, John F. Kennedy Library.

54 "a substantial number of . . ." *Ibid.*

54 "On the whole, I am not . . ." *Ibid.*

55 "Kennedy, I've always believed . . ." John Kenneth Galbraith, *A Life in Our Times* (Boston: Houghton Mifflin Company, 1981), p. 389.

55 "As a military ally the entire . . ." John Kenneth Galbraith, *Ambassador's Journal* (Boston: Houghton Mifflin, 1969), p. 107.

55 "exceedingly half-baked"; "Once there. . ." *Ibid.*, p. 243.

55 "A comparatively well-equipped . . ." Telegram, Galbraith to the president, Nov. 20, 1961, *United States-Vietnam Relations*, XI, p. 407.

55 "key and inescapable"; "the ineffectuality." Telegram, Galbraith to the president, Nov. 21, 1961, Box 195, National Security Files, John F. Kennedy Library.

56 "[T]he only solution must be . . ." *Ibid.*

56 "the arguments in favor of . . ." Taylor Report, Appendix C, "Internal Political Situation in South Vietnam."

56   "the victim of my own . . ." Galbraith, *A Life in Our Times*, p. 474.

56   "very sad and disappointed," Telegram 687, Saigon to State, Nov. 22, 1961, Box 195, National Security Files, John F. Kennedy Library.

57   "Vietnam Not a Guinea Pig . . ." Telegram 702, Saigon to State, Nov. 24, 1961, Box 195, National Security Files, John F. Kennedy Library.

57   "foolish and dangerous." Telegram 708, Saigon to State, Nov. 26, 1961, Box 195, National Security Files, John F. Kennedy Library.

57   "emotional, incorrect, and . . ." *Ibid.*

58   "sham"; "puppet of Nhu." Telegram 734, Saigon to State, Dec. 2, 1961, Box 195, National Security Files, John F. Kennedy Library.

58   "Something must and will be . . ." Memorandum, Hilsman to Rusk, "Coup Plotting in South Vietnam," Nov. 28, 1961, Box 195, National Security Files, John F. Kennedy Library.

58   "Their estimate of U.S. intentions . . ." *Ibid.*

58   "irresponsible gossip"; "agents provocateurs." Memorandum, U. Alexis Johnson to Bundy, "Status of Actions with Respect to South Vietnam," Box 195, National Security Files, John F. Kennedy Library.

58   "concrete measures to improve . . ." *Ibid.*

58   "marathon discussion." Telegram 748, Saigon to State, Dec. 1, 1961, Box 195, National Security Files, John F. Kennedy Library.

59   "closer consultation with . . ." Telegram 756, Saigon to State, Dec. 4, 1961, Box 195, National Security Files, John F. Kennedy Library.

59   "good job." Telegram 727, State to Saigon, Dec. 4, 1961, Box 195, National Security Files, John F. Kennedy Library.

59   "clarified." *United States–Vietnam Relations*, II, p. 147.

59   "To carry the matter . . ." Bundy, unpublished manuscript.

59   "[The Americans] gave the impression . . ." Bui Diem, interview with the author, April 7, 1982.

CHAPTER 4: A Slowly Escalating Stalemate

60   The arrival of the *Core* in Saigon. *New York Times,* Dec. 12,
     1961, p. 21.

61   "there must have been 300 slides . . ." Rufus Phillips, interview
     with the author, June 1981.

61   "He didn't like flip charts . . ." Gilpatric oral history, p. 69.

61   "volunteered." Henry F. Graff, *The Tuesday Cabinet: Deliberation and Decision on Peace and War under Lyndon B. Johnson* (Englewood Cliffs, New Jersey: Prentice-Hall, 1970).

61   "It was as if I had been talking to a devout Catholic . . ."
     Deposition of George A. Carver, Jr., William C. Westmoreland
     vs. CBS Inc., et al., November 1983.

63   "McNamara's band concerts." Paul Kattenburg, *The Vietnam
     Trauma in American Foreign Policy, 1945–1975* (New Brunswick, New Jersey: Transaction Books, 1980), p. 193.

63   "the first team there." Memorandum, McNamara to the secretary of the army and the chief of staff, Dec. 21, 1961, Box
     195, National Security Files, John F. Kennedy Library.

63   "number one priority." "The Strategic Hamlet Program," *United
     States–Vietnam Relations,* III, p. 15.

63   "to win this battle." Robert F. Futrell, *The United States Air
     Force in Southeast Asia: The Advisory Years to 1965* (Washington: GPO, 1981), p. 119.

63   "occupation force." *U.S. News & World Report,* July 25, 1966,
     p. 38.

63   "no alternative to the introduction of . . . " JCS memorandum
     36-42 to the secretary of defense," "The Strategic Importance
     of the Southeast Asia Mainland," *United States–Vietnam Relations,* XII, p. 453.

63   "a planned phase in the Communist timetable . . ." *Ibid.,* p.
     450.

63   "a peninsula and island-type of campaign . . ." *Ibid.,* p. 453.

63 "I am not prepared to endorse . . ." *Ibid.*, p. 447.

64 "If you have seen Mr. Kennedy's eyes . . ." Lawrence Houston testimony, *Alleged Assassination Plots Involving Foreign Leaders* (Washington: GPO, 1975), p. 133.

64 "a major form of politico-military . . ." NSAM 124, "Establishment of the Special Group (Counter-Insurgency)," Jan. 18, 1962, Box 333, National Security Files, John F. Kennedy Library.

65 "infrared target detector"; "hand-held air gun . . ." JCS Memorandum 843-62 to the special assistant to the president for national security affairs, "Summary Report, Military Counterinsurgency Accomplishments Since January 1961," July 1962.

65 "People would look down and see . . ." Charles Maechling, Jr., interview with the author, April 1981.

65 "Why had the gods dumped so much salt . . ." Memorandum, "The Civilian Irregular Defense Groups (CIDG) Political Action Program," March 3, 1965, Lyndon B. Johnson Library.

66 "resistance to corruption angered many . . ." *Ibid.*

66 "They couldn't figure what the hell . . ." William Colby, interview with the author, October 1981.

67 "This struggle . . . must be won by . . ." Memorandum, "A Strategic Concept for South Vietnam," Box 195, National Security Files, John F. Kennedy Library.

67 "Hilsman was a very sharp and . . ." Michael Forrestal, interview with the author, Sept. 2, 1981.

68 "well and efficiently executed"; "inappropriate." Hilsman, "A Strategic Concept for South Vietnam."

68 "This would of course kill everything." Memorandum, "Visit with General Paul Harkins and Ambassador Nolting—17 March 1962," Roger Hilsman Papers, Box 3, John F. Kennedy Library.

69 "Diem's mystical philosophy was too abstract . . ." George Allen, "The Indochina Wars, 1950–75," unpublished contract monograph for U.S. News Books.

69 "became more of a sham than was realized . . ." Maechling interview.

70 "Incidentally, who is the man . . ." Letter, Galbraith to Kennedy, March 2, 1962, *Ambassador's Journal*, p. 311.

70 "Why do large numbers of Americans . . ." Telegram 1173, State to Saigon, Box 196, National Security Files, John F. Kennedy Library.

71 "to get us out of [Laos] whatever . . ." Michael Forrestal, interview with the author, Dec. 8, 1982.

71 "Harriman turned to us, smiled . . ." Stewart Methvin, "Genesis of CIA Involvement in Laos and South Vietnam," unpublished contract monograph for U.S. News Books.

71 "losing horse in the long run"; "should be to support the government . . ." Memorandum of conversation, April 6, 1962, declassified by the U.S. Archivist, Oct. 26, 1983.

71 "of an attempt to reconvene the Geneva . . ." *Ibid.*

71 "operational experiment." Forrestal to the president, April 16, 1962, Box 196, National Security Files, John F. Kennedy Library.

73 "confident the Communists will . . ." Telegram 150, State to Rusk (at Geneva), March 26, 1962, declassified by the Department of State, Oct. 19, 1982.

73 "be prepared to seize upon . . ." Memorandum of conversation, April 6, 1962.

73 "couldn't lead a squad around . . ." Sullivan oral history, p. 23.

73 "In the absence either of an effective . . ." SNIE 58-3-62, "Implications of the Fall of Nam Tha," May 9, 1962.

73 "Now, I agree [political negotiations are] . . ." *Public Papers of the Presidents of the United States: John F. Kennedy, 1962* (Washington: GPO, 1963), p. 378.

74 "The purpose was to signal Moscow and the world . . ." Roger Hilsman, interview with the author, Jan. 26, 1983.

75 "My God, the message has already . . ." Stephen E. Pelz, " 'When Do I Have Time to Think?' John F. Kennedy, Roger Hilsman, and the Laotian Crisis of 1962," *Diplomatic History*, Spring 1979, p. 223.

75 "Well, I can't help it." *Ibid.*

75 "What the hell is going on there?" Sullivan oral history, p. 24.

75 "Tell me about this fleet thing." Pelz, " 'When Do I Have Time to Think?' John F. Kennedy, Roger Hilsman, and the Laotian Crisis of 1962."

76 "urgently"; "continue to help your country . . ." Telegram 28, State to Saigon, July 9, 1962, Box 128, Presidential Office Files, John F. Kennedy Library.

76 "stress in the strongest terms"; "We are aware of the danger . . ." *Ibid.*

76 "It was a relatively useless conversation." Sullivan oral history, p. 32.

77 "[The North Vietnamese] broke the '62 agreements . . ." Notes of the president's meeting at Camp David, April 9, 1968, Lyndon B. Johnson Library.

77 "tremendous progress to date"; "disturbing force." Futrell, *The Advisory Years to 1965*, p. 151.

77 "About one year from the time . . ." *Ibid.*

77 "not worth a damn." Graff, p. 35.

78 "an imaginative officer, fully qualified . . ." Futrell, p. 97.

78 "During one of the first meetings I had with . . ." Paul D. Harkins, interview with the author, Sept. 16, 1981.

78 "If they captured an officer . . ." *Ibid.*

78 "It wasn't dishonesty, intending to deceive . . ." George Allen, interview with the author, Aug. 13, 1981.

78 "premature"; "At best, it appears . . ." INR Research Memorandum RFE-59, "The Situation and Short Term Prospects in South Vietnam," Dec. 3, 1962, *United States–Vietnam Relations*, XII, p. 487.

80 "a slowly escalating stalemate." Current Intelligence Memorandum 02142/63, "Current Status of the War in South Vietnam," Jan. 11, 1963, declassified by the CIA, Nov. 11, 1981.

80 "This suggests either the casualty figures . . ." *Ibid.*

80 Communist losses, recruitment, and infiltration figures. National Security Study Memorandum 1, "The Situation in Vietnam," Feb. 4, 1969, declassified by the NSC, June 22, 1982.

CHAPTER 5: **More Vigor Is Needed**

81 Battle of Ap Bac. David Richard Palmer, *Summons of the Trumpet* (San Rafael, California: Presidio Press), pp. 27–38; General Don A. Starry, *Armored Combat in Vietnam* (New York: Bobbs-Merrill, 1980), pp. 25–28; Futrell, pp. 157–159; Telegram, COMUSMACV to CINCPAC, Jan. 3, 1963, Box 197, National Security Files, John F. Kennedy Library; Joint Staff memorandum for the president, "Resumé of the 2 Jan. 1963 GVN Ground/Heliborne Action," declassified by the JCS, June 18, 1984.

82 "We sat there all day . . ." Interview with John Paul Vann, *U.S. News & World Report*, Sept. 16, 1963, p. 40.

83 "contrary to the facts"; "based on ill-considered statements . . ." Memorandum, "Report of Visit by Joint Chiefs of Staff Team to South Vietnam January 1963," declassified by the JCS, June 18, 1984.

83 "Ap Bac epitomized all the deficiencies . . ." David Halberstam, *The Making of a Quagmire* (New York: Random House, 1965), p. 157.

83 "I am convinced we have taken the military . . ." Letter, Harkins to Diem, Feb. 23, 1963, quoted in CINCPAC 132315ZMAR63, Box 197, National Security Files, John F. Kennedy Library.

83 "They were building strategic hamlets . . ." Hilsman interview.

85 "More vigor is needed . . ." Memorandum, Forrestal to the president, Jan. 28, 1963, Box 197, National Security Files, John F. Kennedy Library.

85 "awesome." Memorandum, "A Report on South Vietnam," *The Pentagon Papers*, II, p. 717.

85 "Our overall judgment, in sum, is . . ." *Ibid.*

85 "The American military mission . . ." Memorandum, "Eyes Only Annex: Performance of U.S. Mission," Jan. 25, 1963, Box 197, National Security Files, John F. Kennedy Library.

85 "the right kind of general"; "on balance . . ." *Ibid.*

86 "It is fashionable in some quarters . . ." Earle G. Wheeler, "The Design of Military Power," speech delivered at Fordham University on Nov. 7, 1962.

86 "a reasonable period of time." Memorandum, "Report of Visit by Joint Chiefs of Staff Team to South Vietnam January 1963."

86 "victory is now a hopeful prospect." *Ibid.*

86 "adequate"; "[W]e are winning slowly . . ." *Ibid.*

86 "victory more remote"; "the North Vietnamese bleed." *Ibid.*

87 "a coordinated program of sabotage . . ." *Ibid.*

87 "covert operational plan for North Vietnam." Memorandum, McGeorge Bundy to the president, "Week-end Reading, January 12–13, 1963," Box 318, National Security Files, John F. Kennedy Library.

87 "There is every reason to think . . ." *Ibid.*

87 "considerable effort." Memorandum, Forrestal to the president, Dec. 11, 1963, Vietnam Country File, Box 1, Vol. 1, Lyndon B. Johnson Library.

87 "non-attributable"; "U.S. military materiel . . ." "Military Pressures Against North Vietnam," *United States–Vietnam Relations*, III, p. 2.

87 "commando type coastal raids." *Ibid.*

88 "plans for possible military action . . ." NSC Action 2465, Box 314, National Security Files, John F. Kennedy Library.

88 "The Laos accords were a bitter disappointment . . ." Dean Rusk, interview with the author, Nov. 24, 1981.

88 "the initiation of military action against . . ." Memorandum, Rusk to the president, June 17, 1963, Box 341, National Security Files, John F. Kennedy Library.

88 "President Kennedy had some very informal . . ." Rusk interview, Sept. 22, 1980.

89 "When you get to the final . . ." *Operation Zapata: The "Ultrasensitive" Report and Testimony of the Board of Inquiry on the Bay of Pigs* (Frederick, Maryland: University Publications of America, 1981), p. 224.

89 "not as a contingency response . . ." Rusk to the president, June 17, 1963.

89 "objective is to be able to meet new . . ." Telegram 158, State

to Vientiane, Aug. 19, 1963, declassified by the Department of State, June 23, 1983.

90 "both visible and hidden meanings." CINCPAC 132315ZMAR63, Box 197, National Security Files, John F. Kennedy Library.

90 "Barring greatly increased resupply and reinforcement . . ." "Phased Withdrawal of U.S. Forces, 1962–1964," *United States–Vietnam Relations*, III, p. 11.

91 "We believe that Communist progress . . ." NIE 53–63, "Prospects in South Vietnam," April 17, 1963, declassified by the CIA, Oct. 26, 1983.

91 "to translate military success . . ." *Ibid.*

91 "To my mind, [the NIE] was not . . ." George Carver, "The 1963 National Estimates," unpublished contract monograph for U.S. News Books.

91 "masked fundamental problems not only . . ." *Ibid.*

91 "The present GVN is not likely to take . . ." ONE draft of "Prospects in South Vietnam," Nov. 19, 1962, declassified by the CIA, Oct. 26, 1983.

92 "pyrotechnic." Carver, "The 1963 National Estimates."

92 "infringements." CIA Information Report TDCS DB-3/654,285, April 22, 1963, Box 197, National Security Files, John F. Kennedy Library.

92 "a reduction in the number of U.S. personnel . . ." *Ibid.*

92 "at least 50 percent of the U.S. troops . . ." *Washington Post*, May 12, 1963, p. 14.

92 "if not brought up sharply"; "rough going." Telegram 1104, State to Saigon, May 17, 1963, Box 197, National Security Files, John F. Kennedy Library.

CHAPTER 6: **Who Are These People?**

94 "a presidential proclamation in . . ." John Mecklin, *Mission in Torment* (New York: Doubleday & Company, 1965), p. 153.

95 "The crowd surrounded the armored . . ." John Helble, interview with the author, Aug. 10, 1982.

96 "Unless Diem is able to reach . . ." Memorandum, "Buddhist

Demonstrations in South Vietnam," June 3, 1963, Box 197, National Security Files, John F. Kennedy Library.

96   "urge necessary measures in strongest terms." Telegram, State to Saigon, June 3, 1963, declassified by the Department of State, Feb. 16, 1981.

96   "dramatic action"; "bloody repressive . . ." Telegram 1100, Saigon to State, June 4, 1963, declassified by the Department of State, Feb. 16, 1981.

96   "satisfyingly swift." Telegram 1104, Saigon to State, June 4, 1963, declassified by the Department of State, Feb. 16, 1981.

97   "Meetings with Diem were normally . . ." William Trueheart, interview with the author, May 1981.

97   "profoundly disappointed." Telegram 1136, Saigon to State, June 9, 1963, declassified by the Department of State, Jan. 15, 1982.

97   "above reproach"; "there is still some . . ." Telegram 1155, Saigon to State, June 11, 1963, declassified by the Department of State, Jan. 15, 1982.

98   "The [South Vietnamese] government . . ." William Colby, interview with the author, May 1981.

98   "dangerously near the breaking point." Telegram 1207, State to Saigon, June 11, 1963, declassified by the Department of State, Jan. 15, 1982.

98   "You could just see the situation . . ." Rusk interview, Nov. 24, 1981.

98   "must fully and unequivocally . . ." Telegram 1207.

98   "ominous warning." Trueheart interview.

99   "precarious." Telegram 1219, State to Saigon, June 13, 1963, declassified by the Department of State, Dec. 14, 1982.

99   "in which [the] U.S. would play no part"; "military support." *Ibid.*

99   "not impressed by the competition." Telegram 1195, Saigon to State, June 16, 1963, declassified by the Department of State, Feb. 26, 1982.

99   "We are receiving just now . . ." *Ibid.*

100 "leading Buddhist officials." Unnumbered CIA Telegram, Trueheart to Hilsman, June 26, 1963, declassified by the Department of State, Feb. 16, 1981.

100 "an ambitious, skillful, ruthless . . ." Memorandum, "Tri Quang and the Buddhist-Catholic Discord in South Vietnam," Sept. 19, 1964, Vietnam Country File, Vol. XVIII, Box 9, Lyndon B. Johnson Library.

100 "You'd ask as tactfully and . . ." Helble interview.

102 "They have never spoken out . . ." Memorandum, "Conversation with Ngo Dinh Nhu on 25 June 1963," June 26, 1963.

102 "If a government is incapable . . ." *Ibid.*

102 "Nhu is in a state of emotional . . ." *Ibid.*

102 "How could this have happened?" Forrestal interview, Sept. 2, 1981.

102 "Religious fervor was an adequate . . ." Memorandum of Conversation, July 4, 1963, *United States–Vietnam Relations, 1945–67*, XII, p. 526.

103 "The chances of chaos in the wake . . ." *Ibid.*

103 "A non-Communist successor regime . . ." SNIF 53-2-63 "The Situation in Vietnam," July 10, 1963, *United States–Vietnam Relations*, XII, p. 530.

103 "the most likely result . . ." Memorandum of Conversation, July 5, 1963, *The Pentagon Papers*, II, p. 729.

103 "Nobody let me know one word . . ." *U.S. News & World Report*, July 26, 1971, p. 68.

104 "Day spent urging, encouraging, warning . . ." Telegram 106, Saigon to State, July 18, 1963, National Security Files, Box 198, John F. Kennedy Library.

104 "closely cooperate." Telegram 107, Saigon to State, July 19, 1963, National Security Files, Box 198, John F. Kennedy Library.

104 "All they have done is barbecue . . ." Telegram 190, Saigon to State, Aug. 8, 1963, National Security Files, Box 198, John F. Kennedy Library.

104 "a strenuous goodbye"; "it would be impossible . . ." Telegram

226, Saigon to State, Aug. 14, 1963, National Security Files, Box 198, John F. Kennedy Library.

104   "My policy of reconciliation . . ." *U.S. News & World Report*, July 26, 1971, p. 68.

106   "many methods of attacking . . ." Current Intelligence Memorandum 0698/64, "Appraisal of General Nguyen Khanh," March 20, 1964, Vietnam Country File, Vol. VI, Box 3, Lyndon B. Johnson Library.

107   "This is the first time . . ." *U.S. News & World Report*, July 26, 1971, p. 68.

CHAPTER 7: **The Point of No Return**

109   "our old mandarin can . . ." Mecklin, *Mission in Torment*, p. 190.

110   "We feel reasonably sure . . ." Telegram 314, Saigon to State, Aug. 23, 1963, declassified by the Department of State, Oct. 19, 1982.

110   "He had a relationship . . ." William Trueheart, interview with the author, June 1981.

111   "The first step"; "and the secret . . ." CIA Information Report TDCS DB-3/656,252, "Major General Tran Van Don Details the Present Situation in SVN," Aug. 23, 1963, microfiche (Washington: Carrollton Press, Inc., 1977).

111   "an army action to remove them . . ." Memorandum, Rufus Phillips conversation with General Le Van Kim, Aug. 24, 1963.

111   "save the boss by getting rid . . ." Paul Kattenburg, U.S. News Books interview, Dec. 3, 1981.

111   "shot in the dark." "The Overthrow of Ngo Dinh Diem," *United States–Vietnam Relations*, III, p. 14.

111   "if Nhu continued in power . . ." Roger Hilsman, *To Move a Nation* (New York: Doubleday, 1967), p. 485.

112   "there would be even more . . ." *Ibid.*, p. 486.

112   "U.S. government cannot tolerate . . ." Telegram 243, State to Lodge, Aug. 24, 1963, Box 198, National Security Files, John F. Kennedy Library.

112 "We must face the possibility . . ." *Ibid.*

112 "absolutely certain." Rusk interview, Nov. 24, 1981.

114 "I told him that at this time . . ." Forrestal interview, Sept. 2, 1981.

114 "Can't we wait until Monday . . ." *Ibid.*

114 "I read the cable and realized . . ." Victor H. Krulak, interview with the author, Dec. 2, 1981.

114 "Our position was that Diem is . . ." Maxwell D. Taylor, interview with the author, Aug. 26, 1981.

115 "The president on the whole . . ." Ball, p. 371.

115 "If Ball, Harriman, and President Kennedy . . ." Rusk interview, Nov. 24, 1981.

115 "somewhat unhappy about the thrust . . ." Transcript, NBC News White Paper, *Death of Diem*, December 22, 1971, Part II, Section VIII, p. 8.

115 "It's about time we bit . . ." Thomas Powers, *The Man Who Kept the Secrets* (New York: Alfred A. Knopf, 1979), p. 164.

116 "I described to him . . ." Krulak interview.

116 "Send it out." Forrestal, interview, Sept. 2, 1981.

116 "the anti-Diem group centered . . ." Taylor, *Swords and Plowshares*, p. 292.

116 "Propose we go straight . . ." Lodge to State, quoted in Telegram 63461, Forrestal to the president, Aug. 25, 1963, Box 198, National Security Files, John F. Kennedy Library.

117 "Agree to modification proposed." Telegram, Ball to Lodge, Aug. 25, 1963, Box 198, National Security Files, John F. Kennedy Library.

117 "High American officials blame . . ." Mecklin, p. 193.

117 "We thought the VOA broadcast . . ." Trueheart interview.

117 "complicated our already difficult . . ." *Alleged Assassination Plots Involving Foreign Leaders* (Washington: GPO, 1975), p. 219.

118 "bailed out." Richardson to McCone, Aug. 26, 1963, *The Pentagon Papers*, II, p. 735.

118   "I am one of the people . . ." Lucien Conein, interview with the author, March 7, 1983.

118   "We are like this." Nguyen Khanh, interview with the author, April 12, 1982.

119   "The U.S. government is . . ." Alfonso Spera, interview with the author, Sept. 29, 1981.

119   "Great indignation was felt . . ." Taylor interview.

119   "McCone made no bones . . ." Colby interview, May 1981.

119   "You're not worth firing . . ." Forrestal interview, Sept. 2, 1981.

120   "I held my ground . . ." Ball, p. 372.

120   "I wasn't for calling . . ." Taylor interview.

120   "annoyed by the waffling . . ." Ball, p. 372.

120   "John, do you want . . ." Roger Hilsman, interview with the author, Dec. 7, 1981.

120   "colored"; "Maybe properly colored." Taylor, *Swords and Plowshares*, p. 294.

120   "The Vietnamese generals haven't got . . ." Memorandum of Conference with the President, Aug. 27, 1963, Box 316, National Security Files, John F. Kennedy Library.

120   "try once again to persuade Diem . . ." *Ibid.*

121   "If you're right . . ." Hilsman, *To Move a Nation*, p. 491.

121   "We should make clear . . ." Memorandum of Conference with the President, Aug. 27, 1963.

121   "An aggressive, arrogant officer . . ." Memorandum, "Biographic Sketches of Leading Figures of New Government of Vietnam," Box 201, National Security Files, John F. Kennedy Library.

122   "Situation here has reached . . ." Telegram, Richardson to McCone, Aug. 28, 1963, *The Pentagon Papers*, II, p. 736.

122   "neutralized"; "widespread fighting in Saigon . . ." *Ibid.*

122   "changed drastically"; "if the Ngo family wins . . ." *Ibid.*

123   "chances of success . . ." "The Overthrow of Ngo Dinh Diem," *United States–Vietnam Relations*, III, p. 19.

123   "I don't believe there . . ." *Ibid.*

123   "FYI State to Saigon 243 . . ." Telegram 3368-63, Taylor to Harkins, Aug. 28, 1963, Box 316, National Security Files, John F. Kennedy Library.

123   "must decide now to go . . ." Arthur M. Schlesinger, Jr., *Robert Kennedy and His Times* (New York: Ballantine Books, 1978), p. 770.

123   "took the tongue-lashing . . ." Gilpatric oral history interview, p. 31.

123   "The president was appalled . . ." Forrestal interview, Sept. 2, 1981.

124   "but this judgment in turn . . ." Telegram 269, Kennedy to Lodge, Aug. 28, 1963, Box 316, National Security Files, John F. Kennedy Library.

124   "Why wasn't I informed . . ." Lucien Conein, interview with the author, Nov. 19, 1981.

125   "We are launched on a course . . ." Telegram 375, Lodge to State, Aug. 29, 1963, Box 198, National Security Files, John F. Kennedy Library.

125   "Such a step has no chance . . ." *Ibid.*

125   "full support." Telegram, Kennedy to Lodge, Aug. 29, 1963, Box 316, National Security Files, John F. Kennedy Library.

125   "I know from experience that failure . . ." *Ibid.*

126   "If necessary, we should bring . . ." Memorandum, Hilsman to Rusk, Aug. 30, 1963, *Chicago Sun-Times*, June 23, 1971, p. 1.

126   "the days come and go and nothing . . ." Telegram 383, Lodge to Rusk, Aug. 30, 1963, Box 198, National Security Files, John F. Kennedy Library.

126   "uneasiness at the absence . . ." Telegram 284, Rusk to Lodge, Aug. 30, 1963, Box 198, National Security Files, John F. Kennedy Library.

126   "I told him what the proposition . . ." Harkins interview.

127   "was again trying . . ." Telegram 1583, Harkins to Taylor, Aug. 31, 1963, *The Pentagon Papers*, II, p. 740.

127 "There is neither the will . . ." Telegram 391, Lodge to State, Aug. 31, 1963, Box 198, National Security Files, John F. Kennedy Library.

127 "There is little doubt . . ." *Alleged Assassination Plots*, p. 220.

127 "So we see we have . . ." Harkins to Taylor, *The Pentagon Papers*, II, p. 740.

CHAPTER 8: **We Must All Sign On**

128 "Pushing a piece of spaghetti." Telegram 383, Saigon to State, Aug. 30, 1963, Box 198, National Security Files, John F. Kennedy Library.

128 "this repressive regime . . ." Memorandum, "Meeting at the State Department," *United States–Vietnam Relations*, XI, p. 542.

128 "were leading themselves down . . ." Kattenburg, p. 120.

128 "At this juncture . . ." *United States–Vietnam Relations*, XI, p. 542.

129 "In from six months to a year . . ." *Ibid*.

129 "I don't think . . ." *Public Papers of the Presidents of the United States: John F. Kennedy, 1963*, p. 652.

129 "With changes in policy . . ." *Ibid*.

130 "I think it showed the degree . . ." William Colby, interview with the author, June 25, 1982.

131 "no more than three hours . . ." Rufus Phillips, memorandum of conversation, Sept. 5, 1963.

131 "They blew up and . . ." *New York Times*, Sept. 1, 1963, p. 2.

132 "I think the president used . . ." Forrestal interview, Sept. 2, 1981.

132 "We have to be tough . . ." Memorandum of conference with the president, Sept. 6, 1963, Box 316, National Security Files, John F. Kennedy Library.

132 "If we have concluded that we . . ." *Ibid*.

134 "cities of hate . . ." Telegram 453, Saigon to State, Sept. 9,

1963, Box 316, National Security Files, John F. Kennedy Library.

135 "only when it was unavoidable." Mecklin, p. 207.

135 "It's wrong for us . . ." Krulak interview.

135 "The shooting war is still . . ." Report, "Visit to Vietnam 7–10 September 1963," Box 316, National Security Files, John F. Kennedy Library.

135 "the breakdown of civilian . . ." Memorandum of conference with the president, Sept. 10, 1963, Box 316, National Security Files, John F. Kennedy Library.

135 "Did you two gentlemen visit . . ." Krulak interview.

135 "I think I can answer your . . ." *Ibid.*

136 "stagger through to win the war . . ." Memorandum of conference with the president.

136 "In 1961, the hatred and . . ." *Ibid.*

136 "[I] would cut off U.S. aid . . ." *Ibid.*

136 "The key missing item was . . ." Memorandum, "Comments on the Necessity for an Advance Decision to Introduce U.S. Forces in Vietnam," Box 316, National Security Files, John F. Kennedy Library.

137 "I'm sorry to differ . . ." Rufus Phillips, interview with the author, June 1981.

137 "OK"; "in the Delta south . . ." Memorandum of conference with the president.

137 "The battle is not being . . ." *Ibid.*

137 "both to promote unseating . . ." Memorandum, "A Policy for Vietnam," Sept. 10, 1963, Box 199, National Security Files, John F. Kennedy Library.

137 "This is impossible." Forrestal interview, Sept. 2, 1981.

138 "authentic appraisal." Telegram 7391, MACV to JCS, Sept. 12, 1963, Box 199, National Security Files, John F. Kennedy Library.

138 "the value of the answers . . ." Telegram 478, Saigon to State, Box 316, National Security Files, John F. Kennedy Library.

138   "The [South Vietnamese] government is obviously . . ." *Ibid.*

138   "Faced with such extreme alternatives . . ." Memorandum, "Possible Rapprochement between North and South Vietnam," Sept. 19, 1963, Box 200, National Security Files, John F. Kennedy Library.

139   "obviously an interim plan." Telegram 63516, White House to Lodge, Sept. 17, 1963, *The Pentagon Papers*, II, p. 735.

139   "I believe that for me . . ." Telegram 544, *ibid.*, p. 747.

139   "launch into a long statement . . ." Telegram 555, Lodge to the White House, Sept. 20, 1963, declassified by the Department of State, Feb. 12, 1982.

139   "should be directly tied . . ." Telegram 544.

140   "I think it was largely a matter . . ." William H. Sullivan, interview with the author, Jan. 25, 1982.

140   "You're not emotionally engaged . . ." William Bundy, recorded interview, May 26, 1969, p. 6, Lyndon B. Johnson Library Oral History Program.

140   "We just desperately needed . . ." William Bundy, interview with the author, February 1982.

141   "the Viet Cong threat could be . . ." Taylor, *Swords and Plowshares*, p. 297.

141   "I became aware for . . ." William Bundy, unpublished manuscript.

141   "The U.S. military family . . ." *Ibid.*

141   "patently deceitful"; "I felt that . . ." Sullivan interview.

141   "It is abundantly clear . . ." Memorandum, "Highlights of Discussions in Saigon 18–20 December 1963," Vietnam Country File, Box 1, Lyndon B. Johnson Library.

142   "Viet Cong progress has been great . . ." Memorandum for the president, Dec. 21, 1964, Vietnam Country File, Box 1, Lyndon B. Johnson Library.

142   "reasonably satisfactory"; "the disturbing probability . . ." Memorandum of conversation with President Ngo Dinh Diem, Sept. 29, 1963.

142   "were most immature, untrained . . ." *Ibid.*

143 "You could just see . . ." Taylor interview.

143 "The military campaign has . . ."; "[But] further repressive actions . . ." Report of McNamara-Taylor Mission to South Vietnam, Oct. 2, 1963, Box 200, National Security Files, John F. Kennedy Library.

144 "cryptic posture." Telegram, Bundy to Lodge, Oct. 5, 1963, National Security Files, John F. Kennedy Library.

145 "The program outlined in . . ." Memorandum, "Meeting in the Situation Room, Vietnam," Oct. 3, 1963, Box 316, National Security Files, John F. Kennedy Library.

145 "Most of the officials . . ." Summary Record of National Security Council Meeting, Oct. 2, 1963, Box 316, National Security Files, John F. Kennedy Library.

CHAPTER 8: **Plausible Denial**

147 "[I] must know [the] American . . ." Telegram 1445, Lodge to State, Oct. 5, 1963, *The Pentagon Papers*, II, p. 767.

147 "He was even more anathema . . ." William Trueheart, interview with the author, April 14, 1983.

147 "No initiative should . . ." Telegram 63560, White House to Lodge, Oct. 5, 1963, *The Pentagon Papers*, II, p. 766.

147 "urgent covert effort . . ." *Ibid*.

148 "Ambassador Lodge made it . . ." NBC White Paper, *Death of Diem*, Dec. 22, 1971.

148 "While we do not wish . . ." Telegram 74228, White House to Lodge, Oct. [9], 1963, *The Pentagon Papers*, II, p. 769.

148 "There's this nice theory . . ." William Colby, interview with the author, May 1981.

149 "Rightly or wrongly, a lot . . ." Bui Diem, interview with the author, April 7, 1982.

149 "Richardson's recall was the . . ." Roger Hilsman, letter to the author, June 1, 1982.

149 "we do not set ourselves irrevocably . . ." *Alleged Assassination Plots*, p. 220.

149 "hands off"; "[W]e certainly . . ." *Ibid*., p. 221.

150　"certainly would not favor . . ." *Ibid.*

150　"Mr. President, if I was . . ." *Ibid.*

151　"Such an approach to the president . . ." *Ibid.*, p. 118.

151　"I think that any of us . . ." *Ibid.*, p. 149.

151　"We cannot be in . . ." *Ibid.*, p. 221.

151　"All right, [if] you . . ." *Ibid.*

152　"For all these reasons, my associates . . ." Telegram 676, Saigon to State, Oct. 10, 1963, declassified by the Department of State, Dec. 15, 1983.

152　"mount such an operation . . ." *Ibid.*

152　"to have such a horrible . . ." *Ibid.*

152　"He was a maverick, a loner . . ." Harkins, interview.

153　"running very much a vest pocket . . ." Telegram, Saigon CIA station to McCone, Nov. 16, 1963, Box 128a, Presidential Office Files, John F. Kennedy Library.

153　"the overture to the opera . . ." *Ibid.*

153　"bend his efforts along that line." Telegram 1991, Harkins to Taylor, Oct. 24, 1963, declassified by the JCS, July 28, 1983.

154　"Lou, don't leave town . . ." Lucien Conein, interview with the author, Nov. 19, 1981.

155　"Real loyalty uncertain . . ." Office of Current Intelligence Memorandum 2703/63, "Cast of Characters in South Vietnam," August 28, 1963, microfiche (Washington: Carrollton Press, Inc., 1977).

155　"absolutely reliable." Trueheart interview, June 1981.

155　"punctilious in carrying . . ." Telegram 1964, Lodge to Bundy, Oct. 25, 1963, Box 201, National Security Files, John F. Kennedy Library.

155　"our involvement to . . ." *Ibid.*

155　"While sharing your view . . ." Telegram 63590, Bundy to Lodge, Oct. 25, 1963, Box 201, National Security Files, John F. Kennedy Library.

157 "The difficulty is of course . . ." Draft of telegram 63590, Box 201, National Security Files, John F. Kennedy Library.

157 "Diem/Nhu give every appearance . . ." "The Overthrow of Ngo Dinh Diem," *United States–Vietnam Relations*, III, p. 39.

157 "When it was evident that . . ." *Ibid.*, p. 40.

158 "to eliminate Dinh if he showed . . ." CIA memorandum, "History of the Vietnamese Generals' Coup of 1/2 November 1963."

158 "No positive action by the . . ." "The Overthrow of Ngo Dinh Diem," *United States–Vietnam Relations*, III, p. 46.

158 "Believe our attitude to coup . . ." Telegram, 79109, Bundy to Lodge, Oct. 30, 1963, Box 317, National Security Files, John F. Kennedy Library.

158 "One of the problems in all this . . ." Trueheart interview, August 1981.

159 "We reiterate burden . . ." Telegram 79109.

159 "Do not think we have the power . . ." Telegram 2063, Lodge to State, Oct. 30, 1963, *The Pentagon Papers*, II, p. 789.

159 "I do not know what more . . ." *Ibid.*

159 "General Harkins has read this . . ." *Ibid.*

159 "I am not opposed to a change . . ." Telegram 2028, Harkins to Taylor, *The Pentagon Papers*, II, p. 784.

159 "[We] should have more information." Telegram 2034, Harkins to Taylor, Oct. 30, 1963, declassified by the JCS, July 28, 1983.

160 "We do not accept as a basis . . ." *United States–Vietnam Relations*, XII, p. 593.

160 "We are sure it will help . . ." *Ibid.*

160 "But once a coup under responsible . . ." *Ibid.*

CHAPTER 10: **Nine, Nine . . . Nine, Nine**

162 "I know there is going to be . . ." Henry Cabot Lodge, U.S. News Books interview, Nov. 4, 1981.

162 "to attend to some other business." Tran Van Don, *Our Endless War* (San Rafael, California: Presidio Press, 1978), p. 101.

162 "intoxicating"; "be sure if any American . . ." Telegram 841, Saigon to State, Nov. 1, 1963, Box 201, National Security Files, John F. Kennedy Library.

162 "Please tell President Kennedy . . ." *Ibid.*

163 "bring all available money." *Alleged Assassination Plots*, p. 222.

163 "buy[ing] off potential opposition." Telegram 2063, Lodge to State, Oct. 30, 1963, *The Pentagon Papers*, II, p. 789.

163 "nine, nine . . . nine, nine." Lucien Conein, interview with the author, Nov. 19, 1981.

163 "What are you doing here?" *Ibid.*

163 "I need a bottle of whiskey." *Ibid.*

164 "family dictatorship"; "more effectively commanded." Telegram 867, Lodge to State, Nov. 1, 1963, Box 201, National Security Files, John F. Kennedy Library.

166 "Ky, Diem's bodyguards are . . ." Nguyen Cao Ky, *Twenty Years and Twenty Days* (New York: Stein & Day, 1976), p. 40.

167 "By this plan, we shall trap . . ." Confidential source.

167 "What are you generals doing?" *The Coup d'Etat of November 1, 1963*, American embassy translation of a series of articles that appeared in the Saigon newspaper *Lap Truong* between June 4 and July 31, 1971, p. 67.

168 "Some units have made a rebellion . . ." "Overthrow of Ngo Dinh Diem," *United States–Vietnam Relations*, III, p. 57.

169 "blasted off the face of the earth." CIA memorandum, "History of the Vietnamese Generals' Coup of 1/2 November 1963."

170 "If you hesitate, you will be lost." Lucien Conein, interview with the author, March 3, 1982.

171 "with honor." CIA memorandum, "The Situation in South Vietnam," Nov. 2, 1963, Box 128a, Presidential Office Files, John F. Kennedy Library.

171 "until Vietnamese have stopped . . ." Conein interview, March 3, 1982.

171 "We can't hold them that long." *Ibid.*

172 "Diem had acted with his . . ." Memorandum of conversation,

William Colby and [officially deleted], Nov. 12, 1963, Vietnam Country File, Box 1, Vol. 1, Lyndon B. Johnson Library.

172 "You use such a vehicle . . ." Nguyen Ngoc Huy, "Ngo Dinh Diem's Execution," *Worldview*, November 1976, p. 41.

172 "He killed forty people . . ." Nguyen Khanh, interview with the author, April 12, 1982.

173 "I can state without equivocation . . ." Tran Van Don, p. 112.

173 "the fate of President Diem . . ." NBC White Paper, *Death of Diem*, Dec. 22, 1971.

173 "It's pretty clear . . ." William Colby, interview with the author, May 1981.

173 "I doubt if 'Big' Minh did . . ." George Carver, interview with the author, Sept. 4, 1981.

174 "heated arguments." Conein interview, March 3, 1982.

174 "My co-conspirators let me down." Lucien Conein, interview with the author, Feb. 16, 1983.

174 "By being perfidious to the end . . ." Carver interview.

174 "VC incident." Lucien Conein, interview with the author, Nov. 19, 1981.

175 "This coup is real." Forrestal interview, Sept. 2, 1981.

175 "Kennedy leaped to his feet . . ." Taylor, *Swords and Plowshares*, p. 301.

175 "It shook him personally . . ." NBC White Paper, *Death of Diem*, Dec. 22, 1971.

175 "The execution of a coup . . ." Maxwell D. Taylor, CBS Morning News, June 17, 1971.

175 "There was a real risk . . ." William Trueheart, interview with the author, August 1981.

175 "particularly penetrating." *Ibid.*

175 "blood on your hands." Margueritte Higgins, *Our Vietnam Nightmare* (New York: Harper and Row, 1965), p. 225.

176 "Oh, come on now Maggie . . ." *Ibid.*

176   "Sheltering this fellow . . ." John Helble, interview with the author, Aug. 19, 1983.

176   "further violence would harm . . ." Telegram 5, State to Hue, Nov. 2, 1963, declassified by the Department of State, Sept. 26, 1983.

177   "I was told that [Can] . . ." John Helble, interview with the author, Aug. 10, 1982.

177   "[Lodge] told me that he . . ." Lucien Conein, interview with the author, Aug. 22, 1983.

177   "I have received assurances . . ." Telegram 930, Saigon to State, Nov. 5, 1963, declassified by the Department of State, Sept. 27, 1982.

177   "Giving him asylum . . ." *Ibid.*

177   "As to Ngo Dinh Nhu and . . ." CIA memorandum, "History of the Vietnamese Generals' Coup of 1/2 November 1963."

Epilogue: A Very Disturbing Situation

179   "a certain euphoria." Furtell, p. 192.

179   "It was the first time . . ." Forrestal interview, Sept. 2, 1981.

179   "It remains the central objective . . ." National Security Action Memorandum No. 273, Nov. 26, 1963.

180   "The situation is very disturbing." Memorandum for the president, Dec. 21, 1963, Vietnam Country File, Box 1, Vol. 1, Lyndon B. Johnson Library.

180   "to rapidly strengthen our military . . ." Vietnam Documents and Research Notes, "The Vietnam Workers' Party's 1963 Decision to Escalate the War in the South," p. 15.

180   "absolutely totally protected against . . ." Telegram 1493, Saigon to State, Feb. 5, 1964, Vietnam Country File, Box 1, Vol. 1, Lyndon B. Johnson Library.

181   "first aid to squabbling politicos . . ." Memorandum to the President, Jan. 27, 1965, Vietnam Country File, Memoranda to the President, Vol. 5, Lyndon B. Johnson Library.

181   "Bob and I tend to favor the first course . . ." *Ibid.*

THE ROAD TO WAR
A VIETNAM CHRONOLOGY,
1945–1965

1945

March 11	Japanese topple French regime in Vietnam.
August	Communist-led Viet Minh forces seize Hanoi.
September 2	Ho Chi Minh proclaims establishment of an independent Democratic Republic of Vietnam (DRV).
September 23	After overthrowing local DRV government in Saigon, French declare the restoration of their authority in southern Vietnam.
September 26	OSS commander Colonel Peter Dewey killed—the first of 58,000 American fatalities in the Indochina wars.
October	U.S. State Department policy statement: ". . . it is not the policy of this government to assist the French to re-establish their control over Indochina by force, and the willingness of the U.S. to see French control re-established assumes that French claim to have the support of the population of Indochina is borne out by future events."

1946

March 6	Ho accedes to French reentry into North Vietnam in return for recognition of DRV as a "free state" in the French Union. Further negotiations to spell out details.
March 18	French forces occupy Hanoi.
April	French and DRV unable to reach any significant agreements. Guerrilla warfare in southern Vietnam continues.
November	Local disputes in Haiphong and other cities lead to clashes between French and DRV troops.
December	Large-scale conflict between French and DRV spreads throughout Vietnam.

1947

February 3	U.S. State Department policy directive: "Frankly, we have no solution to the problem to suggest. It is basically [a] matter for [the] two parties to work out themselves."
March 12	Truman Doctrine proclaims: "It must be the policy of the United States to support free peoples who are resisting attempted subjugation by armed minorities or outside pressures."
June	Marshall Plan, an economic program to rebuild postwar Europe and prevent Communist encroachment there.
December 7	First Ha Long Bay Agreement: Emperor Bao Dai associates himself with French-sponsored nationalist movement. French promise independence in vague terms.
December 24	Ngo Dinh Diem visits Hong Kong American consul and characterizes Ha Long Bay agreement as "continued slavery for my people."

1948

April	Soviet blockade of Berlin.

1949

March 8 — Elysee Agreement confirms Vietnam's status as an independent associated state. French military, political, and economic control remains unchanged.

August — NATO treaty enters into force.

September — Soviet Union explodes its first atomic device.

December — After the success of Mao Tse-tung's revolution, Chinese Communist forces arrive on the Indochina border.

1950

January 30 — Moscow recognizes Ho Chi Minh's government.

February 2 — President Harry S. Truman approves U.S. recognition of Bao Dai government.

February 16 — France requests U.S. military and economic assistance.

May 8 — U.S. announces economic aid and military equipment for French in Indochina.

June — Outbreak of Korean War.

August — The first uniformed U.S. military advisers arrive in Vietnam.

1951

February 1 — By this date, approximately $50 million of U.S. military assistance delivered to Indochina.

August 7 — U.S. National Intelligence Estimate: "The present military situation in Indochina is one of stalemate."

November — John F. Kennedy: "In Indochina, we have allied ourselves to the desperate effort of a French regime to hang on to the remnants of an empire."

1953

July   Panmunjom armistice.

1954

                       U.S. financing 80 percent of French–Viet Minh
                       War.

January 8   At an NSC meeting, CIA chief Allen Dulles an-
                       nounces French garrison at Dien Bien Phu sur-
                       rounded. President Dwight D. Eisenhower ve-
                       hemently opposes sending U.S. ground forces.

March 20   General Paul Ely, French chief of staff, arrives
                       in Washington to confer with U.S. officials.

April   U.S. Army position paper: "U.S. intervention
                       with combat forces in Indochina is not militarily
                       desirable."

April 6   At an NSC meeting, President Eisenhower says
                       there is "no possibility whatever of U.S. unilat-
                       eral intervention in Indochina."

April 26   Opening of Geneva conference.

May 1   Effective this date, Bao Dai gives Binh Xuyen
                       gangsters full control over Vietnamese Sûreté
                       (police).

May 7   Dien Bien Phu falls.

June 1   Colonel Edward G. Lansdale arrives in Vietnam.

July 7   Diem assumes office.

July 21   Conclusion of Geneva conference.

August 3   U.S. National Intelligence Estimate: "If the
                       scheduled national elections are held in July 1956,
                       and if the Viet Minh does not prejudice its po-
                       litical prospects, the Viet Minh will almost cer-
                       tainly win."

September 20   U.S. officials in Saigon inform Vietnamese chief
                       of staff that a coup d'état would necessitate a
                       review of U.S. policy toward Vietnam.

September 27	French-U.S. agreement to support Diem.
October 9	North Vietnam evacuated by foreign troops.
October 22	President Eisenhower authorizes a "crash program designed to bring about improvement in the loyalty and effectiveness of the Free Vietnamese Forces."
October 23	Eisenhower letter to Diem announcing direct U.S. economic aid and military assistance to Vietnam.
November 8	General J. Lawton Collins, special U.S. representative with rank of ambassador, arrives in Saigon.
November 23	U.S. National Intelligence Estimate: "The situation in South Vietnam has steadily deteriorated since the armistice."
December 6	Collins to State: "Diem still presents our chief problem. . . . Time may be approaching rapidly when some thought should be given to possible alternatives to Diem."
December 24	Secretary of State John Foster Dulles to Collins: "Withdrawal [of] our support would hasten [a] Communist takeover [in] Vietnam and have adverse repercussions [throughout] all [of] Southeast Asia. Consequently, [our] investment in Vietnam [is] justified even if only to buy time [to] build up strength elsewhere in area."

1955

March 28	Diem moves against dissident sects.
April 19	Collins to State: "I see no repeat no alternative to the early replacement of Diem."
April 27	Dulles agrees to a change in Saigon.
April 28	Diem moves against Binh Xuyen gangsters.
May 1	U.S. again behind Diem.
July	Diem refuses to meet with DRV about elections.
October 24	Diem wins referendum against Bao Dai.

1959

May | Hanoi's Lao Dong party resolves to carry out reunification struggle by all "appropriate mea sures."

1960

USSR provides North Vietnam with $200 million to cover first five-year plan (1961–1965).

January 25 | Three hundred Communist guerrillas attack South Vietnamese regimental command post in Tay Ninh Province.

April | Anti-Diem Caravelle Manifesto by South Vietnamese politicians.

November 11 | Paratroopers' coup attempt.

December 20 | National Liberation Front proclaimed.

1961

January 19 | Eisenhower and Kennedy meet regarding Laos.

January 20 | Kennedy inaugurated.

January 28 | Kennedy approves Counterinsurgency Plan.

March 9 | Letter from Kennedy to Soviet Premier Nikita S. Khrushchev expressing U.S. determination not to abandon Laos.

March 23 | JFK's televised press conference regarding Laos.

April 17 | Bay of Pigs invasion begins.

April 27 | Kennedy meets with NSC on Laotian crisis. JCS alert CINCPAC "to be prepared to undertake air strikes against NVN, possibly southern China."

April 29 | JFK approves an increase of 100 MAAG personnel and the deployment of a 400-man Special Forces group.

May 2 | Laos cease-fire.

May 10	Ambassador Frederick E. Nolting, Jr., presents his credentials to Diem.
May 11	National Security Action Memorandum 52—formalizes JFK's April 29 decisions and directs Pentagon to study the size and composition of forces for possible combat troop commitment.
May 16	Opening of Geneva conference.
September 18	Communist forces estimated at 1,000 seize the provincial capital of Phuoc Vinh, only sixty miles from Saigon.
October 5	Presidential adviser Walt Rostow to JFK: "As for Vietnam, it is agreed we must move quite radically to avoid perhaps slow but total defeat. The sense of the town is that, with Southern Laos open, Diem simply cannot cope."
	JCS Memorandum: "The time is now past when actions short of intervention by outside forces could reverse the rapidly worsening situation [in Southeast Asia]."
October 18	General Maxwell D. Taylor, Kennedy's military representative, arrives in Saigon.
November 1	Taylor to JFK: proposes introducing a U.S. military task force into South Vietnam.
November 5	U.S. National Intelligence Estimate: American escalation would be matched by Hanoi, air attacks against North Vietnam would not stop its support for the Viet Cong, and Moscow and Peking would react strongly to such air raids.
November 11	Joint Dean Rusk–Robert S. McNamara recommendation to JFK urging that the U.S. "now make the decision to commit ourselves to the objective of preventing the fall of South Vietnam to Communism and that, in doing so, we recognize that the introduction of United States and other SEATO forces may be necessary to achieve this objective." Recommendation defers an immediate U.S. troop decision.

November 24   Saigon daily *Thoi Bao* criticizes "conditions" attached to U.S. aid.

November 27   Nolting instructed that, if his discussions with Diem were "clearly not satisfactory," he should return promptly to Washington.

November 29   Nolting to State: "Believe cool and unhurried approach is our best bet for success. . . . I think it would be a mistake to rush [Diem]."

December 4   Nolting reports Diem's substantive agreement with U.S. policy.

December 11   Two helicopter companies arrive in SVN—the vanguard of the expanded U.S. advisory effort.

December 15   First fifty weapons issued to Rhade volunteers at Buon Enao—the start of the Civilian Irregular Defense Groups program.

December 16   First Secretary of Defense Conference at CINCPAC headquarters.

1962

January 3   On Diem's sixty-first birthday, Ngo Dinh Nhu, Diem's brother and principal adviser, publicly announces his intention of including the entire South Vietnamese rural population under the strategic hamlet program.

                 After severely paring a defoliant proposal, JFK authorizes limited experimental operations.

January 9   Total U.S. military personnel in South Vietnam: 2,646.

January 13   JCS memorandum, "The Strategic Importance of the SEA Mainland," recommends bolstering the Diem regime and discouraging internal factions that may seek to overthrow it. If VC are not brought under control, chiefs see no alternative to the introduction of U.S. combat forces.

January 18   National Security Action Memorandum 124—JFK establishes Special Group (CI).

February 8	U.S. Military Assistance Command-Vietnam (MACV) opens for business in Saigon.
February 27	Dissident South Vietnamese air force pilots bomb the presidential palace.
March 22	Phase II (military) of Operation Sunrise officially kicks off the strategic hamlet program.
April 4	Assistant Secretary of State W. Averell Harriman to Nolting: "Department increasingly concerned over constant implications in press generally of U.S. participation and direction, rather than purely support and training."
	Memorandum from Ambassador John Kenneth Galbraith to JFK raises the danger of U.S. replacing the French and urges keeping the door open for political solution and measurably reducing U.S. commitment to Diem.
April 6	JFK, Harriman, and White House aide Michael V. Forrestal discuss Galbraith memorandum.
April 13	JCS rebuttal to Galbraith memo.
April 15	MACV publishes the first extensive Viet Cong order of battle. Overall regular strength: 16,305.
April 27	Company-size Pathet Lao units attack Royal Lao Army near Nam Tha.
May 3	Pathet Lao overrun Muong Sing Airport.
May 6	Pathet Lao overrun Nam Tha.
May 9	JFK at news conference: "Now, I agree [political negotiations are] a very hazardous course, but introducing American forces, which is the other one—let's not think there is some great third course—that also is a hazardous course, and we want to attempt to see if we can work out a peaceful solution."
May 11	Lao General Phoumi Nosavan's troops abandon Ban Houei Sai.
May 15	U.S. announces forces sent to Thailand because of the deteriorating situation in Laos.

May 16	Pathet Lao announce they will resume negotiations.
June 12	Three Lao factions agree on the formation of a government of national union under the leadership of Souvanna Phouma.
July 2	Geneva conference reconvened to conclude Laos negotiations.
July 23	Geneva agreement on Laos signed.
	Sixth SecDef Conference at CINCPAC HQ: Citing "tremendous progress" in SVN, Secretary of Defense McNamara initiates planning for phaseout of U.S. military involvement in Vietnam by 1965.
September 12	CINCPAC to MACV commander, General Paul D. Harkins: ". . . [W]e want to destroy or drive sick, starved, blistered, and blasted Viet Cong from Zone D so that we scoop them up outside of their nest or prevent them from setting foot in the area again."
September 18	Forrestal to JFK: "While we cannot yet sit back in confidence that the job is well in hand, nevertheless it does appear that we have finally developed a series of techniques which, if properly applied, do seem to produce results."
October	Cuban Missile Crisis.
October 2	JFK approves restricted crop destruction.
October 7	By this date all foreign troops required to withdraw from Laos.
November 7	Army Chief of Staff General Earle Wheeler's Fordham University address: "The essence of the problem in Vietnam is military."
December 31	Total U.S. military personnel in Vietnam: 11,300.
	For the year an estimated 30,000 Viet Cong casualties (21,000 killed in action).
	Viet Cong regular strength estimated at 22,000 to 24,000.

1963

January 2	Battle of Ap Bac.
January 11	CIA Current Intelligence Memorandum: "Though the South Vietnam government probably is now holding its own against the Viet Cong and may be reducing the menace in some areas, the tide has not yet turned. . . . On balance, the war remains a slowly escalating stalemate."
	National Security Adviser McGeorge Bundy submits a "covert operational plan for North Vietnam" to JFK: "There is every reason to think that the execution of this plan will encounter all the difficulties of an operation in a denied area, but there is agreement that it is worth trying."
February 23	Harkins letter to Diem: "I am convinced we have taken the military, psychological, economical, and political initiative from the enemy."
March 13	Lao Dong Party Secretary-General Le Duan supports Chinese side of Sino-Soviet split.
April	MACV Summary of Highlights: "Barring greatly increased resupply and reinforcement of the Viet Cong by infiltration, the military phase of the war can be virtually won in 1963."
April 17	U.S. National Intelligence Estimate: "We believe that Communist progress has been blunted and that the situation is improving. . . . We do not believe it is possible at this time to project the future course of the war with any confidence."
April 20	NSC discussion of deteriorating situation in the Plain of Jars.
April 22	CIA Information Report indicating Diem regime's plan to request reduction of American personnel in Vietnam.

May	JCS direct CINCPAC to prepare plans for "non-attributable" hit-and-run operations against North Vietnam. Conducted by the South Vietnamese, these operations will be carried out with "U.S. military materiel, training, and advisory assistance."
May 8	Hue Buddhist incident.
May 11	*Washington Post* interview with Nhu, who suggests reduction in number of U.S. advisers.
May 15	Buddhist leaders present five demands to Diem.
May 17	U.S.-SVN communiqué affirms present level of American personnel necessary to combat the Viet Cong—Diem indirectly and without loss of face disavows Nhu's earlier remarks.
May 21	Five thousand Buddhists demonstrate peacefully in Hue during a ceremony for May 8 victims.
May 29	State instructs Deputy Chief of Mission William C. Trueheart to press Diem for action on Buddhist grievances.
June 7	Madame Nhu denounces Buddhist monks as Communist dupes.
June 11	First Buddhist fire-suicide.
	State to Trueheart: "FYI—If Diem does not take prompt and effective steps to re-establish Buddhist confidence in him we will have to re-examine our entire relationship with his regime."
June 12	Trueheart tells Diem that unless dramatic action were taken to meet Buddhists' demands, the U.S. would publicly state its "dissociation" from the GVN's Buddhist policy.
June 19	State to Trueheart: urges "hard-hitting approach to Diem. . . ."
June 25	Saigon CIA Station Chief John Richardson meeting with Nhu, who "is in a state of emotional shock and is in a dangerous frame of mind. . . . It is possible that Nhu would lead efforts against Diem. . . ."

Dai Viet approaches U.S. official and reports agreement among Dai Viets and Buddhist leaders for coup; seeks U.S. reaction; offers U.S. opportunity to "advise, comment, or participate."

June 27

Kennedy announces appointment of Henry Cabot Lodge as new ambassador.

July 4

At an embassy Independence Day party, CIA learns ARVN generals are actively plotting.

July 7

Altercation between American correspondents and Vietnamese police.

July 18

Nolting spends day "urging, encouraging, warning, [and] trying to get President Diem to move in [a] constructive manner."

August 4

Buddhist immolation.

August 8

Madame Nhu: "All they [Buddhist leaders] have done is barbecue a bonze."

August 14

Nolting bids farewell to Diem, warning "it would be impossible for the U.S. government to continue our present relationship" if he did not redress Buddhist grievances.

August 21

Martial law decree.

Pagoda raids.

August 22

After a brief stop in Tokyo, Lodge arrives in Saigon.

August 24

DEPTEL 243, the "August 24 cable," sent to Lodge.

August 28

Richardson to Central Intelligence Director John McCone: "Situation here has reached [the] point of no return."

August 29

Lodge to State: "We are launched on a course from which there is no respectable turning back: the overthrow of the Diem government."

August 30

State to Saigon: "Possibility therefore increasingly is that if there is to be a change, it can only be brought about by [an] American rather than Vietnamese effort."

August 31   Harkins to Taylor: Major General Duong Van "Big" Minh has stopped planning a coup.

September 2   *Times of Vietnam* article: "CIA Financing Planned Coup d'Etat."

                 On CBS Evening News, Kennedy cites the need for "changes of policy and perhaps with personnel [in the Diem government]."

September 6   State Department alerts all diplomatic posts to the possibility of Nhu's contacts with the Viet Cong.

September 9   JCS approves OPLAN 34–63, a program of covert action against North Vietnam.

September 10   A White House meeting to hear reports of Marine Major General Victor H. Krulak and senior Foreign Service officer Joseph A. Mendenhall. JFK: "Did you two gentlemen visit the same country?"

September 12   JFK at press conference: "What helps win the war, we support; what interferes with the war effort, we oppose."

September 16   Martial law suspended.

September 19   Lodge to JFK: ". . . [W]e should pursue contact with Big Minh and urge him along if he looks like acting."

September 23   McNamara and Taylor arrive in Vietnam.

October 2   McNamara and Taylor report their findings to Kennedy.

October 5   Buddhist immolation.

                 CIA operative Lou Conein meets with Major General "Big" Minh, who reveals his plans for a coup d'état.

                 Saigon CIA station telegram to McCone recommends not setting "ourselves irrevocably against the assassination plot."

White House to Lodge: ". . . no initiative should now be taken to give any active overt encouragement to a coup."

McCone to Saigon station: "[W]e certainly cannot be in the position of stimulating, approving, or supporting assassination, but on the other hand . . ."

October 6   CIA to Saigon station: "McCone directs that you withdraw recommendations to ambassador."

October 7   Madame Nhu arrives in U.S. to begin a three-week speaking tour.

October 9   White House to Lodge: "While we do not wish to stimulate [a] coup, we also do not wish to leave [the] impression that [the] U.S. would thwart a change in government. . . ."

October 22   A controversial State Department study challenges optimistic military evaluations of the war.

October 23   EMBTEL 768: "Diem/Nhu give every appearance of sitting tight and reacting to U.S. pressure with counterpressure and implying through public statements that they can go it alone."

October 24   CIA CRITIC reports coup attempt by Lieutenant Colonel Pham Ngoc Thao.

October 27   Buddhist immolation.

Ambassador Henry Cabot Lodge spends the day in Dalat with Diem: "Mr. President, every single suggestion which I have made, you have rejected. . . ."

October 29   Lodge to State: "In summary, it appears that a coup attempt by the generals' group is imminent."

October 30   McGeorge Bundy to Lodge: "Believe our attitude to coup group can still have decisive effect on its decisions."

Lodge to State: "Do not think we have the power to delay or discourage a coup."

Bundy to Lodge: "We do not accept as a basis for U.S. policy that we have no power to delay or discourage a coup. . . . But once a coup under responsible leadership has begun . . . it is in the interest of the U.S. government that it should succeed."

November 1–2	Coup d'état in Saigon.
November 8	U.S. recognizes new government.
November 20	Prince Norodom Sihanouk of Cambodia severs all economic and military ties with U.S.
	Special all-agency Vietnam conference in Honolulu.
November 22	JFK assassinated.
November 26	National Security Action Memorandum 273 reaffirms Kennedy commitments and programs to South Vietnam.
December	Ninth Conference of the Lao Dong party Central Committee resolves to step up the tempo of the insurgency.
December 21	McNamara to President Lyndon B. Johnson: "Current trends, unless reversed in the next two to three months, will lead to neutralization at best and more likely to a Communist-controlled state."
	McCone memorandum: "It is abundantly clear that statistics received over the past year or more from GVN officials and reported by the U.S. mission on which we gauged the trend of the war were grossly in error."
	LBJ directs an interdepartmental committee to study OPLAN 34A and select those operations with the least risk.

1964

January 1	U.S. military personnel in South Vietnam: 15,914.
January 16	LBJ approves a progressively escalating program of covert operations against North Vietnam.

January 22	Joint Chiefs of Staff propose a ten-point program of "bolder actions which may embody greater risks."
January 30	In a bloodless coup, Major General Nguyen Khanh deposes South Vietnamese junta.
February 20	LBJ orders stepped-up contingency planning for overt pressures against North Vietnam.
February 21	LBJ publicly warns Hanoi that it is playing "a deeply dangerous game."
February 28 –March 10	Desoto intelligence patrol along the North Vietnamese coast.
March 10	By a large write-in vote, Ambassador Henry Cabot Lodge wins New Hampshire Republican presidential primary.
March 16	After a visit to South Vietnam, McNamara recommends intensifying covert operations but is opposed to launching overt attacks against North Vietnam.
April 30	Rusk visits Ottawa and obtains Canadian agreement for a diplomatic mission to Hanoi by International Control Commission delegate J. Blair Seaborn.
May 2	Viet Cong sappers sink U.S. aircraft ferry *Card*.
May 11	CIA's William Colby reports: "The VC hold the initiative and continue to develop their strength among the population."
May 12	Senator Barry Goldwater, stepping up his attack on the administration's conduct of the war, blames LBJ and McNamara for the stalemate.
May 14	LBJ urgently requests that Lodge present recommendations for "a strategy for moving against the North."
May 17	Pathet Lao, aided by the North Vietnamese, launch an offensive that leads to a quick collapse of government forces on the Plain of Jars.

May 19	LBJ asks Congress for additional economic and military aid to bolster war effort.
May 21	U.S. begins low-level reconnaissance over Communist-occupied areas in Laos.
May 25	Goldwater proposes use of low-yield A-bombs to defoliate forests in Vietnam.
May 26	Goldwater claims misunderstanding on A-bomb use, saying that he repeated, without advocating, an idea suggested by "competent" military people.
May 29	Two hundred Americans of draft age join an ad hoc committee against the war in Vietnam.
June 1	Since Jan. 1, 1964, 36 U.S. deaths in Vietnam from hostile forces; since Jan. 1, 1961, 140 deaths from hostile forces.
June 2	Joint Chiefs express their concern over "lack of definition" of U.S. objectives: "We should not waste critical time and more resources in another protracted series of 'messages,' but rather we should take positive, prompt, and meaningful military action. . . ."
June 6–7	Two U.S. Navy reconnaissance aircraft shot down over Laos.
June 9	U.S. aircraft strike Pathet Lao gun positions and headquarters.
June 11	Deputy Assistant Secretary of Defense William Bundy's draft congressional resolution.
June 18	J. Blair Seaborn visits Hanoi and warns that the U.S. intends "to contain the DRV to the territory allocated to it" at Geneva. If the war escalates "the greatest devastation would of course result for the DRV itself."
June 20	General William C. Westmoreland appointed commander of U.S. forces in Vietnam.
June 23	Ambassador Lodge resigns to run for president.

June 25	Westmoreland requests an increase of U.S. military personnel of 4,200 to "influence the successful planning and execution of the National Pacification Plan."
July 2	McNamara and Taylor order military to prepare a three-phase plan for air strikes against North Vietnam.
July 8	Taylor, the new U.S. ambassador, presents his diplomatic credentials.
July 11	CINCPAC/JCS planners, settling on ninety-four strike objectives in North Vietnam, begin drafting detailed plans for massive air action.
July 15	CINCPAC seeks approval to conduct a Desoto intelligence-gathering patrol along the North Vietnamese coast.
July 31	U.S.S. *Maddox* begins Desoto patrol mission.
	Oplan 34A patrol boats bombard North Vietnamese islands of Hon Me and Hon Nieu.
August	The 808th PAVN battalion, the first complete combat unit trained for infiltration into South Vietnam, departs from North Vietnam.
August 2	*Maddox* attacked by three North Vietnamese PT boats—the first direct combat between U.S. and North Vietnamese forces.
August 3	OPLAN 34A patrol boats bombard North Vietnamese military complex and radar site.
August 4	Infamous second Tonkin Gulf incident.
August 5	U.S. planes conduct reprisal air strikes against North Vietnamese patrol-boat bases and supporting facilities.
	Joint Chiefs instruct CINCPAC to complete as soon as possible detailed operational planning for air action against North Vietnam.

August 6–7	Chinese deploy 36 jet fighters to Phuc Yen airfield near Hanoi. Ten new AAA positions, including 75 light and medium guns, have been established at this airfield since the air strikes.
August 7	Congress passes Tonkin Gulf Resolution.
August 8	Agency for International Development official kidnapped in ambush in Phu Yen Province, the first American civilian official captured by Viet Cong.
August 9	Ambassador Taylor recommends immediate armed reconnaissance missions in Laos panhandle and implementing air operations against North Vietnam. Target date: January 1965.
August 10	Taylor to LBJ: "The best thing that can be said about the Khanh government is that it has lasted six months and has about a 50–50 chance of lasting out the year."
	LBJ signs Tonkin Gulf Resolution.
August 15	In wake of Tonkin Gulf incidents, Westmoreland recommends deploying logistic units, a signal battalion, one Marine and two Army Hawk battalions.
August 21	CINCPAC recommends U.S. advisers should accompany ARVN ground troops in cross-border operations in Laos and concurs with Westmoreland's troop proposal.
August 25	In response to growing Buddhist and student pressure, Khanh resigns from his post as president of South Vietnam.
August 29	CINCPAC reports Viet Cong main-force strength at 34,000; other guerrilla units: 60–80,000.
September 1	JCS rebuff Westmoreland's troop request: ". . . [N]ow is not the time to take the actions requested."
September 3	Weaker and with conditional authority, Khanh returns to assume premiership.

September 6	Taylor to State: "The politicians in Saigon and Hue feel today that the political hassle is their appropriate arena. The conflict with the VC belongs to the Americans."
September 9	At a White House meeting General Wheeler reports that Air Force chief of staff and Marine Corps commandant want extensive U.S. air strikes now. LBJ does "not wish to enter the patient in a 10-round bout when he was in no shape to hold out for one round."
September 12	Hop Tac pacification program kicks off. Elements of ARVN 51st Regiment break off attack to participate in an unsuccessful coup attempt.
September 18	The third Tonkin Gulf incident.
September 20	Rhade tribesmen stage simultaneous uprisings in Special Forces camps in Darlac and Quang Duc provinces.
October	PAVN 95th Regiment leaves North Vietnam for the south and arrives there in December.
October 16	Chinese explode their first nuclear device.
November 1	Viet Cong mortar attack on U.S. air base at Bien Hoa.
November 3	In a landslide, LBJ elected.
November 4	Fifteen-man civilian government headed by Tran Van Huong announced.
November 26	Westmoreland squelches coup attempt by Nguyen Cao Ky.
December 7	LBJ issues plan of action in Vietnam. For the next thirty days, there will be intensified covert operations and Lao air operations and stepped-up high-level U.S. reconnaissance of DRV. When implemented, phase II of plan "would constitute a series of air attacks on the DRV progressively mounting in scope and intensity. . . ."
December 14	Operation Barrel Roll launched—U.S. air strikes in Laotian panhandle.

December 19	South Vietnamese military leaders move against Huong government.
December 20	Ambassador Taylor chastises South Vietnamese military.
December 21	Taylor suggests to Khanh that he resign and leave the country.
December 23	At meeting of senior ARVN corps and division commanders, decision is made to propose that Taylor be declared persona non grata.
December 24	Viet Cong bomb U.S. officers' billet in Saigon.
December 28	Battle of Binh Gia.

1965

January 1	U.S. forces in Vietnam total 23,000.
January 26	Westmoreland requests authority to use U.S. jet aircraft in a strike role under emergency situations. CINCPAC concurs.
January 27	South Vietnamese military ousts Huong government.
	McGeorge Bundy to LBJ: ". . . [B]oth of us [Bundy and McNamara] are now pretty well convinced that our current policy can lead only to a disastrous defeat. . . . The time has come for harder choices."
January 31 –February 6	Viet Cong observe a virtual stand down in celebration of Tet, the lunar new year.
February 7	Viet Cong attack U.S. bases at Pleiku and Binh Dinh.
February 8	Operation Flaming Dart, U.S. reprisal air strikes.
February 10	Viet Cong attack U.S. billet in Qui Nhon.
February 11	Flaming Dart II.
February 13	LBJ decides on a program of measured and limited air action against selected military targets in the DRV. Code name: Rolling Thunder.

February 14	Than Huy Quat accepts the invitation of the South Vietnamese military to form a new government.
February 16	According to a Gallup poll, 67 percent of American public approve of U.S. air strikes; telegrams to White House running 14 to 1 against strikes.
February 19	For the first time, U.S. jets strike targets within South Vietnam. Pham Ngoc Thao launches an unsuccessful coup d'état.
February 21	Unable to rally support among the military, Khanh resigns.
February 25	LBJ approves deployment of Marines to Da Nang—the first U.S. ground combat units in Vietnam.
March 2	First Rolling Thunder strike against North Vietnam.
March 8	Marines land at Da Nang.
March 29	U.S. embassy in Saigon bombed by Viet Cong terrorists.
April 7	LBJ's Johns Hopkins speech proposing unconditional discussions with the North Vietnamese.
April 10	CINCPAC recommends deployment of 173rd Airborne Brigade to Bien Hoa/Vung Tau area.
April 20	LBJ's top military advisers recommend additional deployments leading to total of 82,000 troops.
April 22	MACV confirms the presence of Second Battalion, 101st Regiment, 325th PAVN Division, in South Vietnam.
April 30	Deployment of 173rd Airborne Brigade to Bien Hoa/Vung Tau and Marine Expeditionary Brigade to Chu Lai.
May 5	LBJ sends Congress a special request for an additional $700 million to meet the mounting military costs in Vietnam. House passes 408 to 7; Senate passes 88 to 3.

May 13	U.S. bombing pause begins.
May 18	Bombing pause ends.
May 20	Thao launches another unsuccessful (and feeble) coup d'état.
June 11	With the concurrence of Premier Quat, ARVN generals peacefully take control of government.
	Westmoreland to JCS: "We have reached a point in Vietnam where we cannot avoid the commitment to combat of U.S. ground troops."
June 26	Westmoreland authorized to "commit U.S. troops to combat. . . .."
June 27–30	173rd Airborne Brigade into War Zone D—first major U.S. ground operation.
July 2	Joint Chiefs recommend increase in total troop strength to 179,000.
July 12	Moscow announces a new military and economic aid agreement with Hanoi.
July 27	At NSC meeting Johnson makes the formal decision to deploy 100,000 U.S. combat troops to Vietnam by the end of the year. The U.S. is now fully engaged in a land war in Vietnam.

LIST OF ABBREVIATIONS

ARVN — Army of the Republic of Vietnam
CIDG — Civilian Irregular Defense Groups
CINCPAC — Commander-in-Chief Pacific
CIP — Counterinsurgency Plan
COSVN — Central Office for South Vietnam
CRITIC — Critical Intelligence Message
DIA — Defense Intelligence Agency
DRV — Democratic Republic of North Vietnam
GVN — Government of South Vietnam
INR — Intelligence and Research
JCS — Joint Chiefs of Staff
JGS — Joint General Staff
MAAG — Military Assistance Advisory Group
MACV — Military Assistance Command-Vietnam
NIE — National Intelligence Estimate
NSC — National Security Council
NVN — North Vietnam
ONE — Office of National Estimates
OSS — Office of Strategic Services
PAVN — People's Army of (North) Vietnam
PL — Pathet Lao
PLAF — People's Liberation Armed Forces
SEATO — Southeast Asia Treaty Organization
SNIE — Special National Intelligence Estimate
SVN — South Vietnam
VC — Viet Cong
VOA — Voice of America

INDEX

Titles of Related Interest —

HELL IN A VERY SMALL PLACE:
The Siege of Dien Bien Phu
  by Bernard B. Fall

TET! The Turning Point in the Vietnam War
  by Don Oberdorfer

VIETNAM: Three Battles
  by S.L.A. Marshall

THUNDER OUT OF CHINA
  by Theodore H. White and Annalee Jacoby
  New foreword by Harrison E. Salisbury

THE 900 DAYS: The Siege of Leningrad
  by Harrison E. Salisbury

NORTH AMERICA
  by Anthony Trollope

THE KOREAN WAR
  by Matthew B. Ridgway

MEMOIRS OF
HARRY S. TRUMAN: Volume I
1945 — Year of Decisions

Available at bookstores or direct from

DA CAPO PRESS
233 Spring Street
New York, NY 10013
Toll-free 800-221-9369